Also by C. Britt Beemer and Robert L. Shook

*Predatory Marketing: What Everyone in Business
Needs to Know to Win Today's Consumer*

It Takes a Prophet
to Make a Profit

15 Trends That Are
Reshaping American Business

C. Britt Beemer
and Robert L. Shook

SIMON & SCHUSTER
New York London Toronto Sydney Singapore

SIMON & SCHUSTER
Rockefeller Center
1230 Avenue of the Americas
New York, NY 10020

Designed by Kim Llewellyn

Manufactured in the United States of America

10 9 8 7 6 5 4 3 2 1

Library of Congress Cataloging-in-Publication Data

Beemer, C. Britt.
    It takes a prophet to make a profit : 15 trends that are reshaping American
Business / C. Britt Beemer and Robert L. Shook.
        p.   cm.
    1. Business forecasting—United States.   2. Economic forecasting—United
States.   3. United States—Economic conditions—1981–   I. Shook, Robert L.,
1938–   II. Title.
HD30.27.B44 2001
330.973'0929—dc21

                                                                        00-061889

ISBN 0-684-86546-7

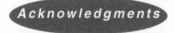
Acknowledgments

This is our second collaboration—we think we're a darn good writing team. But by no means are we the only team members. Several other people contributed to this publication whom we take great pride in acknowledging.

We are grateful to Al Zuckerman, our literary agent, who believed in our idea about how trends affect lives. Bob Bender, our publisher at Simon & Schuster, helped us crystallize our many different ideas. Bob is a marvelous editor who ranks among the best in the business. Like Bob, his assistant, Johanna Li, worked with us throughout the entire publishing process, and she, too, is a real professional. We also appreciate our copy editor, Lynn Anderson, who, like Bob and Johanna, makes us look good.

Maggie Abel, Stormy Bailey, Carla Keaton, Frank Lessor, and Debbie Watts helped in transcribing the hundreds of hours of interviews we conducted. They also assisted in the typing and organization of the manuscript. Maggie, Stormy, Carla, Frank, and Debbie—you're the best!

Without support from the staff at America's Research Group, gathering all the information could not have happened. In particular, we thank Mike Kelly, who worked many extra hours to find what we needed "yesterday." Kathy Hilleshein worked above and beyond in setting up crucial interviews—she's the one who was responsible for making sure the two of us were able to get together to make specific deadlines.

And most important, excellent research depends on excellent telephone interviews. We are especially grateful to ARG's professionals, who did the impossible task of completing thousands of interviews on top of their normal calling schedules.

Children see their world differently because everything is fresh and new. Chloe Jiang Beemer, I dedicate this book to you because I now see my world with a fresh perspective.

—C.B.B.

Many of my previous books have been dedicated to my children, Carrie, RJ, and Michael, as well as to my wife, Elinor. So I dedicate this book to my precious grandchildren in the order from the oldest to the youngest: Natalie, Olivia, Jacob, and Paige (they are ages five through one). May you give your parents as much joy as they have given to Nana and Papa.

—R.L.S.

Contents

A student once said to his professor, Albert Einstein, "These are the same questions you asked on last year's test. Nothing has changed."

Einstein answered, "It is true that all of the questions are the same. But this year, all of the answers are different."

The element of change is at the core of all trends. Past trends and current trends impact future trends, yet you can be assured that future trends will be different. It is those differences that make them difficult to spot. Still, it is possible to read the tea leaves, and those who can will enjoy an advantage over the competition.

In today's high-tech, fast-changing world, trends come and go at an increasingly rapid pace. To recognize their influence, one need only look at the huge corporate graveyard filled with companies that failed to adjust: Studebaker, Eastern Airlines, Railway Express, Gimbel's.

That's a mere handful of former greats that have been laid to rest. A full 40 percent of the *Fortune* 500 disappeared from the list between 1990 and 1995. The common denominator of these enterprises: their inability to anticipate trends in the marketplace.

Wayne Gretzky, the greatest hockey player of all time, was once asked to explain his success. "I skate to where the puck is going to be, not to where it has been."

Businesses should heed this wisdom. To survive in our highly competitive marketplace, business owners must tune into prevailing trends. Unlike hockey, business has some historical perspective;

nonetheless, it's reckless to presume that history will repeat itself. Rather, history creates some useful guidelines.

Trends can be anticipated by studying patterns of the past, thus developing a historical perspective. As founder and CEO of America's Research Group (ARG), C. Britt Beemer has studied consumer behavior patterns for the past two decades. In this capacity, he has conducted more than 4 million interviews with consumers and businesspeople. His impressive list of clients includes General Electric, Kmart, and Barnes & Noble. At ARG, a trend is anticipated by observing consumer traffic patterns. The firm develops research mileposts, noting how consumers respond to certain issues over a period of time. The beginning of a trend is like a tiny beep that gradually gets louder. If it goes from a tiny 3 percent to 7 percent in a few months and then quickly to 10 percent, a trend is probably developing. In general, a single major factor doesn't indicate an upcoming trend. Instead, a lot of little clues signal its arrival.

While ARG produces research mileposts based on regional and national trends, it's possible to calculate do-it-yourself time lines for a small business. This requires keeping good business records and tracking a lot of things that may seem insignificant but that over the course of years will become important information. A retail store might track hourly transactions, the daily number of individual shoppers versus groups, the number of men compared to women in those shopping groups, the average time each customer spends in the store, how frequently each customer shops, and the average shopping time compared to money spent per customer. Obscure but perhaps critical data include a customer's time at the checkout, the store's advertising program, repeat customer business, and so on. In three to five years patterns will emerge, showing management what to expect in the future.

Fifteen major business trends are presented in *It Takes a Prophet to Make a Profit*. These are national and global trends, and, depending on what you do, several of them are likely to impact your business. Consequently, you will be compelled to act on them. One thing is certain: you cannot remain an idle observer. Failure to respond means disaster.

Note that we have selected significant business trends. We purposely excluded those that are obvious and have been repeatedly covered by the media, such as America's physical fitness craze, the attitudes of Generation X, and political issues. Nor are phenomena such as the graying of America included. Living longer, having fewer children, and experiencing other changes are demographics, not trends. These demographics do, in turn, stimulate trends, as you will discover in Trend 7, "More Americans Are Caring for Their Aging Parents."

Many trends are interrelated. *It Takes a Prophet to Make a Profit* illustrates how one trend may spawn others, some of which may surprise the reader. For instance, you will observe how Trend 1, "Americans Have Less Discretionary Time," keeps surfacing in other trends, especially Trend 4, "There Is a Growing Obsession with the Internet," which begs the age-old "chicken or egg" question: Are Americans surfing the Web because they have less time and wish to maximize their communication and shopping experience—or is the Internet actually consuming more discretionary time? And in Trend 11, you'll discover that today's consumers are buying more brand-name products. Is this because they don't have time for comparison shopping?

Likewise, the rising number of adult children taking care of their elderly parents (Trend 7) results in less discretionary time for this group. Another trend that has transpired as a result of the time crunch is Trend 9: the number of dual-income families in America has been on the rise since World War II, and we're now seeing a trend toward single-income families. Finally, a desire to budget one's discretionary time has stimulated a growing number of people to set up home offices and telecommute (Trend 14).

It doesn't take a prophet to recognize that the ability to spot trends is vital to all managers and entrepreneurs. Ultimately, their success or failure rests on business decisions they make concerning the future. These decisions range from the inventory they carry to the messages they advertise. In short, a business thrives by anticipating and then planning what will be, which is why understanding trends is essential.

Americans Have Less Discretionary Time

Back in the 1960s, life was a breeze. Take a look at Rob Petrie, the scriptwriter character in *The Dick Van Dyke Show*. Rob had it made. He rarely deviated from his nine-to-five schedule. When Rob kissed Laura good-bye each morning, the sun was shining. When he arrived home each afternoon, the sky was still light. While Rob had his share of deadlines, there was always time for a good kibitz around the water cooler or with Buddy in their office. Of course, Rob had more time than his modern counterpart—he wasn't constantly sending and retrieving e-mail, voice-mail, and facsimile messages. Nor did he have to contend with teleconferencing and the Internet. But wait a minute—aren't those contraptions supposed to save time? Isn't technology supposed to make life easier? Machines are designed to do our chores and thereby provide us with more free time for leisure and pleasure.

The pace of Laura's life was a tad slower, too. After sending little Richie off to school, washing the dishes, making the beds, and doing a load of laundry, there wasn't much to do until lunchtime. No wonder she was so cheerful when Rob walked through the door each evening. After an unhurried several-course meal, the Petries had plenty of time to chat and watch TV before retiring for a long, restful night's sleep.

True, technology has relieved drudgery and made it possible for us to be more productive. But in many ways it has added to our workload by causing our work to spill over into our personal lives. Today we bring home laptop computers that even accompany us to our country homes and the beach. After dinner, we check our e-mail, send a few replies, and peek at our portfolios on the Internet. We may dally in a chat room, visit a few Web sites, and so on. Then there are the time-consuming software glitches we must contend with.

Even computer illiterates are inundated by a sea of information. We now have cable TV offering more than two hundred channels, daily and weekly newspapers to read, and magazines arriving monthly.

As Americans, we have enjoyed unprecedented prosperity during the past decade, but we have not experienced a corresponding improvement in the quality of our lives. Instead, our growing affluence has compounded the demands on our time. Consequently, Americans feel more stressed and worn out than ever. In survey after survey, Americans emphasize the need to regain control of their lives. Sixty percent of those queried in 1997 by Kurt Salmon Associates, a New York consulting firm, said they had less time for leisure. An astounding 44 percent confessed that, given a choice, they'd rather have more free time than more money.

How we reconcile the growing imbalance between material wealth and what Harvard economist Juliet Schor calls "time poverty," and how we address this problem and its accompanying duress, will shape consumer spending and the American economy for years to come.

Spotting the Trend

This is one trend that practically everyone senses because it affects us all. Even if you're not one of the millions of Americans who are scratching for discretionary time, it's likely you are in contact daily with many who are.

In our 1986 survey, 44 percent of Americans said they had all the free time they needed. In 1992, this number had dropped to 34 percent. By 1999, only 22.2 percent felt no time crunch. Note that in thirteen years, the number of Americans comfortable with their discretionary time dropped by half! These numbers show the strength of this trend.

Twenty-nine percent of Americans say that they never have time to do anything for themselves. They say the culprit is their work schedule. Work consumes their week, so they try to squeeze all their other activities into the weekend. When we cram everything into Saturday and Sunday, the two days set aside for leisure and fun become stressful as well.

Our surveys identified six ways that having less time is affecting Americans. In order of importance they are:

1. Less time for family vacations. Americans love vacations. It is a time when relationships grow. Parents and children bond. Couples fall in love again. Siblings interact in different surroundings and create lifelong memories. Some experts say the loss of vacation time has a negative impact on all family members, making it difficult for them to cohere as a unit. This, they say, causes teenagers to be unruly in school, submit more easily to peer pressure, and develop other social handicaps.

2. Less time to exercise. A steady exercise program requires dedication. In the face of time constraints, exercise routines lose their priority. This is the number one reason why most people cannot schedule regular exercise in their daily lives. Our studies show that only 18 percent of all Americans exercise regularly.

3. Less time to participate in sports that promote camaraderie. Here we mainly refer to social sports for men, such as golf and tennis, and pickup sports such as touch football and basketball. While sports of this nature provide exercise, they are generally more valuable as venues for nurturing male-to-male relationships. Women generally find it easier to incorporate social behavior into work activities than do men. Fewer opportunities for men to establish and nurture male relationships means greater concern about the absence of such relationships.

4. Less time to read. While women typically read more than men, both sexes now claim to have less reading time. When people are tired and budgeting their minutes closely, this is a relatively easy activity to eliminate. In particular, reading for pleasure is curtailed.

5. Less time to watch television. Considering the enormous amount of time Americans spend watching television, this would be an obvious activity to cut back on. The fact that it is not at the top of the list suggests that the average American actually prioritizes TV time ahead of reading, exercise, and vacations.

6. Less time to shop. Last but not least, the average consumer has less time to shop. For many Americans, shopping is a way of relaxing and lifting their spirits. Later, we will discuss how tight shopping schedules impact America's spending habits.

The Overworked American

Americans complain that the number one reason they don't have enough time is that they spend too much time at work. Interestingly, this doesn't automatically equate with bigger paychecks. Hourly workers do receive overtime pay, but salaried employees actually find that their hourly wage is reduced. One salaried systems engineer said her personal records document that she worked 154 hours a year that were not compensated for in her forty-hour-per-week salary. "I figure that's more than nineteen days I donated to my company that I didn't get paid for," she said. She epitomizes the U.S. worker who is spending more time at work and resents it.

The Families and Work Institute reports that we work later and commute farther than workers did twenty years ago. According to a 1998 study, the number of hours worked at all jobs for all employees averaged 46 per week—as compared to 43.6 hours in a 1977 survey. Commuting time now averages nearly 50 minutes a day.

One in three employees brings work home at least once a week. The typical two-career couple worked 247 more hours (6.2 workweeks) a year in 1996 than in 1989.

These figures do not include hourly employees. For the most part, long workweeks are confined to managerial, professional, and sales occupations that carry above-average salaries.

The National Study of the Changing Workforce shows that Americans believe they are working longer, harder, and faster:

• 88 percent reported having to work hard and 68 percent having to work fast, yet 60 percent still can't get everything done.

• 71 percent said they feel used up at the end of the day.

• 38 percent said that stress has caused them minor health problems.

• 37 percent are "somewhat likely" or "very likely" to make a genuine effort to find a new job with another employer in the next year.

Two-career couples are working longer hours, but they're not happy about it. Based on a study by Marin Clarkberg, a sociologist at Cornell University, both sexes feel stressed by the competing demands of job and home. Clarkberg claims that the situation is sometimes worse for women than men because women must often choose between working full-time or not at all. There are few part-time jobs for women with families, and those jobs often pay poorly and do not offer health insurance or other benefits. Clarkberg's research shows that both men and women would like to work fewer than forty hours a week.

As part of the National Study of Families and Households, Clarkberg's findings were that:

• 43 percent of men and 34 percent of women work more hours than they want to. The number is smaller for women because 25 percent of them don't have paying jobs.

- Half of all the women and 20 percent of the men wish they could work part-time.

- Just 14 percent of couples want both spouses to work full-time.

In spite of these figures, the job market remains geared toward the traditional employee who works either full-time or not at all and caters to working husbands with stay-at-home wives.

Something Has to Give

Innovations such as home computers, pagers, e-mail, and faxes were supposed to permit flexible work hours and allow more time for people's personal lives. Somehow, however, the new technology seems to result in people working more, not less! It has simply opened the doors of employees' homes to their employers. Workers are now accessible to their companies twenty-four hours a day, seven days a week.

In a 2000 survey, we discovered that 27.3 percent of dual-income households are saying "Something has to give." They are near a breaking point because they have no relief on the job and can't find time to unwind when not working. We can't compare it to the attitudes of twenty years ago because similar studies weren't done back then. We estimate that the number of Americans who feel this way has increased three- to fourfold.

People are fed up. We asked them, "Would you like to see your children grow up to be part of a two-career family?" Forty-eight percent said no. Parents typically want their children to have better lives than they. This survey clearly says that nearly half of all Americans are not content with their hectic lives. They believe that there must be a better way to live.

We also asked if Americans emphasize material possessions over a higher quality of life. An astounding 83 percent responded, "Yes." Our society has long been thought materialistic, but the number of Americans who feel this way has never been so high. Interestingly, 38.5 percent of Americans say that they are better off financially because both spouses work. Nearly an equal amount, 38.3 percent, state that they are too busy to enjoy life!

One reason why Americans feel so stressed is sleep deprivation. Our 1999 survey reveals that 35.8 percent of Americans catch up on their necessary activities by cutting back on the amount of time they sleep. Furthermore, when asked how much less sleep they now get, a whopping 45.8 percent said they sleep at least two fewer hours each night because sleeping is too time-consuming.

Managers should pay heed to Dr. James B. Maas, past chairman of the Department of Psychology at Cornell University. Dr. Maas says, "For anyone who wants to be successful, sleep is a necessity, not a luxury." In his book *Power Sleep,* Maas emphasizes that even minimal sleep loss has profound detrimental effects on mood, cognition, performance, productivity, communication skills, accident rates, and general health. Given the role of sleep in determining functioning during the day, Maas is alarmed at the extent of American workers' sleep deprivation. He estimates that at least 50 percent of the U.S. adult population is chronically sleep-deprived.

The average adult sleeps between seven and eight hours. For a very few individuals, according to Dr. Maas, six hours of sleep each night is adequate. One or two people in a hundred can get by with five hours. However, many need nine to ten hours of sleep to function at full capacity and be wide awake all day.

Realistically speaking, most of us aren't willing to schedule ten hours daily for sleep. But according to Dr. Thomas Roth at Henry Ford Hospital's Sleep Disorders and Research Center in Detroit, sleeping just one hour extra boosts alertness by 25 percent! And that's just one of the several benefits that comes with proper sleep.

Knowing about the effect of sleep deprivation on their workers, smart managers will realize that long work schedules don't pay off. Not only do they lower morale, they often result in inferior performance. Management should think twice about having employees work overtime. Those extra hours at the office might mean fewer hours of sleep that night. Some may say, "What do I care, as long as they're on time the next morning?" As we know, there's more to being a good worker than simply showing up. Considering how productivity can be affected by loss of sleep, being satisfied by a worker's mere presence on the job is shortsighted.

One company that wants its people to be well rested is the Longaberger Company, headquartered in Newark, Ohio. This is one company that doesn't judge an employee's worth by the number of hours he or she puts in. In fact, the opposite is true.

Founded by Dave Longaberger in the 1970s, this $1 billion company's incredible growth can be attributed to its caring corporate culture. Longaberger strongly adheres to its principles of management, one of which is that the proper amount of rest is essential to employee productivity. As Dave Longaberger stated, "If I see somebody working past five o'clock, I'll say, 'Can't you get your work done on time?' or 'You won't score any points with the boss by staying here late, because I won't be seeing you.'"

It's not that Longaberger feels that overtime is unnecessary. Instead, as he puts it, "I want people to get enough rest so they'll be energized the following day. When people overwork, they burn themselves out, and it shows up in the poor quality of their work. This is why I encourage people who don't get proper rest to take a sick day. By dragging themselves to work, they're likely to do more harm than good!"

It's refreshing to see a business leader who believes people can be more productive by working fewer hours. All too often, managers think that managing people means driving them into doing overtime to increase productivity. On the contrary, overworking is counterproductive to productivity. We think Longaberger has the right idea, and we hope that more companies will pick up on this admirable philosophy in the future.

Another stressful activity that causes wear and tear on America's workforce is a long daily commute. Not only is the extra fifty minutes behind the wheel tiring, it reduces the time available for family or leisure activities. What's more, it totals more than two hundred hours a year, the equivalent of five standard workweeks! A survey we conducted in 1999 reveals that nearly 25 percent of all Americans would consider changing jobs for a shorter commute to work. This is an interesting fact for human resources executives and headhunters to be aware of.

While we're on the subject of commuting, one of the most stressed business groups is those who must travel. Business travelers who miss time with their young children are the most vocal. Today, we are hearing more about company employees who challenge nearly every request to travel overnight and who make an extra effort to race back home to be with their families. At the same time, companies facing rising travel costs insist that they schedule low-fare stopovers and side trips to smaller airports. This is a dilemma that managers must address.

With a record 32 percent of working adults traveling on business in 1997, the *National Business Monitor* says the tension between travel and family is rising. According to a survey of business travelers by the Travel Industry Association and OAG, a travel information and systems concern, business travelers say the rush to get home is the number one priority in picking flights. Today, this factor overrules lower fares and frequent-flyer miles.

On another time-related subject, 44 percent of U.S. employees feel that their employers show disrespect by requiring them to attend unproductive meetings. While the meeting-and-memo frenzy has long been a sore point in business circles, subordinates in corporate America's time squeeze resent it. Good managers do not schedule meetings frivolously; nevertheless, this issue should be addressed in earnest.

Let the Retailer Beware!

Let's take a look at how today's consumer saves time. Our 1999 survey reveals that:

1. They do less comparison shopping.

2. They shop only at stores that are sure to carry their size, color, and so on and have adequate stocks of sale items.

3. They buy more brand-name products.

The number one time-saver, doing less comparison shopping, means two things. First, it means that shoppers tend not to read product labels. It also means that they shop in fewer stores. In our 1980 study, consumers shopped in an average of 3.5 stores for a major purchase such as a large appliance or electronics. In 1990, they visited 2.8 stores; only five years later, 2.1 stores. Today, they visit only 1.5 stores. This means that only 40 percent of America's shoppers will even check a second store before buying merchandise. Thus, a merchant must make sure his store is the first one visited. If it's third, fourth, or fifth on the list, he's in serious trouble.

We also discovered that in 1980, when shopping for a big-ticket item ($500 or more), Americans would look at 2.3 ads and visit 2.8 stores. Today's consumer looks at 4.5 ads and visits 1.5 stores.

In 1999, 38 percent of Christmas shoppers purchased virtually all their gifts at one store. In 1985, only 6 percent went to only one store to do their Christmas shopping.

Closely related to cutting down on comparison shopping is buying more brand-name products. Customers buy products they know and trust because it's easier and quicker. They're willing to spend more money on a product they feel is reliable rather than buy an unknown brand and risk disappointment. This behavior in itself is important, and we'll discuss it in detail in Trend 11.

Now, getting back to time-saver number two: today's consumers are so pressed for time that if they are disappointed by a store, they won't come back. Some become enraged at having to go home empty-handed!

Some complain, "You've wasted my time. You'll never see me in here again!" Most, however, never say a word. They simply don't return. The message to retailers is loud and clear: You'd better get it right the first time. You must deliver what you advertise. In a new store, you'd better have the shelves full before you open the door. Our studies show that customers will go to another store rather than go back to one that isn't adequately stocked. Clothing shoppers also complain when merchandise is misplaced because this, too, slows them down. During recent Christmas seasons, leading department stores hired employees whose only job was to return misplaced merchandise back where it belonged.

Furthermore, our research shows that today's consumers aren't quite as patient as they were ten years ago. In 1990, department store shoppers found it acceptable to wait in line behind three or four people. During the 1999 Christmas season, they would barely tolerate only two customers ahead of them.

Paco Underhill, a noted retail anthropologist, is the founder and head of Envirosell, a firm that researches American shopping habits. Underhill believes that once people decide on which store to shop at, the amount of time spent in the store (shopping, not waiting in line) is perhaps the single most important factor in determining how much they will buy. Underhill states, "Over and over again, our studies have shown a direct relationship. If the customer is walking through the entire store (or most of it, at least) and is considering lots of merchandise (meaning he or she is looking and touching and thinking), a fair amount of time is required."

His research reveals that nonbuyers in an electronics store spend an average of 5 minutes and 6 seconds, compared to 9 minutes and 29 seconds for buyers. In a toy store, buyers spend more than 17 minutes, compared to 10 minutes for nonbuyers.

While there are many considerations that determine how much time a shopper spends in a store, Underhill thinks the interception rate—the percentage of customers who have some contact with an employee—has a strong influence on the buying decision. His research shows that this direct relationship is crucial: The more shopper-employee contacts that take place, the greater the average sale. In his estimation, talking with an employee draws a customer closer.

The new store on the block in today's competitive marketplace gets one chance to win a new customer. Ten years ago, American consumers would give a store three chances before deserting it.

Nowadays, a new store must do four things:

1. *Advertise a service that customers believe they can't get elsewhere.* This can range from being open twenty-four hours a day to having the widest product selection in town.

2. *Offer the right brand names at the right prices.* Brand names are a major factor, in particular for a new store that hasn't established a reputation.

3. *Be properly staffed.* When people discuss their shopping experiences, they tell how long it took to get assistance, to check out, whether the salespeople were knowledgeable, and so on.

4. *Create a good physical image.* Our research shows that the external appearance of a building is responsible for about 45 percent of the company's marketing image. For instance, a huge storefront implies that the store has a great selection. A well-designed, attractive storefront suggests quality because a cheaper store wouldn't be concerned with appearance. In other words, an attractive store translates to "Come buy a quality product from a first-class company."

You may ask, "How does this relate to time-conscious shoppers?" The hurried shopper must decide quickly where to shop based on efficiency. Sometimes this decision is based on impressions rather than information. A good way for a business to attract the time-impoverished shopper is to offer an unconditional thirty-day guarantee on its product or service. If the customer has a problem—any problem—a full refund is available, no questions asked. This is a quick, effective way of attracting first-time customers; the store is making an offer with no strings attached. Customers have nothing to lose but time, and they will exchange their time for this ultimate hassle-free experience. That's because they have the option of exchanging the item or getting a refund.

Remember, too, that today's consumers are presold on where to shop from the moment they leave home. Our research shows that on leaving home to shop, 90 percent of Americans have a definite shopping destination, as opposed to only 70 percent just ten years ago. Time is the main factor here; no longer will shoppers head aimlessly to a mall with the idea of wandering around and window-shopping.

A convenient location is also much more important today. At one time, people were willing to drive as much as ten miles to make a major purchase. Today, they'll drive only within a seven-mile radius.

What Time-Pressed Americans Are Buying

In an age of sound bites and electronic mail, nearly everything moves faster today. In a race against time, pressure takes a heavy toll on our lives. And in all races as well as all trends, there are winners. In prosperous times, when consumers have more discretionary money than time, changes in spending will benefit some businesses while hurting others.

For starters, we can expect an increasing demand for timesaving services, from courier services to domestic help. Businesses that meet this need will prosper.

When we don't have time to do certain chores but have the money to hire someone to do them, that's what we do. This means we eat out more; we pay housekeepers; we hire lawn caretakers. Time-pressured people are willing to pay to have other people do nearly anything for them. Our research shows, for example, that clothing items that were formerly laundered at home are now being sent to dry cleaners'. In particular, commercial laundries are handling more knit shirts, which were once simply tossed into the washer at home.

This is one example of how a business can benefit by performing a service we used to do ourselves. When pressed for time, we'll gladly pay to have a variety of things done. We may "outsource" certain chores. Then there are some things we stop doing altogether. We quit washing our own cars, we forgo weekly manicures, and so on.

Of course, one person's chore is another's pastime. For instance, some people enjoy cooking or gardening and make time to experience these activities as a form of relaxation. Major home remodeling is an activity on the rise, providing recreation as well as bringing the family together and saving money. Companies such as the Home Depot and Lowe's Home Improvement Warehouse have capitalized on this trend.

Most of us, however, take the easy way out. If we can afford it, we pay to have our chores done. As a result, we are seeing more small entrepreneurs who clean gutters and chimneys, pressure-wash sidewalks and driveways, organize closets—and on and on.

Car dealerships are beginning to accommodate time-starved customers. It's not unusual today for service departments to have twenty-four-hour shifts. Customers can drop off their cars at night and pick them up on the way to work the following morning. Many luxury-car dealers such as Mercedes-Benz go one step further. They'll pick up a customer's car and leave a similar model for use in the meantime. The serviced car is usually returned and the loaner picked up the same day. This kind of service commitment at the time of sale is often the tiebreaker for customers trying to decide what car to buy. Sure, it's an added expense, but luxury-car owners are willing to pay for it to save time.

Likewise, upscale department stores such as Nordstrom, Saks Fifth Avenue, and Neiman-Marcus offer one-on-one shopping services. In these stores, a knowledgeable employee will accompany a customer to different departments to select specific merchandise. Or a customer may simply describe a particular gift and allow a personal shopper to make the selection. While these services provide many benefits, they primarily save time for busy customers.

A host of businesses that cater to time-conscious consumers have surfaced, such as small shops that offer packing and shipping services. They're a one-stop convenience for people who don't have the time to find a box for an item, wrap it, and ship it. Our research shows that these companies do 75 percent of their business during November and December.

More and more companies have started outsourcing work because their in-house people can't meet their deadlines. For instance, rather than hiring and training full-time help, an accounting department may job out the year-end budget planning. A consultant earning $125 an hour gets more for his time if he makes his rounds and hires an answering service to handle his calls while he is out. Some companies outsource work because it eliminates paying overtime and employee benefits. As time grows scarcer, we will see more outsourcing.

To get more bang for their buck, business travelers now select hotels with fully equipped business centers and exercise facilities. They save on cab fares and courier fees when the hotel has not only a good restaurant but also a twenty-four-hour business center. It's not just the hotel with the nicest rooms that wins—it's the one that enables guests to use their time most productively, whether that means enjoying a healthy breakfast or working out on a treadmill.

There's still more. Upscale hotels are even offering activities to accommodate families of their business guests. At the Ritz-Carlton in Boston, conference planners boast about their most popular suite—the $725-a-night junior presidential, designed for guests two to four feet tall—with an adjoining room for parents or a nanny. Like other hotels in the chain, it has a program called "Ritz Kids."

And at the Loew's Coronado Bay Resort in San Diego where 70 percent of the guests are business travelers, the hotel is constantly expanding its list of baby sitters, pediatricians, and activities—like classes on explorers, pirates, and nautical rope-tying—for its youngest clientele.

In a booming economy, many overworked parents have been struggling to find more time for their children—so they are taking them along on business trips. The number of youngsters on such trips more than tripled over the 10 years through 1998, according to the Travel Industry Association of America.

Popular products that allow us to do two things at once range from car phones to baby strollers designed for joggers. Sounds wonderful, doesn't it? Mom gets back into shape, and baby has a joyride!

Fast, Convenient Food

Feeding ourselves has long been our favorite pastime. Because most of us eat every day, we have addressed this everyday activity as a separate subject. For starters, dining out has always been more popular with singles. Some single people feel it's not practical to prepare food for one, and eating out allows them social contact as well. These days, however, more two-career couples are eating out because preparing meals is time-consuming. Restaurants everywhere, from fast-food restaurants to fine dining establishments, are beneficiaries of this trend.

Not surprisingly, fast-food restaurants have cornered the lunchtime market because working people are demanding faster service than ever. Operations that get their customers in and out in a short time outrun their competition. With many workers on flextime, the lunch hour has stretched from 11:00 A.M. to 2:00 P.M. or longer, so McDonald's and Burger King now stop serving breakfast at 10:30. Fast-food restaurants, however, are losing customers for the evening meal, in part because so many eat fast food for lunch and want to eat more leisurely and perhaps more healthily in the evening. For health-conscious people, grocery stores are now selling prepared food to take home, ready for heating and immediate serving. This enables time-starved individuals to save extra time: they don't have to spend time cooking *or* eating out!

At full-service restaurants, speed is crucial at lunchtime. But getting diners in and out quickly is easier said than done. This is especially true with restaurants that serve a three- or five-course meal. Interestingly, some sit-down restaurants have it down to a science and can now serve customers nearly as quickly as the fast-food chains. Many full-service restaurants offer limited menus at noon, cutting down on preparation time and kitchen staff, or offer a buffet at an attractive price for diners who would prefer to eat quickly. The winners are the restaurants that can satisfy people who have less than an hour to eat and get back to the office.

Americans today want their food served at fast-food restaurants faster than ever. So for this reason, the drive-thru window is enjoying growing popularity. Not long ago, drive-thru was a hole punched through the wall to supplement dining-room sales. But today, almost 65% of fast-food revenues are coming through that hole. Between 1997 and 2007, sales of meals to be eaten off premises are expected to grow three times faster than on-premise sales, according to the Franchise Finance Corp. of America.

No wonder the fast-food chains are racking their brains for faster ways to dish out food at their drive-thrus. The chain that most consistently offers the fastest service will attract more customers. Regular drive-thru customers know that a six-car lane at one chain is likely to move faster than a three-car lane at another. By some estimates, increasing drive-thru efficiency by 10 percent boosts sales at the average fast-food restaurant by $54,000 per year. In 1999, the average fast-food restaurant did about $560,000 in sales.

The competition for market share in the fast-food industry has driven the chains to keep score based on the length of time it takes for a customer to move from the menu board to departure. The top five performers in 1999 were:

Company	Time
Wendy's	2 minutes, 30 seconds
McDonald's	2 minutes, 47 seconds
Checkers	2 minutes, 49 seconds
Burger King	2 minutes, 51 seconds
Long John Silver's	2 minutes, 52 seconds

Source: Sparagowski & Associates

Even chains that never have put much stock in drive-thru operations, such as Starbucks and Dunkin Donuts, have begun building them. As the competition flares up, we anticipate even faster times than those mentioned above. In a nutshell, fast food is getting faster than ever!

A study by NPD Group on Eating Patterns in America found

that the average American consumed 917 home-cooked meals and 139 restaurant meals in 1998. This compared to 933 home-cooked meals and 122 restaurant meals in 1990, which is a 14-percent increase. Fast-food restaurants accounted for more than 80 percent of the growth in restaurant meals during the last five years of the study.

NPD Vice President Harry Balzer, who has been monitoring national eating patterns for 20 years, believes consumers are more concerned with their time and money than they are with maintaining a balanced diet.

"After years of attempting to eat our way to better health, with the only tangible result being a heavier American, we are back at looking for the easiest and cheapest way to take care of feeding ourselves," he said.

Though people are eating out more, they are entertaining less. And many of those who give parties are having them catered. Again, time is the main issue. People who work full-time don't have the time to prepare their own meals, let alone cook for company. What's interesting is that in the past people would have affairs for thirty or more guests catered. Today, it's not unusual to have parties for a dozen or fewer guests catered.

Speaking of dinner, a new player has entered the food scene: the take-home meal. Pizza delivery companies, neighborhood delis, and even grocery stores offer a quick, hot meal at a reasonable price. Boston Market was a forerunner in this area. Although the company has since been through tough times, in its concept it was right on target.

And pizza isn't the only food that can be delivered. Especially in major metropolitan areas, everything from Chinese food to cold cuts can be ordered from home. Companies have evolved that do nothing but manage home delivery service for twenty to thirty local restaurants. Upscale grocers have installed kitchens to prepare meats, broil chickens, and package ready-to-heat vegetables and casseroles.

Supermarkets sell ready-to-go sandwiches so consumers can

eat lunch on the run. The busy consumer pays a premium for this, but he doesn't waste time buying separate ingredients such as bread, meat, and cheese and making a sandwich. So many people are eating on the run that Bobby Calder, a marketing professor at Northwestern University, says, "Consumers now see eating as something to be done while you do something else. Everybody wants to save time by multitasking. You don't just sit down and eat. You eat while you work, while you're watching TV, while you drive."

The automobile, traditionally a favorite place to snack, is fast becoming a dining room on wheels. Nowadays, a car is hardly worth driving unless it has cup holders in both the front and back. Some new cars even come with refrigerated glove compartments. And within a year, the Samsung Corporation plans to market the first car and minivan microwave, which will plug into the cigarette lighter.

Speaking about eating on the run, we heard about one company that has come up with a line of portable meals that don't require forks, spoons, or even plates. Breakaway Foods in Columbus, Ohio, has six IncrEdibles egg or pasta meals that come in tubelike, push-up containers that can be popped into the microwave and eaten on the run. These are meals for people who don't have much time to prepare them—or eat them!

Only 24 percent of Americans regularly eat breakfast, lunch, and dinner and nothing else, according to a 1996 survey by Roper Starch Worldwide. That's down from 33 percent in 1985. Polls indicate that a majority of American families still eat dinner together or at least they say they do. But walk down the aisles of supermarkets and convenience stores, and you'll find that "portable" foods are taking up a lot more shelf space than before.

Note that snacks line the shelves in stores such as 7-Eleven. More and more foods are popping up that can be eaten with one hand, such as sealed tacos and stuffed breadsticks. Likewise, fast-food restaurants report that 50 percent of their sales are now at the drive-thru window. In some markets McDonald's is testing the McSalad Shaker, a salad in a plastic container that can fit into a car cup holder. As a customer drives off, he can pour in the dressing, fasten the top, and shake it up. Movie snacks are no longer just popcorn and candy: some theaters now serve actual meals at their concession stands; moviegoers can now snack on anything from turkey breast sandwiches to smoked salmon while watching the latest blockbuster. Book retailers such as Barnes & Noble and Borders aren't the only stores to offer gourmet coffee and snacks to shoppers; furniture stores are getting into the business, too—Ikea now has a cafeteria, and Crate and Barrel sells coffee.

In the workplace, some of today's cubicles look more like food pantries than offices—they're stacked with treats such as chips, nuts, rice cakes, and dried fruit to provide snacks for the hungry. Food has become a requisite at almost any staff meeting. All-day grazing has largely replaced the old-fashioned business lunch, for which workers actually had to leave the office.

According to health experts, all this increased snacking is contributing to the rising number of obese and overweight people. According to the National Institutes of Health, 52 percent of Americans are now overweight—the highest rate ever. Consequently, the beneficiaries of this trend are health clubs and stores that sell exercise gear. And of course, working out to lose weight takes up even more of the overweight, overworked consumer's discretionary time!

Downtown Revivals

Alan Schonberg is the founder and chairman of Management Recruiters International, the world's largest headhunter firm. He told us this interesting tidbit: "A big factor in recruiting people today is a shorter commute time. In some markets where there has been a downtown renaissance, executives are excited that they can save two hours a day by living in a luxury high-rise and having the option to walk to the office."

Schonberg points out that empty-nest couples in particular are attracted to urban areas with great shopping and lots of nighttime activities such as fine dining and theater. While New York, Chicago, Boston, Philadelphia, and San Francisco have long been favorites for big-city living, Minneapolis, Charlotte, and Winston-Salem have revitalized and repopulated their downtown areas. Even Detroit, which never had a downtown residential area, is now making an effort to develop one.

Even in areas that have been known to roll up their sidewalks after dark, old warehouses are being turned into lofts for city dwellers who can't afford expensive apartments, town houses, or condominiums. Cities such as Indianapolis, Pittsburgh, and Columbus, Ohio, are starting to imitate Chicago's Printers Row, a section in what was recently considered a blighted neighborhood where converted lofts provide spacious living. Two companies that cater to this trend are Crate and Barrel and Restoration Hardware.

As more people move downtown, we can anticipate new businesses popping up nearby. After all, these new urban dwellers will require grocery stores, hair salons, entertainment centers, you name it. Facilities for child care and pet care, spas and convenience stores will take root. If enough people relocate, what once thrived only in the suburbs will soon succeed downtown.

Time-Savers That Don't Work

We know that people can save time by shopping on the Internet— but not for all products. Book purchases, for example, can be made via the Internet with ease. Amazon.com reports that the average order by businesspeople is more than double the average purchases at brick-and-mortar stores. We are told that executives order multiple copies of books at one time.

"It's so much more convenient than going to the bookstore," one CEO commented. "I just have my secretary punch up Amazon.com and charge books to an account already established with my credit card number."

This is how a busy person can save time on the Internet—and the type of product that works. When it comes to saving time, some products and services are better suited for the Internet than others, for example, purchasing airline tickets, making hotel reservations, and even buying and selling stocks. But items such as jewelry and furs that shoppers want to see and touch aren't likely to sell as well. Nor is clothing that must be tried on for size.

With $440 billion in annual grocery sales in the United States, several on-line companies are eager to sell food via the Internet. Peapod.com with 1998 sales totaling $57.3 million, is the leader, even though it lost $21.5 million that same year. Peapod's competition includes ShopLink.com, HomeGrocer.com, NetGrocer.com, and HighPoint.com. Of course, the big advantage of grocery shopping in cyberspace is that it saves time and also allows customers to compare prices and nutritional content. For certain products such as charcoal briquettes, canned goods, and toilet paper, the Internet appears to be just the ticket for time-starved consumers. But while it may be ideal for ordering stamps and filling prescriptions, it leaves a lot to be desired when it comes to buying tomatoes and bananas. The reason: most people want to pick their own fresh meat and fruit. They want to be able to squeeze a cantaloupe, and a banana that looks ripe to one person may look rotten to another.

While the average consumer visits a brick-and-mortar supermarket 2.2 times a week, fewer than a million U.S. shoppers have bought groceries on-line, industry figures show. One main reason is its cost. In Columbus, Ohio, for instance, where Peapod.com has teamed up with Kroger since 1995, its members can choose from three payment options: $11.95 for each delivery; a $4.95 monthly fee and $6.95 for each delivery; or a $24.95 monthly fee for unlimited deliveries of orders totaling $60 or more each. This service is particularly attractive to the disabled and the infirm, but that segment is rather small. It's also convenient for active, affluent customers, who can afford the additional cost. But there are still people out there who have to tap the melons and eyeball the meat they intend to buy. Because they find themselves still having to go to the supermarket to select their perishables anyway, these shoppers are unwilling to pay a premium to have their nonperishable groceries delivered.

The deliveries themselves are also problematic. Typically, a customer is told, "Your order will be delivered between noon and 5:00 P.M. Or would you prefer it in the morning, between 8:00 A.M. and noon?" Busy people don't have time to sit around waiting for groceries. Another potential problem is that perishables might be delivered to the door or the garage when nobody's home to store them in the refrigerator.

Of course, grocery ordering and delivery are as old as the corner store delivery boy. In New York, for example, members of the pampered crowd can have just about anything brought to them, including groceries. Still, a long list of grocers has tried and failed to fill grocery orders made by phone, fax, or computer. So while Web grocery shopping is now available, it's a rehash of an old concept that never really took off.

It's not just grocers; practically everyone is working overtime trying to come up with a way to tie in his or her business to the Internet. Note, for example, the recent proliferation of cybercafés. These coffee shops offer computers that are hooked up to the Internet, allowing their customers to "kill two birds with one stone." They can eat, sip a trendy beverage, and be on-line at the same time. Sounds like a perfect combination for time-pressed consumers, doesn't it?

One main problem, however, is that most people don't like the idea of eating and typing at the same time. According to Daniel Kite, the owner of three Screenz cybercafés in the Chicago area, "Coffee and food will get people to stay longer, but it won't bring them in." Food and beverage sales account for only 13 percent of his revenues.

Other cybercafés attempt to appeal to hurried businesspeople who might want to check their e-mail and portfolios over the Internet at lunch, but in fact, most diners don't want to be burdened with electronics while eating. Even lonely business travelers aren't very interested in going to a cybercafé because they're already exposed to so much Net access on the road. In fact, it's everywhere they turn: "They can check e-mail or surf the Web from their hotel rooms, the airport, or even the stationary bike in a health club."

Then, too, true technophiles, the people who live on the Net—the people who *would* want to surf the Web while they eat—often already carry notebook computers or portable Web devices.

Still another problem is that it takes a person with a fair amount of computer skills to dilly-dally with one in public. That's because the software differs from one cybercafé to the next, so rarely does it resemble what the consumer is used to. Do you see where we're going with this one? The market isn't as large as it first appears. So while in theory the combination of two of our favorite pastimes seems like a good way to save time, in practice it just doesn't work.

Remember all those do-it-yourself frame shops that popped up across the country a few years ago? Well, there aren't so many anymore. That's because although people saved money making their own frames, it cost them too much time to do so. Consumers got wise and realized that a store-made frame was only a little more expensive—and, for some customers, put together a whole lot better. When it comes to spending time to save money, most people are demanding in deciding which is more valuable.

Special Comforts for the Very Busy

"I'm bushed," people are saying. "No way I'm making dinner. The only thing I'm making tonight is reservations."

The problem goes beyond not having time. More people eat out because they come home exhausted. Even when there's time to fix dinner, they're just too tired. So indirectly, those long hours at work are taking a toll; people may be earning more and then spending the extra money on eating out. It's not just that eating out saves time; it also gives the cook a needed break.

That tired feeling we're hearing so much about has people shelling out their hard-earned dollars for comforts they formerly wouldn't purchase. They splurge on self-indulgent products and services to reward themselves for their hard work. Their rationale is not saving time but alleviating their exhaustion and restoring their energy. That way they can raise their tolerance for stress and reduce their fatigue. In early 1999, we looked at Christmas gifts husbands gave wives. Service gifts such as maid service, manicures, pedicures, and spa visits had increased from 4 to 8 percent over 1997 and 1998. While the total number is small, the increase is significant.

Today, we're seeing husbands plan short getaway vacations as gifts to their wives—practically unheard of in the 1980s. Single and married women are also treating themselves to long weekend trips in order to get some well-deserved R and R. A couple of days' pampering at a spa with facials, mud baths, and massage is just the ticket to make them feel like a million dollars—and ready for combat on Monday morning. Men are taking similar trips to fantasy sports camps, and both sexes are taking three- and four-day gambling junkets and cruises.

Cruise lines are cashing in by offering three-day trips for those who don't have time for a week out. Of course, the big attraction of a one- or two-week cruise is that, by design, it's time-efficient. Look at the timesaving features of a cruise: passengers can visit several exotic ports, sometimes five or six in a week. There's no checking into and out of hotels every day. Packing and unpacking and traveling by cab, bus, train, or plane to the next stop are eliminated. Instead, while passengers sleep, they sail to another tourist spot. How's that for efficiency? No wonder that in an era when time is so precious, cruises are so popular.

Time Is Money—Cashing In On The Trend

To cash in on this trend, anything you can do as a businessperson that saves time for your customers is right on the money. If you're in the retail business, this means having the right store staffing levels at high peak shopping periods so they can be there for your customers who need assistance. You need more than an adequate number of people on the floor to greet customers; you need well-trained, knowledgeable people who can answer questions, make suggestions, and solve problems. Not only does this make for a good shopping experience, it permits customers to make the right buying decisions—promptly. Misinformation delays your customers' decision-making process—and if you waste their time, they will walk out and not come back!

As a way of competing against the big boys, we recommend that small store owners employ high-quality employees who can cater to customers. While it's difficult to hire and train top salespeople, it's feasible when it's done one at a time—and on a one-to-one basis, personally trained by the store owner. This is an edge that small shopkeepers in a niche market can enjoy over their big national competitors.

Another way to save customers time is to have well-planned directional signage. This is critical for "big-box" retailers. Also, it is essential that the checkout counters run smoothly. Here too, people must be trained to operate the registers.

Finally, a company must service customers properly on the phone. We're sure you've had the frustrating experience of being put on hold when making an airline reservation or dealing with customer service over a billing error. The time spent pushing buttons to answer questions asked by a computer is enough to drive anyone up the wall! If you're one of those people who dread spending your precious time talking to a computer, make sure you don't subject your customers to this insufferable frustration.

The Gap Between the Haves and the Have-Nots Is Widening

The good news is that America has more rich people than ever. The richest 2.7 million, the top 1 percent, average $516,800 in after-tax income. The bad news is that this 2.7 million at the top have as much money as the bottom 100 million Americans. According to a 1999 analysis by the Center on Budget and Policy Priorities, a nonprofit organization based in Washington, D.C., each group has $620 billion to spend. New data just released by the Congressional Budget Office shows that the ratio of rich to poor has more than doubled since 1977, when the total assets of the top 1 percent matched those of the bottom 49 million. The study shows that the income disparity is so great that four of five households, or about 217 million people, take home a thinner slice of the economic pie now than in 1977. The average after-tax household income of the poor, adjusted for inflation, has dropped 12 percent since 1977. This means that America's poor are getting a smaller slice of pie while the pie itself is growing. Note that the income of America's richest households increased from an average of $234,700 in 1977 to $516,800 in 1999.

It's no wonder that the number of millionaires—households with a net worth of $1 million or more—increased from 3 million households out of 99 million in 1995 to 4.1 million out of 102 million in 1998. That's a jump of 36.6 percent in three years. In 1998, 275,000 households were considered very rich, each having a net worth of $10 million or more. This is a 44.7 percent increase since 1995. Comparing the haves and the have-nots in 1977 and 1999, the Center on Budget and Policy Priorities reported that the after-tax income of the richest 1 percent of the population rose by 115 percent while that of the middle-income group increased by 8 percent. Adjusted for inflation, the incomes in the middle were virtually flat over twenty-two years.

Not only are there more millionaires, but they're getting rich at a younger age today. According to a study by Professor Edward Wolff at New York University, of the heads of the wealthiest households in the top 1 percent by assets, only 0.7 percent were 35 years or younger in 1983. Today, in the year 2000, this age group totals 5 percent of the elite 1-percent-by-assets group.

Not all this wealth resulted from higher incomes; the stock market helped the rich get even richer. While the net worth of the nation's richest 10 percent grew, the remaining 90 percent of the population lost ground. The middle class in particular is overmortgaged due to consumer spending and home buying.

Since the rich had proportionately much more invested in the stock market, their net worth has grown by nearly 20 percent annually since 1989. The median wealth level in America (the level at which half of all households have more, and half less) rose to $54,600 in 1989 from $52,000 in 1983 and $36,200 in 1962, but it fell to $45,600 in 1995. It did, however, manage to rebound to $49,900 in 1997. All these figures are adjusted to 1995 price levels.

While the highest percentage of Americans in the history of our country now owns equities, most shareholders own less than $10,000 each in stock and mutual funds. Previously, their biggest investments were their homes, which since the 1970s had increased in value, often outpacing the stock market. But in the 1990s, home values did not increase, causing homeowners' net worth to shrink, and only in 1995 did it recover. Today, though home prices are up, mortgage debt and home equity loans have risen faster, further reducing homeowners' net worth. When consumers' spending goes up faster than their earnings, middle-level families must borrow or dip into liquid savings.

Whatever savings Americans do have are imperiled by hospital bills. In 1989, 33 million Americans under age sixty-five had no health insurance; by 1996, 41.3 million were without it.

In our September 1999 survey, 44 percent of Americans thought the middle class is disappearing. Forty-three percent think that the United States will eventually consist of haves and have-nots. Sixty percent think the rich are getting richer and the poor are getting poorer, and 54 percent think this is a dangerous trend. In summary, more and more people believe the American Dream no longer exists!

The Widening Gap: Danger Lurks

If America's rich and poor continue drifting further apart, here's what Americans believe will happen:

More crime	35%
More control for the rich	24%
More envy	14%
Class war: rich versus poor	9%
More social unrest	8%
Power in the hands of a few	5%
More racism	5%

While crime rates in general have declined, 89 percent thought the gap between the haves and the have-nots would increase violence. When a large majority feel they are excluded from privileges others have, riots may occur. Admittedly, this sounds alarmist, but history demonstrates that when the middle class is discarded, revolution occurs.

Such disparity is global; the inequality between rich and poor countries is vast. The United Nations has reported that 20 percent of the global population accounts for 86 percent of consumption.

In its annual Human Development Report in 1998, the United Nations said that global consumption doubled in the last ten years and increased sixfold in the last twenty years, and that Europe and North America now spend $37 billion yearly on pet food, perfumes, and cosmetics. According to U.N. figures, that sum would provide food, water, sanitation, and basic education for all those now without it, with $9 billion left over.

A child born in New York, Paris, or London will consume, pollute, and waste more in his or her lifetime than fifty children born in a developing country. But poor children are more likely to die from air or water pollution.

The United Nations says that the world's 225 richest people are worth more than $1 trillion—the annual income of the Earth's poorest 47 percent, about 2.5 billion people. In America in 1999, there were 268 billionaires, 79 more than in the previous year, making it the first year that more than half the *Forbes* 400 richest people are billionaires. Together, the four hundred have a net worth of $1 trillion—greater than the gross domestic product of China.

What About Wealthy Entrepreneurs and Entertainers?

No other period in U.S. history has experienced such enormous creation of wealth as the 1990s. While the gap between the haves and the have-nots has widened, so has the gap between the rich and the superrich.

At the top of the growing list of America's billionaires is Bill Gates, whose net worth, exceeding $100 billion, makes him the richest man in the world. What makes the 1990s superrich so different is that so much has been accumulated so quickly—by so many young people. *Fortune*'s September 27, 1999, cover story on the forty wealthiest Americans under age forty casts a bright light on the Internet era's unprecedented intersection of youth, technology, and serious money. Michael Dell of Dell Computer headed that list with $21.5 billion in assets. In last place at number 40, Gregory Reyes, CEO of Brocade Communications, owned assets worth $243 million. This under-forty group averaged more than $1 billion in net worth, with their median wealth in excess of $400 million.

What makes the *Fortune* list so interesting is how the path of the superrich has changed. It's no longer necessary to spend years climbing the corporate ladder. Decades of experience at a craft are not necessary, nor are polished people skills. You don't need a privileged background, well-heeled social contacts, or even a college degree.

Owners of Internet-related start-up companies don't account for all of the vast fortunes amassed in the 1990s. Some superstars in the entertainment field also have mega-incomes. In 1998, Jerry Seinfeld, the number-one moneymaking entertainer, earned $267 million for the sale of his television show's syndication rights. Other celebrities who earned big bucks in 1998 were Steven Spielberg ($175 million), Oprah Winfrey ($125 million), Tim Allen ($77 million), Michael Jordan ($69 million), and Michael Crichton ($65 million). Many more names appear on the list, including thousands of professional athletes, movie and TV personalities, models, authors, and so on.

Since most Americans put in long, hard hours for their pay, we wondered how they feel about entertainers who earn an average worker's annual income in just a few hours. For example, a star pitcher might make $3,000 for each pitch hurled toward home plate; a best-selling author might receive $20,000 for each written page; a major speaker might pull in $100,000 for a one-hour speech. In our 1999 survey, 61 percent of Americans did not resent such superstars—entertainers and professional athletes included— but 35 percent did, and 4 percent had no opinion. Of those with a grudge, only 22 percent consequently watch fewer sporting events.

When we asked about Bill Gates, 75 percent thought that he had earned the money and was entitled to it. Only 19 percent resented him, and 6 percent had no opinion. Likewise, only 39 percent thought that the stock market boom during the late 1990s caused too many people to get rich too fast. This seems to contradict the 60 percent who believe the rich are getting richer and the poor poorer. These numbers indicate that Americans are not currently concerned about the middle class disappearing but are saying, "I hope I can keep up!"

We concluded from our research that most Americans do not envy billionaires who create their wealth by founding companies and taking risks. Nor do they resent people who profit from special talents. Athletes, for instance, have a limited time to generate wealth before their bodies wear out. Depending on the sport, this might happen in their late twenties or early thirties. Likewise, models and actors often lose their beauty at a relatively young age and consequently their careers are ended.

According to the majority, the risk takers and entertainers are living proof that the American Dream is alive and well. And Americans don't want to lose that dream.

Greed at the Top in Corporate America

While most Americans don't resent fat-cat entrepreneurs and entertainers, they are offended when CEOs and other top corporate executives are compensated with huge salaries, bonuses, and stock options. In 1998, a William M. Mercer survey reported that CEOs' pay increased almost 30 percent over the previous year. The New York comptroller's office says that in the same year, Wall Streeters collected around $12 billion in bonuses, up 25 percent in 1996. For perspective, consider that the average white-collar worker got a 4.2 percent salary increase that same year. According to the AFL-CIO, back in the 1960s, the ratio of CEOs' to factory workers' pay was about 44 to 1; today it's more than 300 to 1.

As emphasized in Trend 1, America's workforce lacks discretionary time and complains about overwork and stress. A 1999 study released by the International Labor Organization disclosed that the number of hours Americans work each year is increasing in comparison to other industrial nations, where they are declining. This trend has put Americans in first place, in number of hours worked, at 1,966 hours each year, zipping past the Japanese by about 70 hours. On average, Americans work 350 hours, or about nine full workweeks, more per year than Europeans. And a 1999 study by the Economic Policy Institute reports that over the previous decade "the typical married-couple family with children put in 256 more hours of work—six additional full-time weeks—than it did in 1989." Consequently, America has kept inflation down because millions of workers are clocking 50, 60, and 70 hours of work each week, even though they're not receiving overtime pay.

For good reason, the nation's workers are steamed about CEOs and top management who are lining their pockets with seven- and eight-figure compensation plans. According to a 1999 study by the Economic Policy Institute, the annual income for the median American family was $44,468 (using the latest data from 1999, adjusted for inflation)—less than $300 above the 1989 figures. That's not much of a raise over ten years. The authors said, "The booming economy has thus far failed to lift the economic prospects of middle-class workers beyond where they were before the last recession. Despite their substantial contribution to the growing economy, wages for these workers have been stagnant or declining, manufacturing jobs are disappearing at an accelerated rate, and the share of non-college-educated workers with employer-provided health coverage has declined." Families faced with constant education and health care worries may well wonder what all the celebrating is about.

Jared Bernstein, a labor economist with the Economic Policy Institute and one of the authors of the report, said, "If you look at the business cycle over the last ten years, you will see that despite some positive results in the most recent years, folks are just about back where they started." He added, "When productivity is increasing on average, and workers at the middle of the wage scale—who certainly make a non-trivial contribution to that growth—when their wages are not keeping up with it, that's evidence of an unfair distribution of economic growth. And if it's not going to the middle, we know it's going disproportionately to the top.

"I look at it this way: If the pie is growing faster, then the bakers of the pie ought to get a bigger piece."

Workers aren't getting their fair share. What about investors? Graef Crystal, who edits a San Diego–based newsletter on executive compensation, conducted a study for *The New York Times*. Mr. Crystal looked at the performance of 383 large companies where the same chief executive had held office from 1993 to 1997. An investment of $100 in the stock of those companies at the end of 1993 would have grown to $202.20 four years later, for an annual return of 19.2 percent. If the pay of the companies' chief executives had risen at the same rate, their average compensation would have roughly doubled, from $2.78 million in 1993 to about $6 million four years later. In fact, according to Mr. Crystal's analysis, the executives' pay climbed 38.1 percent a year, to an average of $10.1 million.

In 1997, the nation's highest-paid CEO was Travelers Group's Sanford Weill, who received more than $400 million in total compensation. His salary was just a shade over $7 million; the overwhelming bulk of his gains came from stock options and the stock market. Travelers stock rose 25 percent in 1997, increasing the company's market capitalization by $38 billion. Was Weill worth so much money? Four hundred million dollars may seem like a bargain to some investors when compared to the $38 billion increase in market value. Consider Occidental Petroleum CEO Ray Irani, who in 1997 received more than $100 million in compensation even though Oxy stock was a so-so performer; its total average annual return over the last five years was 11 percent, compared with 23 percent for the Standard & Poor's 500-stock index.

In contrast, most shareholders would consider GE's Jack Welch a bargain. One of the recent great builders of stockholder wealth, Welch received just over $40 million in 1997, a year when his company gained $119 billion in market capitalization. Likewise, Intel's Andy Grove received $3.3 million in salary and total compensation of over $50 million in 1997, another bargain compared to the $13.5 billion market capitalization increase Intel enjoyed that year.

It's debatable whether any executive who's not a principal company owner is worth such a salary, because though he may create wealth, he does not risk his own. In a 1999 survey we conducted, only 22 percent of Americans believed a CEO's salary should double when a company's share price doubles.

Nonetheless, with the chasm between what CEOs receive and what employees and investors get, we were prompted to find out what America thinks about top management compensation packages. Our 1999 survey revealed that 65 percent think they are grossly excessive, 21 percent do not, and 13 percent had no opinion. When asked if any *Fortune* 500 company CEO should be paid more than $10 million, only 19 percent answered yes; 66 percent said no, and 15 percent had no opinion. When asked what they thought this group of CEOs should receive, 68 percent thought a total compensation package should not exceed $2 million.

While it's debatable whether CEOs who receive jumbo-sized compensation packages at companies making hundreds of millions and billions of dollars, there is certainly a strong case against dishing out this kind of dough to CEOs at companies that operate in the red. A case in point is what William F. Farley received during his fourteen years at the helm of Fruit of the Loom. From 1984 through 1998, Farley was paid $60.6 million, including salary, bonus, and the present value of his granted stock options. During the same period the company lost $247 million, and it filed for Chapter 11 bankruptcy in March 2000. In addition to the compensation package, Fruit of the Loom guaranteed $103 million in personal loans to Farley from 1994 to 1999. But that's not all. During his reign, Farley's private management companies charged in excess of $100 million in management and investment banking fees.

Any criticism of his pay, Mr. Farley says, is purely subjective. "People are free to say whatever they want to think about its adequacy," he said. "I think my compensation was fair and obviously the board did."

It was interesting to observe that the attitudes most Americans have toward professional managers do not extend to entertainers and entrepreneurs. True, it takes special talent to act, sing, or sink a basketball. But talent is also required to head a multibillion-dollar international corporation.

The Rationale for Exorbitantly High Pay

There are several reasons why major corporations shell out big bucks to CEOs and senior managers. One reason is to compete with other companies. If a company doesn't match the going rate, it risks losing its top people to another company.

There is also the "ego factor": if a CEO is paid less than his peers, his ego is bruised. Many companies in the Dow Jones Industrial Average, for instance, have pledged to keep their executives' pay well above the median of their peers'. For instance, Philip Morris's goal is to compensate its executives in the "upper quadrant." The same goes for Coca-Cola, while IBM shoots for the seventy-fifth percentile. American Express uses the third quartile as its reference point.

GTE's proxy states that the company's pay philosophy is to be 10 to 15 percent above "a median grant posture" of its comparison group for long-term incentive pay. From 1993 to 1997, GTE stock rose an average rate of 17.8 percent a year; the pay of chief executive Charles R. Lee rose an average of 75.8 percent a year, from $2.15 million to $13.35 million.

Options are sometimes used to motivate underperforming executives, and at other times to reward good past performance. But options used simply to keep an executive at par may have nothing to do with performance.

Just how are these pay packages determined? Generally, stock option committee members rely on the advice of a small coterie of compensation consultants. The problem is that the selection and hiring of these consultants are typically controlled by management itself. If executives do not agree with their consultants, they can replace them with others whose opinions are more in tune with their own. Obviously, consultants should be hired by the board of directors' compensation committee. Some believe that for complete effectiveness, the compensation committee should consist entirely of independent outside directors and be approved by the entire board.

While this may work in theory, independent board members are generally appointed by the CEO, who can also influence their removal by recommending other board members in the company's annual proxy report.

The Envy Factor

Envy among the affluent is a timeless theme, one that writers such as Jane Austen and others have examined. But it is exacerbated today by widespread media coverage of the world of business, and the proximity of new wealth.

Though most people don't begrudge Bill Gates his billions, it appears that high-wage earners are taken aback by the new super-rich who seem to have fallen into their wealth by being in the right place at the right time. Retired senior executives, for instance, see their replacements accumulate more wealth in a single year than they made during their entire careers. Attorneys see partners at major New York law firms pull in millions of dollars a year. And what about the enormous fees paid to lawyers for class action suits against the tobacco companies and others?

Imagine living in Silicon Valley where many of your neighbors, most of them under age forty, made millions of dollars in the last few years—and you didn't. The Internet capital in this community has made hundreds of lucky people independently wealthy for the rest of their lives. If you're one of the new millionaires in the area, life is beautiful. But you live across town and know you're as smart as those Internet employees. You're making a good living, but it's unlikely you'll ever accumulate that kind of wealth. Chitchat at cocktail parties goes something like "So-and-so got acquired, so-and-so bought a house." No one knows anyone else's bank balance, of course. But people do know the size of various IPOs and acquisitions, and, combined with a lot of semi-educated guessing, they can extrapolate a figure to envy.

One young Internet employee, not yet thirty, describes working in the Valley: "When you go to a company like this and see every motorcycle is a Ducati and see the rows of BMWs, and everyone has the Rolex, you realize people don't think of one million, five million or even ten million dollars as a lot of money. The scale is different."

Think about what housing must be like for Valley residents not affiliated with an Internet company. The average Santa Clara County home is $400,000, the highest in the country—and prices keep skyrocketing, faster than in any other metropolitan region in the United States. Flush with cash, high-tech people push the prices higher and higher. As a result, many professionals, including doctors, accountants, and lawyers, are being priced out of the Valley. Anyone who doesn't already own a house or doesn't have stock in an Internet company is at financial risk.

On a more whimsical note, a 1999 scientific survey taken by Yankelovich Partners for Adam & Eve, a North Carolina purveyor of adult-oriented magazines, videos, and paraphernalia, say that rich people even engage in more sex. They report that 61 percent of Americans earning $35,000 or less are sexually active compared to 89 percent of those earning $100,000 or more. Overall, 73 percent of those surveyed said they were sexually active, split evenly by gender. So much for the popular saying that money can't buy you love.

An Open Invitation to Unions

Back before unions, there was a pervasive us-versus-them attitude between management and workers. The segregation of white-collar from blue-collar workers was clearly intentional. Workers considered managers uncaring and callous. And managers felt that workers lacked motivation and took no pride in their work. They contributed their backs, never their brains. Little if any responsibility was delegated to workers, who understood what was expected of them and rarely did anything more.

When Henry Ford set up the first mass production lines, he employed mostly European immigrants who had difficulty reading English. There were many who spoke only in their native tongues. The Ford Motor Company operated on the premise that a few employees would do the thinking while the vast majority did as they were told. Ford was no different from most American manufacturers. Across the country, workers were treated as brainless, interchangeable parts. They received no respect from managers and in turn had no respect for their bosses. This adverse relationship, plus horrendous working conditions, was the breeding ground of unions, beginning in the coal mines of Pennsylvania and West Virginia.

Corporate America and the unions have learned from the past; in recent years harmony between management and labor has grown. Unions in most industries are far weaker than in the 1960s—today they represent only 13.9 percent of the workforce, down from more than 30 percent in the 1960s.

When workers feel polarized by management, they are attracted to unions. Management should know that such an environment invites labor leaders to unionize the discontent workforce. When the compensation paid to top managers is disproportionately high, workers feel cheated and morale suffers. Our studies show that 59 percent of Americans believe morale plummets when a CEO's mega–salary figure is announced. During the 1997 UPS strike, union officials were quick to highlight the $2 million salary of their CEO. The union made an issue of the colossal compensation package, making a strong case that these earnings had come at workers' expense. As you may recall, UPS was hiring part-time employees rather than paying overtime to full-time employees.

This survey also revealed that 40 percent of the people interviewed believed it's easier for a union to establish itself in a nonunion shop when the CEO is paid exorbitantly.

Advice to Corporate America

Knowing that such animosity is a problem, management should be more sensitive to this issue. Certainly, there are pros and cons to high salaries, and some people undoubtedly believe that certain CEOs' performances warrant big compensation. In particular, this can be justified when a company's market capitalization increases by billions of dollars. Considerable compensation is required to attract and retain people with the special skills needed to run a huge corporation.

We doubt this book will persuade many CEOs to downsize their paychecks, but we do suggest that companies communicate to their workforce why their CEOs make so much money. Most importantly, a company should communicate to its employees and stockholders how the compensation package was determined, especially if it was designed to meet certain company objectives. Likewise, we recommend releasing pertinent information regarding the company's outstanding performance over the previous period. In the case of Jack Welch, who accepted $50 million from GE the same year that the company's market capitalization increased by $119 billion, we think the bargain was fair. Nor do we think Jack Welch would be very easy to replace, a factor that should also be explained.

CEOs and senior management must spend less time in their ivory towers and more time walking the floors meeting their employees. Aloofness creates an adversarial atmosphere between management and labor. Senior managers must constantly communicate with their employees. They must listen to their subordinates and invite them to participate in decision making during a project's early stages. Employees who are involved in implementing change also support it.

Management must also recognize the constant struggle people endure between their hectic work schedules and their personal lives. Trend 1 is that the lack of discretionary time is a significant source of stress. To mitigate such pressure, management must make the workplace more flexible and supportive, and acknowledge that a rich, rewarding family life increases a worker's long-term productivity.

Our research shows that this management style works best in today's competitive workplace. When there is respect for employees by those at the top of the corporate ladder, it is reciprocated from the bottom. In such a caring environment, there is less ill will when CEOs and top executives are handsomely rewarded.

As discussed, many Americans respect the self-made wealthy, in part because they are risk takers. One CEO who has the respect of employees, shareholders, and the investment community is John Lauer, who in 1995 retired as president and COO of BFGoodrich. Lauer chastised U.S. companies for paying too much to their CEOs. Then he signed on as CEO of Oglebay Norton, a Cleveland shipping company that also mines and sells sand for industrial use. Lauer faced a dilemma: should he take the big bucks or practice what he preached?

"I can't write this doctoral paper, I can't believe this and have these kinds of values, and then the first crack out of the box go sell myself down the river," the fifty-nine-year-old Lauer said.

So when Lauer joined Oglebay in December 1997, he structured his contract so that he would receive no salary. He reluctantly agreed to accept a bonus if the company met certain performance goals. He also bought $1 million of the company's common stock out of his own pocket.

The Oglebay Norton board also granted Lauer options on 384,000 company shares, which he can buy from 2001 through 2005 at $38 a share, 20 percent higher than when he signed on. As of September 1999, the stock's fifty-two-week high price was $29.12; the low was $17.93. Three cheers for Mr. Lauer for putting his money where his mouth is. We hope other CEOs will follow his good example, and we wish him well.

Catering to the Affluent

Obviously, the creation of immense wealth provides opportunities for businesses that cater to such consumers. Everything from expensive jewelry to multimillion-dollar homes is selling at a record pace. America's affluent are spending thousands of dollars on top-of-the-line bicycles, luxury boats, private jets—you name it, the people who can afford the best are buying it.

As mentioned, you don't have to work for a start-up company to profit from the Internet boom. Real estate agents, custom home builders, swimming pool contractors, and interior decorators are obvious beneficiaries of the nouveau riche. So are the retailers of fine wines, whole-house sound systems, expensive cars, and sports equipment. In the service industries, everyone from travel agents to financial consultants is cashing in.

Never before have there been so many wealthy Americans with so many big houses that need tending. Consequently, there is a demand for household managers to manage homes for the superrich. Household managers in Manhattan command salaries of $60,000 to $120,000 a year. Schools to train such people are springing up in different parts of the country, they command tuition of around $7,000 for an eight-week course in the elegant care and feeding of the rich.

The demand for household managers is a result of the increase in the number of people who can afford a butler—it's estimated that as many as 55,000 households in the New York City area have a net worth of at least $10 million. The demand is also due to the growing number of large houses in America. When the Census Bureau began measuring home size in 1984, only 7 percent of new houses were larger than 3,000 square feet (often considered the size of the threshold for household help). By the second quarter of 1999, 17 percent of new houses were at least that big and many were much, much bigger, according to the National Association of Home Builders, whose surveys also show that the largest and most expensive of these houses are concentrated in the Northeast. Their owners are screaming for good help.

In New York, Washington, and Los Angeles, placement agencies that specialize in servants for the rich say that the demand for experienced household managers exceeds the supply. There are many people in America who are so wealthy, they can buy anything they want. There are literally hundreds of affluent communities across the country, from Aspen to Palm Beach.

On the flip side, there are also opportunities for those who cater to the have-nots. Most obvious are retailers of secondhand merchandise, such as pawn shops, resale merchants, and discount and off-price retailers that offer good value. Mass-marketing retailers that open large stores in the suburbs but neglect the inner city are missing a good opportunity.

There is a trend in the automotive industry that we find interesting: during the 1990s, cars lasted longer because Americans increasingly expect their cars to keep running a long time and shun brands that fail to do so. New-car buyers expect to resell their vehicles within several years for at least half of what they paid. As used cars become more reliable, they no longer carry a stigma.

One explanation of this trend is the rising income inequity: fewer Americans can afford new cars, while those who can afford them are choosing more expensive models, fully loaded. Affluent buyers increasingly demand compact disc changers, powerful engines, and other amenities. Dealers have begun to stock cars with every possible option, even though they are less affordable to the average buyer.

As the gap between the haves and the have-nots widens, we anticipate that others will profit as the have-nots buy what the haves sell or discard.

Henry Ford once said, "Poverty is not a man without a dime; it's a man without a dream." As a nation, we must make sure the American dream is attainable for everyone.

Community Involvement Enhances a Company's Reputation

Walk into most downtown areas and shopping malls across America, and you'll notice the absence of big-name department stores. In the 1950s in New York City alone, thirty-one major department stores thrived. This number has dwindled to just eight. Famous department store chains that have closed their doors are Allied Stores, parent of Gimbel's and Jordan Marsh; Associated Dry Goods, parent of Lord & Taylor and Joseph Horne's; and Carter-Hawley-Hale, parent of Neiman-Marcus and Broadway Stores. In Cleveland, Halle's is gone; in Washington, D.C., Woodward & Lothrop has closed; in Philadelphia, Garfinkel's and Wanamaker's have shut down; and in San Francisco, I. Magnin is no longer in business.

In their heyday, these department stores dominated their respective marketplaces. They reigned supreme, and their leadership was unchallenged. When it came to fashion, department stores set the trends. They were often the heart and soul of the downtown shopping area. Suburban shoppers and residents from surrounding towns made regular pilgrimages to these cherished establishments. These big stores were more than companies—they were institutions.

A department store's stalwart reputation was the force that lured customers through its doors. After decades of being first-string players, many grand retailers became complacent. Their competition, however, did not remain idle. The more convenient big-box stores, which specialized in electronics and appliances and were located in the suburbs, changed the complexion of retailing and became known as "category killers." Department stores were unable to compete in selection because they had less space and no room to expand. They were unwilling to lower their prices because these hard-line inventories yield low profit margins. For years, most Americans purchased their TVs and refrigerators in department stores. Big appliance retailers created a dilemma: customers could no longer judge the value of the entire department store based on the price of certain hard goods. With this barometer gone, they could not determine whether the store was a low-, medium-, or high-priced place to shop.

Customers who expected a department store to compete in this category became disillusioned. The "ideal department store" ceased to exist. Later, the big-box stores went into everything from sporting goods to books, offering a greater selection and better prices than the department stores. Department by department, the department stores lost their competitive edge.

Department stores also believed that no competitor could ever be more trendy and fashionable than they were. This, too, proved untrue. Specialty stores such as The Limited, The Gap, and Benetton entered the scene. Having their clothes manufactured in low-wage countries, they were able to knock off fashions at lower prices in a matter of weeks. Then large discount stores such as Wal-Mart, Kmart, and Target began proliferating in the suburbs and surrounding towns, and they undercut department store prices. Finally, when MasterCard, Visa, and American Express started offering perks to their cardholders, the department stores' credit card customer base, their core strength, disintegrated.

The well-established department stores began to fade, and a host of unfamiliar retailers sprang up across the land. Some have since become household names, such as Home Depot, Circuit City, Best Buy, and Office Max. The department store's drawing card—

its reputation—was diminished. Meanwhile, new retailers lined up and quickly became the in places to shop.

This same phenomenon also occurred in nonretail industries. Dozens of new companies have stepped into the limelight—Microsoft, Intel, and Dell Computer are all relative newcomers compared to old-economy companies. Some of the high-tech firms that have sprung up and flourished in recent years are now among the nation's most highly regarded companies. Americans have stopped evaluating a company based on its longevity, once a sign of stability and reliability. The criteria for measuring a company's reputation have changed. People are rethinking how they assess the integrity of a company.

Measuring a Company's Reputation

Companies with weaker reputations are less likely to get consumers' business. But, as we know, shady enterprises don't always fall by the wayside. Some people are willing to patronize them because of their low prices, convenient locations, better selections, and so on. A company's reputation was traditionally determined by its staying power. Some firms boast about theirs. We've all seen the signs: "Now in our 75th year," "Founded in 1918," "Family-owned for three generations."

Withstanding the test of time is interpreted as proof of reliability because it means that customers keep coming back. Certainly, this measurement has some validity, but many new companies are rising stars. Today, mature business must rely on more than longevity to stay afloat.

Reputation still counts, more today than ever before. Our survey shows that in 1987, 32 percent of Americans rated a company by its reputation. In 1999, 52 percent rated reputation as a very important component for why they gave a company their business. In twelve years, buying based on a company's reputation has gone up 60 percent—a huge increase.

In 1986, 46 percent of Americans believed that all or three quarters of a store's reputation was based on how well it handled returned purchases. In 1999, 70.6 percent were similarly influenced by a company's return policy. No longer is a company's age considered more important than its return policy.

In 1999, we asked, "Have you ever stopped shopping at a store where a friend had a bad experience?" Thirty-nine percent said yes, compared to 31 percent in 1990. This is nearly a 30 percent increase in nine years. When asked whether a store's reputation or its prices was more important, 50 percent believed that reputation was equally or more important. Our research also shows that an equal number of Americans consider a store's reputation as important as the merchandise it sells. In summary, our surveys indicate that people will always care about a company's reputation, but how they evaluate it has changed.

What's Good for the Community Is Good for the Bottom Line

In the mid-1940s, cartoonist Al Capp introduced millions of readers to the colorful characters of the comic strip "Li'l Abner." The comic strip featured Daisy Mae, Earthquake McGoon, Fearless Fosdick, and Evil Eye Fleagle, who all became nearly as well known as Li'l Abner himself. At the time, business magnates were stereotyped as self-serving and ruthless. Capp gave us the greedy, unscrupulous General Bullmoose, the nation's richest, most powerful man. His credo was "What's good for General Bullmoose is good for America!" Today, some leaders of commerce are also our top philanthropists. They recognize that charity not only benefits the community but also adds to their own bottom line. A modern-day General Bullmoose might be heard declaring "What's good for America is good for General Bullmoose."

For the record, we believe that most American corporations give generously to the community because it's the proper thing to do. We believe their hearts are in the right place. However, our 1999 research indicates that generosity is also very good for business. In fact, corporate giving ranked equal to or even higher than many more traditional things companies do to project a positive image. For instance, 56 percent of Americans stated that they would spend more with a company that was active in its community than with one that was not. An almost equal amount—55 percent—said they rate a company's charity involvement as an important factor when deciding where to buy. This is close to the 60 percent who praised a company that paid top salaries to its employees, which, in the 1980s, would have seemed far more important. Sixty-eight percent said it was very important for a company to hire locally, traditionally a critical factor in determining public opinion.

Our research disclosed what Americans think are very important community activities for companies:

Sponsoring their child's sports team	82%
Giving profits to local charities	70%
Helping needy children at Christmas	68%
Assuming leadership in a local crisis	61%
Having a college scholarship fund	57%

Other commitments that scored high were the following: (1) Being a major supporter of United Way: 46 percent; (2) Working the phones for MS/Easter Seals: 46 percent; (3) Hiring more minorities: 45 percent; (4) Having a leadership position in Rotary/Kiwanis/Lions Club: 42 percent.

What does all this mean? It demonstrates that, contrary to what some believe, *nice guys do win!* This research also confirms that time and money spent on community causes enhance the bottom line. The results of our study surprised us somewhat—in years past, community involvement wasn't even a consideration for patronizing a company.

What Was the Root of This Trend?

Americans' monitoring of corporate philanthropy is a recent development. We believe this trend began when federal cutbacks occurred after the Republicans gained control of Congress in 1994. It became apparent that funds for certain programs were dwindling or disappearing. Consequently, these programs' responsibilities had to be shouldered by another source—and corporate America stepped up to the plate.

Giving back to the community became important for the business sector, and businesses that assumed leadership were viewed favorably by the American people. Because so many companies look alike to outsiders, corporate giving became a new criterion in how consumers decide who gets their business. One recent survey revealed that stores in the same category look alike to 73 percent of consumers. Only one can get any given order; consequently, many consumers look closely at corporate giving as the tiebreaker when deciding where to shop.

The 1990s have been called the decade of "shopper share." Shopper share is a way of evaluating how many people walk into a company to buy something compared to how many people walk into its competitors. Say that 100 people go to buy a particular product. Twenty-five go to one store, and the store sells to 40 percent of them, or 10 customers. That store thus has a 10 percent market share, but started with a 25 percent shopper share.

We predict that this will be the decade of "consideration share." Consideration share is based on the percentage of shoppers who think about shopping at a store before leaving home. Today's rushed consumers usually have an exact place where they intend to buy a specific product. If a store is not on their mental target list, it has a serious problem. Consumers must be aware of a store before they leave home. A store is in trouble if they say, "I've heard of ABC Company, but I don't know enough about it to shop there." Having a high profile in the community is increasingly vital to attracting consumers.

Customers Care That Your Company Cares

We asked the specific question "Do you believe that a company active in community affairs takes better care of customers?" Seventy-eight percent of the respondents answered yes. Seventy percent ranked customer service as very important or most important in determining which company gets their business. In terms of significant attributes, respondents said a company's involvement in charities was:

Most important	9%
Very important	26%
Important	29%
Somewhat important	25%
Not important	11%

In other words, the average American believes that a company that nurtures its community will also look out for its customers. Does this make sense? Consumers think so, and we do, too.

To further gauge the value of community involvement, we asked consumers buying a $100 item if they would drive an extra ten minutes to a store that was a good corporate citizen. An astonishing 53 percent responded that they would. We were surprised that America's time-conscious consumers would go so far out of their way. We all know how important location is to a retailer. Yet when we asked consumers if they thought a store's reputation was more important than its convenience of location, 41 percent said yes and 20 percent thought reputation and location were equally important.

Benevolence alone is reason enough for community involvement. Our 1999 research proves that community involvement is not only virtuous but a great generator of revenue.

The Public Is Always Judging a Company's Actions

It's one thing for a company to talk about community involvement or its appreciation of customers and employees, but words alone are not enough. A company must continually be vigilant of its public image. A good reputation takes years to build but can be lost overnight.

This thought was on our mind when we asked the following questions in 1999:

Question	Percentage Who Answered Yes
Have you stopped shopping at a store where a friend had a poor experience?	39%
Have you stopped shopping at a store that sold pornographic magazines?	24%
Have you ever not purchased from a company accused of discrimination?	23%
Have you ever not purchased from a company accused of environmental wrongdoing?	22%
Were you less likely to buy gas at Exxon after the oil tanker spill?	22%

All of the above questions directly relate to a company's reputation—not a customer's firsthand experience. Notice that 39 percent said they would not shop a store if a friend was dissatisfied—an especially high figure considering that this was not a personal experience. The responses of 22 and 24 percent for the last four questions reveal that a company making just one bad mistake can be devastated by the ensuing bad publicity.

The Trust Factor

We asked, "Do you think that a company that is active in the community can be trusted?"

Yes	78%
No	15%
Don't know	7%

Every businessperson should pay close attention to these data.

A Good Place to Work

We believe that a company actively involved in the community enhances its bottom line because its employees become more productive and loyal.

An amazing 88 percent of the people we interviewed said they feel good about their company's community presence. Eighty-six percent claimed it made them more loyal. Eighty-eight percent say it's something they talk about with their family and friends. A whopping 95 percent boasted that their bosses' civic activities made them proud to work for the company. Only 15 percent of the employees we surveyed thought their company executives were too active in community affairs.

To recruit and retain good employees in a tight labor market, many companies should emphasize community involvement. Top job candidates are often already active in volunteerism, so working for a company known for its community leadership appeals to these people. By encouraging employees to serve the community on company time, the company saves them valuable discretionary time of their own.

Even shareholders of publicly owned companies favor giving back to the community. We asked, "Do you think companies are too generous with contributions?" Eighty-one percent favored American companies' altruism.

If you weren't already convinced that good corporate citizenship tips the scales, this research should win you over. Community involvement not only generates new customers, it also yields a more productive and loyal workforce. If General Bullmoose were around today, we think he'd be heading the local United Way campaign!

Get Involved!

It's hard to imagine that anyone who has read up to this point could remain passive about community involvement. This trend clearly shows the payoff. Our July 1999 research quantifies what we've long suspected: charity is a two-way street. By giving, the giver becomes a recipient, too. But a giver's motivation should stem from his sincere desire to help and not from his desire to profit. We believe it's always better to give for the right reasons; giving should come from the heart. Furthermore, Americans are savvy: they'll notice wooden nickels in the collection plate.

In the event that you have to explain your charitable activities to your shareholders, employees, or spouse, tell them about this research. When your company continues to give during tough times, it enhances the company's reputation. Stress to the doubters that in time it will generate revenue as well as boost morale and productivity. It's a win-win situation. The community wins, the company's employees and shareholders win, and the company itself wins.

These benefits apply across the board, from mom-and-pop operations to the *Fortune* 500. Whether you are just starting up or firmly entrenched, it's important to get involved. It's never too soon and never too late to start giving back to the community.

Even small entrepreneurs on a budget can make a difference. Don't forget that 37 percent of Americans think very favorably of companies that support children's sports teams. Put your name on your teams' uniforms, T-shirts, and programs, and put signs in your store to inform the public and remind your employees that you're the team sponsor. Remember, Little Leaguers are future customers. Of course, depending on what you sell, teenagers represent a major consumer group in their own right. And remember that

82 percent of parents whose children's activities are sponsored by your company say that they are more likely to give their business to you.

We recommend that you go beyond what's expected of a sponsor. Really get involved. Go to local games and wear the team colors or one of the T-shirts you had printed. Why not have a picnic or a pizza party to celebrate the end of the season? Take that extra step and supply trophies. Even if the team has a losing season, you can still recognize the most valuable player, the most improved player, the player with the best team spirit, and so on. Both the kids and their parents will love team sponsors that promote positive values of this nature. And they'll never forget you—or your company.

If you don't have much money to donate, donate your time and resources. For example, you might offer to chaperon a weekend scouting retreat. Donate your parking lot to the local Scouts' car wash one Saturday and pay them to wash your car first! Offer space in your warehouse or parking lot for the PTA to hold a rummage sale. Find space for the local hospital to conduct a blood drive or check customers for hypertension, or even have it bring in its mobile mammography unit. This is something every business can do regardless of size, in every small town and large city across America.

You can also make a contribution of your product or services. For instance, a restaurant owner might offer to serve as chef for a fund-raising event. He might donate the food as well as prepare it. Not only is this a good way of being philanthropic, it's a good way of promoting his restaurant. The people who attend the event are good candidates to patronize the restaurant because they experience a pleasurable meal the owner prepared. If preparing a several-course meal is beyond your budget, you can volunteer to make the dessert. Likewise, you can offer in-kind services to charitable and civic organizations by volunteering to do whatever it is you do: accounting, legal work, advertising, and so on.

If you own a small business, to keep from spreading your resources too thin, you might choose one charity each year to support—this way you can make a difference. You might want to select a high-profile local charity that sponsors an event such as the March of Dimes 10K Run and encourage all your employees to participate. Not only will this give your company some visibility, it will be a boost for employee morale. If a disaster happens to strike your locality, allow your people to volunteer their time (on company time) to the American Red Cross or another disaster service provider. You might also consider making your company a pickup point for the Marines' Toys for Tots program or a similar program in your area and encourage your employees to be involved.

If you want more alternatives, talk to any school principal or clergyman. There is always a need for a caring sponsor in the community. Or you can log on to the Web site www.helping.org. This is a nonprofit organization set up by America Online that provides names, phone numbers, and addresses of charities seeking volunteers in local communities across the country. There is no shortage of needs out there; people are crying out for you and your company to give a helping hand. There are dozens of wonderful organizations that can use volunteers, ranging from the American Cancer Society to your city zoo.

It's also important to invite your employees to participate. Allow them to be involved in your causes, and get involved in theirs. Encourage them to be active during company time when you can. You'll score points with your people as well as with outsiders.

In addition to being active in such organizations, you can give your support by running promotions where a certain percentage of sales goes to a specific charity. Our research shows that 70 percent of consumers are more likely to buy when a charity will benefit from their purchase. Seventy percent of the people who respond to advertisements of this nature believe the company fulfills its promise. Keep in mind that 53 percent of shoppers said they'd go ten minutes out of their way to buy from a caring retailer. According to a 1999 Cone/Roper Cause Related Trends Report, a national survey of consumer attitudes to marketing of causes, nearly two thirds of consumers say that when price and quality are equal, they would likely switch brand or retailer to one involved with a good cause. And 68 percent said they would happily pay more for a product associated with a good cause.

Of course, big corporations can also get involved in supporting the community—and in a big way. In 1999, Wal-Mart, which has mounted major programs aiding children, education, family issues, and local communities, was named by consumers as the nation's most socially responsible company, knocking McDonald's from a post it had held since 1993.

"We're particularly proud to have Americans recognize Wal-Mart as a good corporate citizen," commented David Glass, CEO and president. "It is even more heartening to know that Americans care that we share their concern for, and commitment to, the people and issues they face in each of our communities."

With its donations to worthy causes amounting to $127.9 million in 1998, Wal-Mart has found that its efforts are valued by its workers as well as shoppers. "It definitely boosts employee morale and also raises customers' feelings that we're giving back to the local communities we serve," said Laura Pope, a spokesperson. Almost all of Wal-Mart's charitable initiatives are managed locally by individual stores. "When we go into a community, we're part of that community. For the employees to be involved has a positive impact on them, not just the store," Pope said.

Wal-Mart and McDonald's, the world's number one retailer and the leading fast-food chain, head the list of socially responsible companies. Interestingly, they are also the world's most successful companies in their respective industries.

Recall that 78 percent of Americans believe that a company active in the community can be trusted. A company receiving bad publicity can often regain the good favor of the public by extraordinary giving.

Some business owners don't want to make a major commitment to their community because they're afraid that if lean times force them to cut back on contributions, their customers might desert them. Don't worry about it. American consumers are both smart and sensitive. They understand that a caring company in dire straits must protect its interests. Our surveys reveal that only 15 percent of Americans would be less likely to buy from a company that was forced to cut back on its contributions. In other words, once your customers are convinced you care, they will continue to care about you.

There Is a Growing Obsession with the Internet

You may wonder why we're including a trend about the Internet in this book. Unless you've been comatose, you've seen or heard literally thousands of news articles covering the Internet. On radio and TV, in the workplace, at lunch—everywhere you go, people are talking about the Internet.

But because the Internet is the biggest thing in commerce since the invention of the printing press, we can't exclude it. Those of us who use the Internet on a daily basis hardly recall life without it. Anyone lacking Internet skills must feel insecure these days. We predict that it's only a matter of time before those without Internet proficiency will be labeled illiterate. If your company is not already on the Net, you should do something about it immediately; otherwise, it's destined to go the way of the dinosaur.

Just how big is this trend? Consider this fact: the Internet is growing faster than all other technologies that preceded it. Thirty-eight years after radio came out, it had 50 million listeners. Television took thirteen years to acquire the same-size audience. The Internet hit the 50 million user mark in only four years. In 1994, only 3 million people were connected. By 1999, 67.5 million U.S. computers were on-line for a total of 92 million users, up 50 percent from the previous year. The numbers are increasing at such a rapid rate that by the time you read this book, many of our Internet numbers will be obsolete.

Eventually, Net service will be as common as phone service. The personal computer is less than twenty years old, yet 48 percent of U.S. households have at least one. Sixty-eight percent of American children live in a house with a PC. The percentage of schools with Internet connections zoomed from 65 percent in 1996 to 85 percent in 1998.

Additional multitudes will soon be sending e-mail messages from the new "smart phones" and personal organizers that are adding both e-mail and Internet functions. While many of us aren't familiar with these latest products, an estimated 2.4 million Americans owned one in 1999; that number is expected to jump to 7.7 million in 2003, according to Jupiter Communications. The e-mail devices look like souped-up beepers, with a large screen and tiny keyboard. Unlike simple two-way pagers, which have been around for years, these devices often work with corporate e-mail systems and include calendar and address-book functions.

Most impressive, in 1996, America Online members averaged only fourteen minutes a day on-line; in 1998, they were on-line for fifty-one minutes. According to Nielsen, those AOL minutes come at the expense of television: users say they're watching less TV. And AOL subscribers aren't techies—they're regular, slightly upscale folks who happen to own computers.

It's a New World Out There

A word to the CEO of Rip Van Winkle Enterprises: you have no choice but to go on-line. A plumber who is not on-line is on his way down the drain. Many people say they find e-mail so compelling that they lose contact with their friends who do not have it. If you do not understand that, you are probably already losing suppliers, customers, and job candidates.

Think electronic commerce is a niche market? Sure, the money's small today. E*trade is just a pimple on Merrill Lynch's nose—today. But just months after Merrill's executives derided Internet brokerage, they embraced it. Ninety-two million users is hardly a niche market. And what about the millions of students who are developing skills to meet the challenges of the era of Internet technology?

All one needs to do is look at the investment community, where a lot of smart people are betting their futures on the Internet. Huge investments by venture capitalists in high-technology companies are a clear sign that something big is going on. Consider the market value of Yahoo!, a company that has been public for three years. Its market capitalization has grown from $34 million to $27 billion— more than that of the entire U.S. steel industry. And Microsoft is worth more than General Motors, Ford, and DaimlerChrysler combined!

According to IBM CEO Louis V. Gerstner, Jr., the Internet has become "the ultimate medium for business." He predicted that consumers and investors will be dazzled over the next few years by the ways bedrock U.S. companies such as Ford, Wal-Mart, and First Union will harness the Internet. IBM already attributes 25 percent of its revenue to electronic business channels. Silicon Valley upstarts may be in the headlines now, Gerstner said, but ultimately the Internet presents a gigantic opportunity for established companies such as IBM.

Who's On-Line?

Everyone who can afford it. As computer prices have kept on dropping, the Web has become open to all. In 1995, 21 percent of Americans had computer access both at home and at work. Our July 2000 research showed that this number has more than doubled, to 52.1 percent. We found most impressive in this trend that nearly six times as many people spend time on the Internet than did two to three years ago.

We surveyed people to find out how they use the Internet in their homes. The five top uses are:

To get information	88%
To communicate via e-mail	76%
To improve personal skills	64%
To do work-related projects	51%
To learn about products before shopping	43%

Other areas of at-home Internet use include: purchasing items (33 percent); playing games with children (32 percent); helping children with schoolwork (28 percent); everyday banking (28 percent); investment transactions and stock purchases (28 percent); meeting people (23 percent). At the bottom, 14 percent have used the Internet to find a different job.

While the survey shows 28 percent helping their children with schoolwork, only one third of those surveyed had children. Of those who have children, 84 percent use the Internet to help them with schoolwork.

Adults employ the Internet for practical personal and work-related uses. Seventy-six percent of Americans think they are more efficient at their work because they use the Internet. They are watching less television, surfing the Web instead. Also, 41 percent said that they do less shopping the traditional way. When we asked if they plan to shop on-line more in the future, 40 percent said yes. To date, only a third of the population with Internet access actually purchase products on-line. These purchases account for only a small percentage of actual retail sales, but the percentages keep growing exponentially.

About 51 percent of Internet users at America Online are women, up from only 16 percent in 1994. In a 1999 Nielsen Media Research study, women made 29 percent of all Internet purchases in June 1998; by April 1999, they accounted for 38 percent. No wonder Internet companies are sprouting up to cater to women. One such company is Oxygen Media. Its founder and CEO is Geraldine Laybourne, the former head of cable television operations for the Walt Disney Company and ABC who pioneered Nickelodeon, the children's cable network.

"The traditional media have missed the boat with modern women," Laybourne stated. "There is nothing that serves women the way ESPN serves men or Nickelodeon serves kids. We want to create a brand on both television and the Internet that brings humor and playfulness and a voice that makes a woman say, 'You really understand me.'" It's estimated that 80 to 85 percent of total household spending is controlled by women, so capturing their attention and loyalty is essential.

According to a 1999 survey by NFO Interactive, women who shopped on the Internet said they planned to spend 20 percent more time on-line in the next year.

In the past year, the number of small businesses on-line increased by 17 percent to 3 million, according to Cyber Dialogue, a New York market research firm. "The real drama is not so much in the sheer numbers of new small businesses on-line but the growing dependence on being on-line," said Thomas E. Miller, the company's vice president. About 56 percent described the Internet as "essential" to the success of their business. Of the 33 percent who sold on-line, half said that their on-line sales were meeting or exceeding their expectations. And of businesses taking orders on their Web sites, the majority said their on-line operations brought in 23 percent of their total sales.

"In addition to selling on-line, entrepreneurs are comparison shopping for business suppliers on-line just like consumers, and nearly half of all on-line small businesses expect to save costs by using the Internet," said Cyber Dialogue's Mr. Miller. The most popular sectors shopped by small businesses offer computer products, office supplies, books and travel services.

Students use the Internet in school and at home, so it's no surprise that high school seniors are also researching colleges on-line. In a 1998 survey by Art & Science Group, a Baltimore college marketing consultant, 78 percent of 500 higher-ability students had visited individual college Web sites. That compares to 58 percent in 1997 and 4 percent in 1996. These sites provide information about curriculum, tuition, and other expenses, and even a virtual campus tour. Most schools offer substantial archives of photos or videos and even interactive chat rooms where students, faculty, and admission officers can advise recruits. Visits can be scheduled on-line, and sometimes applications can be filed on-line. (In 1999, the Massachusetts Institute of Technology did away with paper applications altogether.) Web tours allow electronic visits to schools when travel is too complex or expensive.

Internet activity isn't confined to working adults and students. Grandma and Grandpa are surfing the Web, too. In 1997, people over fifty were the second fastest growing group on the Internet, trailing only sixteen- to twenty-four-year-olds, according to Nielsen Media Research and CommerceNet. But the study found that the over-fifty group still accounted for only 17 percent of users. And only 25 percent of people over sixty own a computer, compared with 50 percent of those under sixty, according to Microsoft and the American Society on Aging.

Nevertheless, high-tech companies view aging Americans as one of the last largely untapped U.S. markets. With this in mind, Microsoft, Intel, and America Online are distributing instructional videos on computer use and sponsoring seminars and Web sites that cater to seniors.

As the baby boomers mature, the numbers of senior citizens on-line will climb. As the computer-literate age and have more discretionary time, they will find the Web ideal for communicating with children and grandchildren, shopping, tracking investments, you name it. A 1997 survey conducted by Media Metrix determined that PC users over fifty-five averaged 130.2 minutes per day, compared with 117.8 minutes for all age groups.

Why People Shop On-Line

Certain on-line advantages to both seller and buyer are making traditional brick-and-mortar retailers shake in their boots. Most obvious is a vast product selection that traditional retail outlets can't carry. For example, eBay offers more than 2.5 million items for auction at any given time and lists 300,000 items daily. Due to shelf space and inventory constraints, no retailer in the world could match its diverse choice of goods. In supermarkets, shelf space is so scarce that food manufacturers often pay "stocking fees" for their products. Considering that building and expanding physical stores is so capital-intensive, adding a new product generally means dropping an old one. In cyberspace, extra shelf space can be created effortlessly and inexpensively.

While a typical bookstore carries an inventory of about 40,000 books, Amazon.com, for example, offers all 1.5 million books in print in the United States. Even a Barnes & Noble or Borders superstore carries only about 150,000 titles. (Both retailers, however, have on-line bookselling operations.) The on-line bookstores also have access to more than 8.5 million hard-to-find and out-of-print books.

A record store generally carries about 9,000 titles and a record superstore about 60,000; CDnow.com offers 325,000 titles to its shoppers. Likewise, Beyond.com hawks 48,000 software titles, compared to a traditional retailer's inventory of about 2,000.

Trend 1 demonstrated that Americans with less discretionary time prefer to shop at their convenience, which they can do at on-line stores twenty-four hours a day, 365 days a year. There's no driving to the mall, looking for a parking space, standing in line, or coming home empty-handed.

With the rise of self-service retail stores such as Wal-Mart and Kmart and the demise of fully staffed department stores, Americans have become self-reliant shoppers. Even prestigious department stores have reduced their numbers of knowledgeable salespeople, and today's enterprising consumer is accustomed to making independent purchasing decisions.

In addition, few retailers can offer the point-of-purchase information available to Internet shoppers in search of superior selection and good value. For example, a customer can read *The New York Times Book Review* at barnesandnoble.com or, for that matter, download a music demo at Amazon.com. The information available to an Internet customer is virtually endless.

Net Sales

The total 1999 U.S. Internet retail revenues forecasted by the Direct Marketing Association totaled $11 billion, or about 0.2 percent of the nearly $3 trillion in sales rung up that year, up from $5.9 billion in 1998.

The percentage of total Internet sales to both consumers and businesses is expected to increase about 50 percent annually through 2004, whereas total retail sales are expected to grow only about 3.6 percent a year. So while Internet sales make up a minuscule percentage of total sales, their exponential growth rate is impressive.

What's selling on the Net? Obviously, some products are better suited than others. The first products that met with some success were computer-related: hardware and software for the "techno-elite." This was predictable since they were using computers to access the Internet. In 1996, Forrester Research calculated that gift items such as flowers and things the firm calls "boy toys"—PCs, pornography, CDs—made up slightly more than half of all on-line consumer purchases.

Investors have also turned to the Internet as a vehicle for financial information and trading. An early 1999 Gallup survey for PaineWebber revealed that 44 percent of on-line traders, or 15 percent of all investors, had invested in Internet stocks. By June 1999, 18 percent of American investors had traded securities over the Internet. Compare this with the total retail sales of all U.S. goods sold on-line, and it becomes obvious that trading securities is one of the Internet's hottest commercial uses.

The Internet is also revolutionizing the travel industry, giving travel agents a major headache. Today, many travelers bypass travel agencies when booking airline reservations, car rentals, and lodging. On-line travel sales totaled only $654 million in 1997, but Jupiter Communications reported that such sales represented 28.2 percent of total Internet travel sales in 1999, and that by the end of 2002 7.6 percent, or $12.6 billion, spent on leisure and unmanaged business travel will be transacted on-line. While saving money is the primary reason for making on-line bookings, there is also a powerful psychological benefit: handling their own reservations gives people a sense of control.

As mentioned, it's hard to beat buying books on-line. Amazon.com has an easy-to-use site and a hacker-free track record. With so many books at discounted prices and overnight delivery, why bother going to a bookstore? The on-line shopper is privy to the same information available in a retail store, and then some. With a click of the mouse, book reviews, readers' comments, and even authors' comments appear onscreen.

Practically any tangible goods that traditionally sell via catalog sell well on the Internet. There's no reason why an electronic photograph can't be the equivalent of a printed one. And when video is used to demonstrate a product on-line, it is superior to a print catalog. Some clothing retailers even have customer service staff who provide real-time sales assistance. Consumers can't interact with a catalog! Yes, they can call a toll-free 800 number to ask questions, but they can't see custom color combinations over the phone. On-line selling also has a cost advantage over catalog selling as postage costs for mailing catalogs escalates.

U.S. catalog sales came in at about $93.2 billion in 1999, up 9 percent from $85.2 billion in 1998. Combined catalog and Internet sales accounted for 3.5 percent of total retail sales in 1998. The Direct Marketing Association estimates that by 2004 the two direct marketing avenues will generate 6.3 percent of retail sales. An estimated 84 percent of catalog companies have Web space as well. Evidently, the industry's thinking: if we can't beat 'em, let's join 'em.

The reasons behind the Internet spending spree vary widely. Customers big and small like the convenience of buying on-line. When cybermarkets work properly, appointments, lines, and surly clerks become a thing of the past. Web sites, at least in theory, are always open and ready to serve.

Just about everything can be sold on-line. Products that must be fitted for size, such as apparel and shoes, are obvious exceptions.

Yet, once a cybertailor has your measurements, even custom-made garments can be purchased on-line.

The list of items being bought on-line ranges from watches to groceries to sporting goods, health and beauty items, and pet supplies. Even big-ticket items such as automobiles are being bought on-line. In a 1999 survey by J. D. Power and Associates, 40 percent of recent car and truck buyers had used the Internet to help them shop, up from 25 percent the previous year. The same report showed that more than twenty-five thousand purchasers a month had used an on-line buying service, twice as many in the first quarter of 1999 as in the first quarter of 1998. The percentage of new-vehicle purchasers using the Internet increased from 1.1 percent in 1998 to 2.6 percent in 1999.

One advantage of buying a car on-line is that there is no haggling with a salesman. A separate J. D. Power survey showed that 26 percent of those buying a 1994 to 1999 model in January 1999 used the Internet to locate and purchase a vehicle. It's believed that used-car buyers get a greater advantage from using the Internet, as they can find a specific model in the wider inventory placed with new-car dealers, used-car lots, auctions, and private sellers. Thus newspaper classified sections and other traditional media advertising used cars will be greatly impacted by the Internet.

Shopping to finance or refinance a home can be as trying as buying a used car. Loan officers can be pushy and rude and overwhelm buyers with paperwork. Nowadays, all a mortgage shopper need do is click on a home loan Web site to instantly compare the terms of several lenders. They can even apply on-line and hear from a loan officer within twenty-four hours. According to the Mortgage Bankers Association, more than three thousand lenders now offer e-mortgages, up from only sixty in 1996. While loans originated on-line are relatively few, the field is expanding so fast that the trade association estimates that by the year 2003, almost one out of every four mortgages will originate on the Internet.

There was a time when the sturdiest, most prestigious building in town was the local bank. Banks believed they had to project a strong image to make their customers feel secure. Times have changed. Faraway banks are now diverting their construction budgets to outsourcing companies such as nFront in Norcross, Georgia. It can build a full-service "Internet branch" for a bank from scratch in three months for $50,000.

Everything from antiques to baseball cards is sold at auctions on-line. There is a limitation: the customer is buying something that auction site employees have never seen or handled. Hence, the facilitators of a sale won't guarantee that consumers will get what they bargained for. All the same, eBay and uBid are plenty active.

In September 1999, bookseller Amazon.com repositioned itself as an Internet shopping bazaar, opening its popular Web site to merchants large and small for a minimal fee. The initiative, called zShops, sells 500,000 new products, almost quadruple the inventory of the average Kmart. Merchants pay $9.99 a month for space on the site and distribute their own goods. They pay an additional 4.75 percent of the total sale if they have Amazon process their credit card purchases. For another percentage, Amazon will let any merchant offer one-click shopping. Customers use credit information stored in the Amazon data bank to purchase through other merchants. Amazon charges the card and deposits the money directly into the seller's account. The seller is responsible for shipping and quality control.

Amazon's on-line mall will add a new dimension to Internet shopping, as its innovative search engine has the capacity to locate specific goods on the Net. Most existing search engines, by comparison, don't handle shopping queries well; for instance, "tennis balls" is likely to yield countless references to sports stories, fashion reviews, even obscure hits involving orthopedic medicine and engineering.

Brick-and-mortar stores are nervous about the Internet's encroachment, but people need such stores because of an innate desire for human contact. Shopping is one of America's most popular social activities. The Internet user's sterile environment can never satisfy this basic human need.

Business-to-Business

In the beginning stages of e-commerce, the excitement focused on retail sales, and little was mentioned about online business-to-business transactions, now referred to as B2B. Perhaps that's because it's not nearly as glamorous. Most of us can relate to the business-to-consumer market because we're all consumers. But as more and more coverage has been given to the business-to-business market, more and more people are realizing that this is where the greatest potential of business transactions is certain to be.

Manufacturers and merchants have found that on-line connections with consumers, on one hand, and corporate customers and suppliers, on the other, can expand their sales reach, reduce costs, and shorten reaction times. Some of the most decisive moves are being made in the auto industry, where once cumbersome supply chains are streamlined as never before.

It was the February 25, 2000, announcement made by General Motors, Ford, and DaimlerChrysler that set the world straight on the enormity of B2B potential. That's when the three huge automakers said they would combine forces to create a single Internet marketplace through which to do their buying.

The three automakers plan to eventually take their joint venture public, and, as for equity, some Wall Street analysts are already estimating that the Big Three's exchange could, as a publicly traded company, have a market capitalization of more than $30 billion.

Analysts say most B2B exchange revenue will come three ways: from recurring subscription and maintenance fees from participants, from a small commission on each transaction, and from equity stakes in the new exchanges. Together, the amounts should be huge.

Consider a few hypotheticals. Total B2B transactions are expected to rise from $145 billion in 1999 to $7.3 trillion in 2003, according to the Gartner group, a consulting firm. A cut of, say, 0.25 percent of that in transaction fees would yield nearly $20 billion in annual revenue, with much more growth to come.

"There is probably at least a trillion dollars in market cap up for grabs in the B2B industry," said Andrew Roskill, an analyst at Warburg Dillon Read. "At the end of the day, there are probably only going to be a few winners in each vertical industry sector, but those guys are going to command a very high premium."

Even in much smaller, out-of-the-way markets, the Internet is changing the face of commerce. Neoforma, a Santa Clara, California, medical supplies distributor, uses its Web site to reach remote customers, such as the government of Oman. In Lakeville, Massachusetts, Ocean Spray Cranberries uses on-line technology to give its growers faster, more reliable information about its supply needs and pricing policies.

Business-to-business e-commerce has virtually exploded. In 1998, businesses ran up $43.1 billion of Internet invoices with other corporations, according to Forrester Research. For 1999, the firm estimates that this figure leaped to $109 billion.

The firm projects that business-to-business e-commerce sales will skyrocket to $1.3 trillion by 2003—an annual growth rate of 99 percent! This is twelve times the sales it expects from the on-line consumer market. This $1.3 trillion figure pales in comparison to the Gartner Group's $7.3 trillion projected for B2B transactions in 2004.

Given this huge potential, companies known as "vertical portals" are entering the marketplace. These are characterized as "digital trade magazines with fat classified ad sections." These young companies have Web sites that focus narrowly on a particular industry: plastics, steel, even bull semen. They provide users with services such as news, research reports, a chat room, and e-commerce for similarly inclined colleagues.

VerticalNet, based in Horsham, Pennsylvania, operates forty-three different portals in the meat and poultry industry, and in bioresearch and solid waste. Many of its sites involve some kind of e-commerce by either auction or straight sales. One VerticalNet site is Water Online; cofounder Michael McNulty generated it while selling ad space to *WaterWorld*, a trade publication aimed at sewerage engineers. McNulty thought it made sense to offer a cyber-forum where engineers could discuss problems and get feedback, as well as bid on projects. With such a precisely targeted market, McNulty predicted that advertisers would shell out big bucks. He was correct. Water Online has 1,300 advertisers that each pay $6,000 a year. E-commerce fees are now yielding 5 percent of the company's revenues and are projected to make up 50 percent by 2002.

COW, the Cattleofferings Worldwide Web site, is another example of a vertical portal. At its beginning in 1995, COW provided mainly on-line classified ads for cattle. As an estimated 35 percent of U.S. farmers are now on-line, the time was right for COW to evolve into one of the first e-business sites to support real-time farm auctions. Entire lots of cattle are bought and sold via video feeds and downloadable images. Farmers can also buy chemicals, grain, and feed on the site. In 1999, the site clocked 40,000 visits a month.

Today, every American industry is represented on-line. Large corporations are using the Internet to build relationships with strategic partners. The business-to-business Internet market is making it possible for buyers and sellers around the globe who have never met to engage in business on a daily basis.

Superior Service

Whether business to business or retailer to consumer, many services are best delivered via the Internet. On-line retailers are better able to focus on customer needs. Traditional retailers can, at best, make only an educated guess at those needs and then try to accommodate the majority.

On-line retailers, however, can personalize the shopping experience for each consumer by gathering customers' profile information, tracking their movements through the site, and segmenting shoppers' preferences. This results in a huge pool of customer data that is unavailable to traditional retailers. In time, an on-line retailer can use these data to personalize each shopper's experience.

E-mail notifies a customer, for example, that a particular shipment has arrived that would interest her, based on her history of past purchases. Somebody who bought a computer within the past twelve months, for example, is a good prospect to buy a scanner or a faster modem. The proud new owner of an expensive set of golf clubs might be intrigued by a five-day travel package featuring major courses in Scotland. And a homeowner five years into a mortgage might be interested in refinancing when interest rates drop.

Through its inventory database, when a customer is cybershopping, a retailer can spot a specific customer who buys a certain style of clothing. The merchant can then let him or her know about an arrival of similar merchandise that's available at a special price. Or an on-line janitorial supply company can track order cycles to remind customers when they're running low on disinfectant.

Estée Lauder has had about 600,000 hits on its Clinique Web site, asking for information. The company e-mails a monthly newsletter with new product information and skin care tips. In March 1999, the company ran a multimedia promotion of its "Stop Signs Visible Anti-Aging Serum." The company mined its database and sent a product sample to every woman who had indicated on the site that she was worried about wrinkles or was over thirty-five. A few weeks later Clinique e-mailed sample recipients a sales offer. Good marketing and good service yielded about an 8 percent return on on-line sales.

One huge advantage Estée Lauder and other on-line retailers have realized is the low cost of communicating with customers by e-mail. They can literally contact their entire customer base by e-mail within minutes. They can upload coupons or rebate offers to test a specific market segment at a fraction of the cost of direct-mail postage or telemarketing.

Customers can also communicate with merchants faster and more cheaply. They can place orders, make inquiries, and voice complaints. An on-line company has boundless borders—it can do business all over the world. If you are a buyer, your selection of merchandise is greatly enhanced. And if you're a seller, you have virtually a worldwide marketplace in which to peddle your goods.

According to a 1999 study by Bizrate.com, a Los Angeles firm that tracks customer satisfaction in e-commerce, the level and quality of customer service most determined whether a customer returned to a particular merchant, beating out on-time delivery, price, and other concerns.

As on-line competition heats up, the winners will be the companies that provide the best service. This means that companies will still need to cultivate the human touch. Customers lured on-line with low prices and easy ordering still expect prompt, professional customer service. They want their orders filled on time, complaints addressed, and questions answered.

E-commerce is not all a bed of roses. At present, few companies with an Internet presence have perfected their Web sites. Nor are they providing an incredible shopping experience for their customers. Many glitches are causing problems, ranging from customers' having to navigate confusing, poorly constructed sites to getting hold of customer service when something goes wrong. Fulfillment problems are also commonplace. We have heard many complaints about slow delivery of orders as well as incorrect invoicing. There is also the problem of delivering merchandise to a customer who is not at home to receive it. Returning purchases is also a problem. For instance, what happens when Jon orders a book on-line and has it shipped to his mother in another state? What if Mom doesn't like the book or has already read it? How can she exchange or return it if there's no brick-and-mortar bookstore in her area? If she's not an Internet user, how can she communicate with the seller?

Web shoppers, according to Internet business evaluators Bizrate.com, most value return policies that include 100 percent money-back guarantees, no restocking fees (which can amount to up to 15 percent of a purchase if packaging has been damaged), free shipping and no advance authorization required. During the 1999 Christmas season, Extraprise Advisors, an Internet consulting firm in Boston, studied 50 well-known Web sites for their return policies. They examined 30 "click-and-mortar" sites, those with offline stores as well, and 20 "dot-coms," companies with no off-line businesses or partnerships. Seven of the 20 dot-coms that Extraprise studied required the consumer to pay for shipping, along with six of the 30 click-and-mortars. Of all 50 of the Extraprise sites, 13 didn't explicitly state their policies on-line, requiring telephone calls or e-mail for clarification.

Another concern about e-commerce is that so far, many companies selling on-line have been operating in the red. For example, Amazon.com sells some merchandise at low margins in order to lure customers. If the shopping experience and product line at Amazon are so compelling, why does the company continue to make such offers?

We're big believers in the Internet's future, but the combination of the brick-and-mortar with a strong Web site will ultimately win.

Coming Attractions

The Internet is still an embryo; compare it to the early days of television broadcasting, when for several hours a day all you could see was a test pattern in black and white. Live video on the Net is still quite primitive, but its availability to those equipped to view it is important. This technology will be perfected over time; we can only imagine the enormous impact it will have on everything from sales presentations to service calls in real time!

In a 1997 survey, adults and teenagers told us how they think people will make purchases in the year 2020:

	Adults	Teenagers
Shop in person	48.0%	40.0%
Shop via the Internet	44.8%	46.0%
Shop via television	38.6%	42.4%
Shop by telephone	37.2%	39.8%
Shop using debit/ATM cards	36.2%	32.2%

Even in 1997, shopping on the Internet ranked first among teens and second among adults in their forecasts of the future. Although we haven't conducted a more recent survey, it's certain that a higher percentage would predict that shopping on-line will prevail as the favored shopping mode of 2020. It's interesting that the perceptions of these two age groups are not far apart.

Today's Internet is the ultimate communication medium. Time zones are unimportant because messages travel around the clock, independent of what time it is where the sender or recipient is. Communications can be easily saved as data files or in print. Response can be efficient—and quick. Most attractive is that the Internet is cheap, very cheap—cheaper than long distance, cheaper than a stamp. And it's speedy. It's like comparing a bicycle to a rocket.

The United States has the jump on the rest of planet Earth because most computer programming has originated here. Most software is written first in English. As a result English has become the international language of e-commerce. Much like movies, music, and television, the Internet promotes American culture.

We've all heard about Japanese trade barriers. The Internet offers a crucial tool companies operating overseas need: a cheap toehold in the market to gauge how they might make significant inroads.

To date, the Internet hasn't had the effect in Japan that it has in the United States, mainly due to the high connection cost of a local telephone call. In 1999, about 14 million Japanese were on-line, but Access Media International, a New York Internet research firm, projects that 27 million will log on by 2001, with the volume of e-commerce jumping to 1 trillion yen ($8.5 billion) from 200 billion yen ($1.7 billion) today. This means that there will be opportunities for small and midsize companies that formerly avoided doing business in Japan.

The Internet is quickly edging out the telephone in communications. It's well accepted internationally, and far superior to telex, fax, and even voice mail. In the on-line job market in January 1998,

17 percent of *Fortune* Global 500 companies were actively recruiting on the Net, according to research firm iLogos.com in Ottawa. Just a year later, that figure was 45 percent. Forrester Research projects that employer spending on on-line recruiting will mushroom from $105 million in 1998 to $1.7 billion in 2003. An estimated 2.5 million résumés have already been posted on various on-line job sites, and at least 28,500 job boards, such as Monster.com, HotJobs.com, and CareerMosaic (which has a partnership with Fortune.com), bring employers and candidates together. Of course, bringing them together is only the first step of the hiring process, which relies primarily on human contact. But it's a very important first step.

These days, even old-line industries are realizing that cyberspace is crucial to their future. Few expect their chiefs to design Web pages or be power Web surfers. But they want leaders who recognize that a workable Internet strategy goes straight to the bottom line. As a consequence, all cutting-edge companies are placing a premium on hiring key people with Internet skills. We expect to see managers who lack these skills passed over for top-level positions.

At the other end of the spectrum, as PC prices fall and more adult children give "hand-me-up" computers to Mom and Dad, legions of seniors are signing up for computer and Internet courses. Hundreds of Web sites have sprung up catering to this market, with information on travel, retirement venues, health issues, and elder care. Once on-line, older computer users often become avid shoppers. One study found that over-fifty users were 30 percent more likely than their juniors to order goods and services over the Net. The varying content on seniors' sites reflects a basic fact: like users of any age, retirees mine the Internet for information on their own interests, sports, and hobbies.

Research clearly indicates that both young and old are on-line; women and men are equally active. Whether business-to-consumer or business-to-business, all visionary companies see the Internet as a valuable tool. Those with a wait-and-see attitude are certain to regret that they resisted change.

Even Amway, the direct-selling giant that prides itself on people-to-people selling, is going on-line. In 1999, the cleaners, cosmetics, and vitamins company formed a sister division, Quixtar.com, so its customers can shop on-line. In doing so, Amway joined the ranks of direct sellers Tupperware and Avon. As senior vice president Ken McDonald said, "We're going to have the ability to combine high-tech . . . with high-touch, which is what the independent business owners [Amway's million-plus distributors] provide."

Perhaps you're interested in investing in Internet companies but can't make up your mind where to put your money. If so, we recommend considering companies that serve Internet companies. These companies will piggyback on the success of Internet industry, so you don't have to pick a specific Internet company to come up with a winner. For example, UPS and Federal Express are two firms that should benefit by delivering packages purchased by on-line shoppers. Of course, there is a slew of companies that provide service to Internet companies, which include Agilent Technologies, a firm that specializes in providing enabling services to high-growth markets within the communications, electronics, life sciences, and healthcare industries. Akamai Technologies is another company that services Internet companies. One of its specialties is to help Internet companies prevent Web site crashes due to demand overloads. And then there's Research in Motion Ltd., a Canadian company that manufactures and designs wireless products for the mobile communications market. Included in Research in Motion's product line are wireless handheld e-mail devices that receive and send messages from the new "smart" phones and personal organizers. These devices sell for about $400, but users also have to pay a monthly service fee. Likewise, paper companies that make the packaging will profit. So will other companies that provide fulfillment, warehousing, and consulting services. Some consultants, known as "applications services providers," take existing technology and customize it to meet customer needs; they will also benefit from the Internet. If you want to invest in a technological provider to the Internet industry, you could put your money into a company that makes digital fiber-optic cable systems. And don't overlook the business-to-business Internet companies—in the long run, we believe they have more potential than retailers catering to consumers.

In conclusion, we like what Intel chairman Andy Grove has to say: "Today we are preoccupied with Internet companies. In five years that label will be meaningless because all companies will be Internet companies." He adds that the Internet-based marketplace "is causing a huge re-engineering of business. It is doing to commerce in the 1990s what Japan's quality and just-in-time practices did to the manufacturing industry in the 1980s. It matches buyers and sellers, so that buyers can become infinitely informed without ever talking face to face."

We agree with Andy Grove that the Internet will be an important tool for every company. To make sure your Web site is current, you must stay ahead of the competition, and this means always being considered state of the art. If it takes bringing in outside experts to get you there, so be it—bring them in! Remember, too, that people use the Internet to get information; with this in mind, make sure your Web site provides clear, accurate information. And don't forget, the Internet has a strong appeal to young people—they're the ones most likely to use it. So focus on young people—they are the future.

When the day comes when everyone is doing business on-line, the most successful companies will be those that do it best. Their sites will be superior in providing information about such things as security, return policies, and shipping costs. The sites that fail will be those that make shopping a chore because of poor organization. As usual, the cream will rise to the top.

American Companies Can't Expect Employee Loyalty—They Must Earn It!

Gone are the days when people always bought the same make of automobile, voted a straight party ticket, or spent a lifetime working for the same company. These days, Americans expect to have five or six different jobs during their working lives.

In years past, an employee who was disloyal to the company that paid his wages was akin to a traitor or an unfaithful spouse. Then, in the mid-1990s, came corporate downsizing, massive layoffs, rightsizing, reorganizations, and mergers and acquisitions, and American workers emerged with a different attitude toward their employers. As thousands of companies frantically restructured to cope with their slipping market shares, they tore up the old notions of paternalism. People got the message: Don't plan on a one-company career anymore. Acquire all the skills you can. Prepare to change jobs, employers, even industries. Forget about loyalty. If you don't take care of yourself, no one else will.

Corporate America continued to proclaim, "People are our most important asset." But its real message was easily read between the lines: "People are also our most expendable asset." Clearly, downsizing and rightsizing fundamentally altered the employer-employee relationship. Job security is a thing of the past. In their zeal to be efficient, corporations devalued the human spirit. Workers who have remained on the payroll feel lucky to have a job, even if their workload has increased by 50 percent. Employee loyalty became the proverbial baby thrown out with the corporate bathwater.

Continual restructurings, even in boom times, sap morale. Layoff announcements—and the fear they generate—have a profound effect on a workforce. What's worse is that top management thinks it's doing a better job, while employees' views of management deteriorate.

Not long ago, most people were wary of leaving a job, whatever its faults. They had too much at risk, such as seniority and benefits. But the recent era of prosperity and low unemployment changed all that. Now, for the most part, people do not lose their jobs; their jobs lose them.

In November 1999, the Labor Department reported that unemployment had fallen to 4.1 percent, the lowest in nearly thirty years. The following January, it dropped to 4 percent. Unemployment for adult women fell as low as 3.5 percent, the lowest since 1953. The pendulum has swung in the other direction. No longer can a company expect an employee's loyalty simply because it signs his paycheck. Loyalty must be earned. And in this booming economy, employers are hustling to figure out how to retain good people. They know how expensive turnover is because recruiting and training are so costly. With turnover near 20-year highs, companies are pouring millions of dollars into efforts to increase employee loyalty. The payoff is clear: Replacing an employee costs roughly 1½ times a year's pay. Also, companies with highly committed employees tend to post sharply higher shareholder returns, says a Watson Wyatt Worldwide study. In addition, low morale saps productivity, and discontented employees are less likely to go the extra mile for customers.

It was estimated that at the end of 1998, there were at least 350,000 job openings nationwide for programmers, systems analysts, and computer scientists and engineers, according to Virginia Polytechnic Institute and the Information Technology Association of America. According to the association, by the end of 1999, one of every ten information technology jobs remained open.

Consequently, stock options are becoming a big recruiting tool. Fifty percent of junior technical employees now have stock options, up from 35 percent in 1997.

To seal a deal, recruiters may offer overseas airline tickets, increased vacation time of four to five weeks for starting employees, or eleventh-hour signing bonuses as high as $20,000. Other perquisites now seem commonplace: many employees are allowed to redesign their offices, work at home, dress casually, or even bring pets to work.

Why Employees Are Less Loyal

To determine why employee loyalty has declined, we asked, "What is different in 1999 that has made you less loyal?"

Company doesn't let me know what's expected of me	40%
Management has changed	20%
Opportunities for advancement are fewer	18%
Company doesn't treat me as well	14%

It's not surprising that 40 percent are confused about what their company expects of them. The problem goes beyond poor communication. Some confusion can be attributed to management changes. With mergers and acquisitions as well as cutbacks in management, subordinates feel less secure about what's going on in the executive suites. They begin to think there are fewer opportunities for advancement. And why shouldn't they, especially when middle management positions have been eliminated? Workers are not only unsure about whom they report to, they see fewer rungs above them on the corporate ladder.

It should come as no surprise to downsized companies that their remaining employees feel dumped on. Had management rewarded them amply for taking up the slack, they might feel differently. Instead, workers feel threatened, believing that if they don't keep apace, they will be the next to go. Similarly, seeing their peers get the boot is demoralizing, especially as top management's bonuses have been padded with the recouped salaries of those laid off.

Management changed the rules. Workers were stunned when American companies did whatever was necessary to survive and succeed: shutting down plants, eliminating layers of management, and relocating manufacturing far away in South America or the Pacific Rim.

Meanwhile, the U.S. economy has flourished due to technology that has maximized efficiency. In fact, many companies now get a lot more from employees who work the same hours. This greater productivity has enabled companies to keep their prices down and still remain profitable.

To put the entire blame on corporate America would be unfair. It is human nature to resist change, and the nation's workforce is no exception. Advances in technology—in particular, technology that alters job descriptions—are threatening to most people. This form of change makes people feel powerless. Furthermore, today's technology changes so quickly that people feel they can hardly keep up—and they worry that they will ultimately be replaced by a machine. As we know, this fear is well substantiated. Technology determines which U.S. companies will live or die. It also determines the fate of each individual in the workplace.

A fifty-five-year-old worker may resist retraining. What should an employer do with such an employee? From a company's viewpoint, the best decision may be to buy him out. A younger replacement will be trainable, will probably accept a lower salary, and certainly will have fewer accrued benefits.

The message to America's workforce is "Keep improving your skills." Those who have seniority may see this as treasonous. Fourteen percent of those we surveyed feel that this is mistreatment. In today's competitive workplace, however, no one can remain idle. Standing still is tantamount to moving backward.

In the same survey, we followed up by asking people why they are less loyal to their employer today. The top four reasons:

1. **My wages don't keep up with my standard of living.** People resent seeing the CEO and other senior managers receive exorbitant compensation while their own salary does not keep pace with inflation.

2. **My responsibilities have increased because coworkers were discharged by the company.** People who stayed aboard said that downsizing meant additional work for them, as they had to replace the output of workers who were let go. Hence, they feel overworked and underpaid.

3. **My company does not reward performance and recognize long-term employees as it used to.** People don't feel appreciated anymore.

4. **My benefits are less today than they were.** People complain that company benefits have been reduced. In particular, health insurance has a higher deductible and fatter premiums, and HMOs are hostile service providers.

Our survey reveals that average Americans are not content with their jobs; nor are they the loyal employees their companies would like them to be.

The New Loyalty Paradigm

Just as companies have taken stock and taken responsibility for doing what's right for business, employees have asked, "What's in it for me?" That's fair enough. In a tight job market, workers can afford to be more opportunistic. It's understood that the idea of a company taking care of employees is dead. People realize they must take responsibility for their own professional and personal needs, for developing their skills and balancing their work with their interests outside the office.

A new American employee has evolved. No longer do workers bank on sharing their employer's good fortune. Lifetime employment is a thing of the past—no longer expected, also no longer desired. Today's worker is a free agent. Jobs are easy to come by; if one doesn't work out, there's always another one around the corner that might even pay more.

Nowhere is this more evident than in Silicon Valley where quitting has become so fashionable that the turnover rate for companies there has reached an estimated 25 percent a year. The average 32-year-old American has already worked for nine different companies. Workers today fantasize not about landing a "dream job," but about having a "portfolio career"—one dream job after the other.

Today's employer offers something to the employee and vice versa. It's a fair and honest exchange. The company offers a good working environment and a competitive wage. The employee gains skills and job marketability. Both parties benefit from the exchange. But the relationship is impersonal.

The new notion of loyalty is more arm's length. "The company is responsible for providing the environment in which people can achieve their full potential, and employees are responsible for developing their skills," says Raymond V. Gilmartin, CEO of Merck. "That's the key to our ability to attract and retain talent, and it defines the new employment relationship as I see it today."

Perceiving that employees no longer "mate for life," some companies apparently feel little obligation to them, even during good economic times. This myopic view can come back to haunt a company, especially in a tight job market. When a company's employee loyalty is low, it doesn't take much for somebody else to steal away its people. And turnover is costly.

What It Takes to Take a Walk

What would it take for another company to hire one of your employees away from you? In our 1999 survey, we first asked people if they would join another company for the same pay and benefits. Twenty percent said they would. If the salary was the same but benefits were better, 34 percent said they'd leave. And if pay was better but benefits were the same, 46 percent said they'd leave.

Then we asked how much more salary would another employer have to pay them to leave. The results were as follows:

At a Salary Increase of	Percentage of Employees Who Would Leave Their Present Employer
0–5%	12%
6–10%	20%
11–20%	32%
21–30%	16%
31–50%	15%
51–75%	4%

Note that 32 percent of all employees would leave their current job for a salary increase of 10 percent or less. Sixty-four percent would leave for 20 percent or less, and for 30 percent more, a company could hire away 80 percent of a competitor's employees.

The bait doesn't have to be big, which tells us two things: (1) Americans aren't terribly loyal to their employers, so it doesn't take much to lure them away. (2) There's more to winning Americans' loyalty than a paycheck.

What Makes Employees Loyal

If you think loyal employees are valuable, so far this trend is a real downer. Don't despair, there is hope. Our survey also reveals four things a company must do to instill loyalty among its employees. In order of importance, we were told:

1. Give raises. When in doubt, pay on the high side. Chances are you'll get your money's worth. Having a reputation as the employer paying the best wages is okay. Also, reward your people with raises—it's good business. Raises should be tied to performance. One way to accomplish this is to pay a base salary with a year-end bonus to those who performed exceptionally well. To be effective, a compensation incentive plan must be executed carefully.

2. Give special recognition. Everybody likes recognition, so acknowledge people when they perform well. We all respond to praise; pour it on when it's deserved. We could write a book on how to do this. Special attention can range from a pat on the back to a banquet in Hawaii. Feature employees in a company newsletter and give awards at company events; public praise is an outstanding way to let people know you appreciate them.

3. Say thank you. If you're way up the ladder, you can never thank good employees enough. It's so easy, and it doesn't cost you a penny! It's hard to imagine a boss who doesn't express gratitude. But we all know there are a lot of them out there.

4. Give promotions. When people deserve promotion, give them their due. High achievers crave advancement. Good pay notwithstanding, it's challenge and the ensuing success that motivate many. Successful companies elevate their star performers. Furthermore, good people won't stick around if there's no room to move up—instead, they move elsewhere!

A hefty raise is the best way to induce loyalty among employees. Note, however, that it's only one out of four ways of earning loyalty that is money-related.

We also asked the question with a different twist: "Why are you loyal to your company?" The response to this question was:

Good working environment	90%
Good pay	89%
Good fringe benefits	82%
Supervisor/CEO listens to me	70%

Just look at the importance of a good working environment: while pay is important, if employees don't feel comfortable, it's hard for them to be loyal to the company.

We also learned that 65 percent of all U.S. employees believe their company is a good corporate citizen. Only 22 percent said their company was not, and 13 percent didn't know. In Trend 3, we discussed how community involvement enhances a company's reputation. It also enhances employee loyalty. In the same survey, 65 percent appreciate their company having a mission statement. Most said they felt their company lived up to its mission statement. It seems that employees are loyal to companies that do the right thing. It confirms what we believed all along: doing the right thing is good for business.

Employees admire companies that communicate where they stand. Many companies claim to prize trust, life balance, employee development, and other lofty goals, and they enumerate them in policies and value statements. But a company must walk the walk. When its stated values clash with its actions, its employees will become cynical and disillusioned, and morale will suffer. If you're going to announce your company's values to your employees and the ensuing world, be sure you mean what you say. Be committed— and show it. Values, or deeply held principles and beliefs, can be powerful motivators that, when shared, form a foundation for corporate culture.

Corporate America did not score well when we asked, "Do you feel profits are fairly distributed to employees?" Forty-five percent responded no; 41 percent said yes; 14 percent expressed no opinion. Again, it's Trend 2, the widening gap between the haves and the have-nots. When top management appears to receive unreasonably high compensation, employees become disgruntled.

Employee Loyalty and the Bottom Line

If the biggest paycheck won employee loyalty, the company with the deepest pockets would have all the best workers. Fortunately, there are other ways of attracting and retaining good people.

As noted, people want a good work environment. This goes far beyond plush offices and mood music. It means treating people with respect, regardless of their rank. It means listening to what they have to say and inviting them to participate during the early stages of new projects. Good leaders share their vision. When companies inform their employees in advance of where they want to go, management's dreams become their dreams and they are given direction.

Another way of showing employees they are valued is by investing in their education and growth. At brokerage firm Edward Jones, which ranks number eleven on *Fortune*'s 1998 "100 Best Companies to Work for in America," new brokers are sent to seventeen weeks of classes and study sessions at a cost of $50,000 to $70,000 each. "We consider training an investment rather than an expense," explains Don Timm, a principal at the Saint Louis company. "If we don't prepare our people well, we have not served them." At many companies, the best employees clamor for education and training because they realize it's a prerequisite to promotion—at their present company or some other. We discovered that companies that don't invest in their employees may lose them to another company that will.

Here's what *Fortune* revealed about the 1998 "100 Best Companies":

SAS Institute (No. 3): The company offers a thirty-five-hour workweek, company-provided child care at $250 a month, a free on-site medical clinic, and twelve holidays a year plus a paid week off between Christmas and New Year's.

MBNA (No. 6): When a child is born or adopted, the company contributes $2,500 toward the child's education.

Ingram Micro (No. 68): Former chairman Jerre Stead maintained his own twenty-four-hour toll-free phone line—and yes, he personally answered calls from employees.

Lenscrafters (No. 61): The company's Gift of Sight program donates thousands of pairs of glasses to Third World countries. Each year, each employee receives a free eye examination and a free pair of glasses.

Herman Miller (No. 87): The company's annual report includes all company employees' names.

Honda of America Manufacturing (No. 90): Every new employee has a tree planted in his honor on the company grounds.

Applied Materials (No. 92): The company cut executives' pay by 10 percent when it announced layoffs in 1998.

Notice that some of these are relatively small or inexpensive policies. Not everything has to be pricey to be appreciated.

Employers must be willing to shed old ways. You may consider making flextime the norm. According to the Texas Transportation Institute, auto travel in Los Angeles takes 51 percent longer during rush-hour traffic. On an annual basis, that's an extra eighty-two hours a year! Think what this would mean to those employees so strapped for discretionary time!

Fortune's 1999 "100 Best Companies" also cited some unusual perks:

- **American Century:** Every employee gets a $650 ergonomic chair.

- **Capital One:** Vacation days are available on half-hour notice.

- **CDW:** When CDW became the world's No. 1 reseller of computers, everyone got a free three-day trip for two to anywhere in the continental U.S.

- **Eli Lilly:** All Lilly drugs (including Prozac) are free.

- **Pfizer:** All Pfizer drugs (including Viagra) are free.

- **Intel:** Eight-week sabbatical is available after seven years.

- **MBNA:** Employees get a limo on their wedding day, plus $500 and a week of paid vacation.

- **Microstrategy:** All employees go on a one-week Caribbean cruise in January.

- **Qualcomm:** If your kid plays on a sports team, Qualcomm will kick in $250 of support.

- **Rodale:** You can have your own gardening plot on company land.

On the principle that it takes many attractions to retain the best, dozens of companies are also generously distributing so-called soft benefits, according to human resources surveys. These comforts promote the elusive work/life balance that is every bit as important to hardworking employees as the job itself. Hence the proliferation of seemingly frivolous perks such as on-site haircuts, shoe repair, and free breakfast. In reality, this frees up time ordinarily allocated to errands and chores. This free time can be devoted to family—and work.

Physical fitness centers and day care are always welcome, but how about dog care? The American Board and Kennel Association estimates that of more than 8,500 kennels nationwide, 500 specialize in day care. And that means far more than a cage, a bowl of chow, and a rubber ball. Centers may offer massages and baths, swimming lessons, off-leash exercises, even pedicures. For employees who think of their pets as family, day care is vital to their pets' mental health. As one dog lover put it, "Imagine what goes on in the mind of a puppy that's in solitary confinement all day." Consequently, don't be surprised to see companies offering pet care. Will it build employee loyalty? We think so.

What else boosts employee loyalty? Having fun. Ken Alvares, who runs worldwide human resources at Sun Microsystems (No. 69 on the 1999 *Fortune* list) said, "Our goal is to keep people so busy having fun every day that they don't even listen when the head-hunters call." It's working: Sun's turnover, at 11.6 percent, is about two thirds lower than the competition's.

Sun is onto something. Fun is not frivolous anymore, if it ever was. Interim Services, a Fort Lauderdale–based temporary staffing company, and Louis Harris and Associates recently identified 1,006 "peak performers" in U.S. companies. They asked those star managers what kind of workplace they'd be most reluctant to leave. Fully 74 percent said, "One that promotes fun and closer work relationships with colleagues." Over and over again, people at the "100 Best Companies" talk about how much fun they're having. "This is just a great bunch of people—very comfortable, very team-oriented. Just coming to work in the morning is fun," said Joyce Chung, director of business development at Adobe Systems (No. 56) in San Jose.

Perhaps nobody is better at promoting fun than Southwest Airlines. When the company's CEO, Herb Kelleher, hires employees, he looks for three things that he considers a must: enthusiasm, a sense of humor, and a great attitude. Southwest encourages laughter and fun, and it hires only individuals who are able to laugh at themselves. Southwest people have fun:

- *At the ticket counter.* You might be asked to take off your shoes and count the holes in your socks. The person with the most holes gets a drink coupon for the flight. Or you might be asked to take out your wallet and count your credit cards. The person with the most credit cards gets a coupon for a drink.

- *On the plane.* The pilot might announce, "We have a little problem. It's nothing to worry about, but our plane will be delayed due to a small problem. Our automatic bag smasher is broken. So we are personally smashing all your bags by hand on the tarmac. Please be patient."

- *In a pilot's announcement.* Another pilot might say in a child's voice, "Hi, my name is Bobbie, and I'll be your pilot today. We're going to go real high, and real, real fast, too."

There's a story about a passenger who nearly missed his Southwest flight. While the aircraft waited, flight attendants stuffed the smallest crew member into an overhead compartment above the nearest unoccupied seat.

Finally, down the aisle came Mr. Late Passenger. When he opened the overhead compartment to store his briefcase, the flight attendant looked down at him and asked, "May I take that for you, sir?"

Southwest employees are considered among the most loyal in the U.S. workforce. Why? They enjoy themselves at work. Incidentally, Southwest has a twenty-five-year history of profitability. Who says you can't have fun and make money at the same time? The good news is that any company—big or small—can emulate Southwest.

Equally important is for employees to have a sense of purpose. Everyone wants to make a difference. Companies that enable people to feel they contribute meaningfully generally retain their employees. People want to go home feeling good about themselves at the end of the day.

We think every company with at least twenty employees should have a newsletter. It doesn't have to be elaborate; a two-page photocopy will suffice. It's an inexpensive way to communicate with employees and a great vehicle for acknowledging their achievements—and what better way than before their peers and family? Small-business owners should consider a newsletter that makes everyone feel like a family member rather than an employee, featuring birthdays and hire dates and announcing events such as births and weddings. When interestingly written, such newsletters are read word for word. Be sure to mail copies to employees' homes so their families can read them, too.

It all boils down to showing employees that the company cares for them. Every time a company stretches a little, people appreciate it. We heard about one company that has a part-time, on-site psychologist who counsels employees with personal problems. Furthermore, it's on company time. How do employees feel about this service? One summed it up: "I love this company because I don't feel like a piece of equipment here. It's a good feeling to work for people who truly care about me." We learned that the company shells out $25,000 annually for this service. But its employee turnover rate was 8 percent, less than one third its industry's norm.

Interestingly, in today's tight job market, many companies are complaining that workers are not available to hire. However, this is not a problem for all companies. The typical 100-best company on

Fortune's 1999 list had 5,125 employees. It added 646 new jobs in 1999—and received 16,829 job applications! Evidently, companies with super reputations have no problem attracting people. So in addition to enabling the company to attract the cream of the crop, having a reputation for being a great place to work also reduces the high cost of employee turnover.

In a similar approach, Marriott International offers a twenty-four-hour, toll-free hot line manned by social workers who assist employees with almost any problem: how to maintain a budget, how to handle a child's expulsion from school, what to do if their house burns down. The hot line costs about $1 million annually. But it saves Marriott about $4 million in absenteeism and turnover.

As mentioned, employees are motivated by their company's involvement in the community. We recommend their involvement, too—on company time. We know of one advertising agency that allows its people to donate pro bono services to local charities. The company gains a loyal employee; the community benefits, too.

If it's not in your budget to be a major philanthropist, don't despair. Generosity takes many forms. We know of one retailer that closes one day a year; all employees spend that day working for a charity of their choice. Spouses and children are invited to participate; it might involve sprucing up a playground or remodeling a senior center. Later that evening, a dinner is held for everyone where employees are recognized for their achievements during the year, including their community involvement. A tremendous amount of camaraderie evolves from doing this.

How to Profit from This Trend

One obvious big winner with this trend is the temporary employment industry. The demand for temps has never been so high. Reflecting this demand, in November 1999 temporary workers totaled 3.1 million, or 2.4 percent, of America's 129.3 million employees. Few other groups of workers have grown as rapidly in the 1990s.

When employees leave for better positions, the temp agencies are frequently called to fill the vacancy. It's difficult to replace permanent workers quickly in today's shrinking pool of available help. Many companies are so desperate for workers that they hire temps and keep them for extended periods. This means substantial fees for temp agencies.

Never before have temps had it so good. Companies treat them with tender loving care, because unhappy temps easily find work elsewhere, and temps who perform well are ready-made candidates for permanent hire. Here's what some of *Fortune*'s 1999 100 Best Companies are doing for their temps:

- Wegman's, a supermarket chain based in Rochester, New York, provides college scholarships.

- Starbucks offers full benefits to employees who work as little as twenty hours a week plus stock options—as well as a free pound of coffee every week.

- Merrill Lynch offers health insurance to employees working as few as eighteen hours a week.

- Federal Express makes part-timers who work as little as seventeen hours a week eligible for health insurance.

We know of one company that provides used cars and trucks for its high school temps so they have transportation to and from work. This same company also gives college scholarships to promising hires. One of its first employees to graduate night school is now a supervisor—and a dedicated, loyal employee.

Another resource for labor-strapped employers is older workers. Why not? Today's seniors are healthier and living longer. Our life expectancy today is seventy-six years, or eleven years past the traditional retirement age of sixty-five, and those who have already reached age sixty-five can expect to live well into their eighties. Employers who have tapped this resource say that these workers have a strong work ethic that is often missing among younger employees. "You can depend on them to show up on time," said one employer, "plus they're courteous and eager to do a full day's work."

According to the Social Security Administration, 92 percent of Americans sixty-five and older receive monthly Social Security checks; 41 percent receive pension benefits from an employer. Some work because they want to supplement their incomes. Others work to remain active and involved. If you plan to add seniors to your payroll, keep in mind that most of them want part-time work, no nights or weekends, and the flexibility to take several minivacations during the year. Don't expect someone who signs up to work twenty hours a week to be willing to put in forty.

To tap into the senior workforce, you'll have to be creative in your hiring process. You're not likely to find seniors registered at a temp agency. Nor do they regularly read help-wanted ads. Many aren't actively looking for work but will jump at the right opportunity. For this reason, we recommend networking. Ask your employees and customers if they know anyone who might like to work part-time. Make suggestions: "How about your dad? What about an aunt or uncle? Or your grandpa?"

Also try recruiting at places where seniors are active and energetic, such as bingo parlors and churches, even physical fitness facilities.

While we're on the subject of recruiting, we recommend that companies spend a lot of time interviewing job candidates and carefully selecting those individuals who are "good fits" with the corporate culture. This requires spending extensive time with each prospect—no easy job, but in the long run it will pay big dividends because it will reduce turnover. In Silicon Valley, an area known for its high turnover, Calico Commerce, a maker of software products to help companies sell products over the Internet, understands how this works. Calico has made a concerted effort to seek out employees considered likely to fit into its culture, placing a premium on recruiting graduates directly from college or business school.

Calico, a startup company with 330 employees that went public in 1999 and saw the price of its stock fall 80 percent in the spring of 2000, has experienced a turnover of only 12 percent. That's impressive considering the high rate of turnover in Silicon Valley, where stock options are widely used as carrots to recruit and retain employees.

Calico also fosters an atmosphere of openness. Young companies often share more information with their employees than bigger, older businesses; the gulf between management and the rank and file tends to widen over time. CEO Alan Naumann realizes the value in being open with employees. He shares lots of information with employees, holding monthly company-wide meetings to discuss where Calico stands in relation to its competitors and its internal goals. In addition he hosts a monthly group breakfast for employees who have birthdays that month and solicits feedback from the group. That level of disclosure and communication goes a long way in building loyalty.

Obviously, it's a good time to work for a temp agency or a headhunting firm. If you're looking for a good business idea, you might consider starting a seniors' temporary employment agency. We think it's a good niche. There's a demand for temps and a large supply of senior citizens to fill that demand. Also, publicly traded employment firms are also worth investigating as an addition to your investment portfolio.

Speaking of investments, consider checking out *Fortune*'s "100 Best Companies" for 1999. The total annualized stock market return for the 49 companies on the list that have been public for ten years compares well to the S&P 500. These companies averaged a 37 percent return over the past three years compared to the S&P 500 averaging 25 percent. Their five-year return was 34 percent compared to the S&P 500 average of 25 percent. And their ten-year return was 21 percent compared to the S&P 500 average of 17 percent for the same period. This confirms that a loyal workforce is good for the bottom line.

Employees' creativity and inspiration can be tapped by rewarding them for money-saving suggestions. When an employee suggests an idea that saves the company $100 a month in copier paper, the bright employee can be rewarded with a cash award. If it's a suggestion that saves money year after year, the employee can be given an annual bonus for the duration of her employment. The company wins a loyal employee and encourages the participation of other employees.

One perk that keeps gaining popularity is the company physical fitness center. A recent survey of 1,544 employers nationwide by William M. Mercer, a consulting firm based in New York, found that 41 percent of large companies (those with more than 750 employees) had fitness facilities.

Such facilities are not only good for morale, they will also contribute to a company's bottom line. When a handful of progressive companies began building gyms for employees in the 1970s, it was viewed as a kind of philanthropy by a benevolent employer. More and more, it's seen as good business to promote fitness and defuse stress. Studies suggest it trims medical costs by keeping injury and illness down.

In a study published by the President's Council on Physical Fitness and Sports, Phoenix-based exercise physiologist Larry Gettman reviewed a number of cost-benefit analyses and found activity programs saved $1.15 to $5.52 for every dollar spent. Dr. Gettman, a director for clinical analytical services for McKesson HBOC, a pharmaceutical-supply management and health-care-information-technology firm, says he found less absenteeism among active workers, and "less absenteeism means you're more productive."

A company can also win employees' loyalty by making sure its customers receive good-value products and services. This will also be good for its employees' self-esteem, which in turn will give them pride in their work—and it will show up in the quality of their workmanship. Medtronic, a Minneapolis-based medical products company that manufactures pacemakers, excels in this area. Each year, the company invites six people with pacemaker implants to an annual gathering attended by its eight hundred local employees. The implant guests address an audience of Medtronic people and tell them how their lives have been improved by the pacemaker. Patients' doctors are sometimes present to explain complicated medical procedures. Medtronic employees leave knowing that their jobs are saving lives and benefiting *real* people. Hence they are motivated to do good work to fulfill their mission. Your company doesn't have to manufacture a life-saving product to accomplish what Medtronic does; having customers speak to your employees about how they benefit from your product or service can be equally inspirational. Incidentally, Medtronic also made the list of the hundred best companies to work for in America.

As discussed in Trend 3, employees also derive immense pride when their employer gives back to the community—especially when they're also involved. Slumberland, the number-one retailer in the twin cities, gives away a thousand mattresses to the needy each year around Christmastime. Slumberland employees participate: they deliver the mattresses to families in need, so they witness firsthand how recipients appreciate the company's benevolence. As we mentioned earlier, when people are proud to work for a company, it shows in the quality of their work.

Studies show that there is a direct tie between employee loyalty and customer loyalty. Research by Mercer Management Consulting confirms that this tie is seen best when customers and employees interact, particularly in management consulting, financial services, casinos, and telecommunications. The clearest evidence of this interaction is the ripple effect created when a valued employee leaves. In a dramatic example, when a popular dealer changes casinos, many high rollers leave, too. We suspect this is because of the personal relationships that have formed. Thus many customers' loyalty is to an employee, not to a firm.

As a rule, we have found that most companies focus solely on either employees or customers, one at the expense of the other. Company A, for instance, may be sales- and marketing-driven, while Company B is driven by human resources. For maximum effectiveness, a company must integrate the two to ensure the loyalty of both employees and customers.

On a final note, the simplest advice and easiest to implement to create employee loyalty is: *be nice.* That's right—just be nice to your employees. Being a tough guy might have worked a decade ago when corporate America was downsizing and laying off workers by the millions. But that era, exemplified by Albert J. Dunlap, the roving chief executive nicknamed Chainsaw Al who boasted about how many people he had dismissed to raise the stock price of his companies, is over.

The American workplace has evolved to a kinder, gentler state. With unemployment at a 30-year low, bosses realize that they have to do more than pay good salaries and offer lavish perks to their employees if they want to keep them. They also have to be nice to them.

And now comes a Gallup Organization study that shows that most workers rate having a caring boss even higher than they value money or fringe benefits. In interviews with two million employees at 700 companies, Gallup found that how long an employee stays at a company and how productive she is there is determined by her relationship with her immediate supervisor. "People join companies and leave managers," said Marcus Buckingham, a senior managing consultant at Gallup and the primary analyst for the study.

In a 1999 survey of 2,293 employees by the Hudson Institute, 56 percent said their company does not care about their careers. In the same survey, a nearly equal number—55 percent—said they do not have a strong loyalty to their company.

In another 1999 survey by Spherion and Louis Harris Associates, 40 percent who rated their boss's performance as poor said they were likely to look for a new job. Only 11 percent who rated their boss's performance as excellent said they were likely to look for a new job. The same Spherion study revealed that the odds were that people who felt negatively about their bosses were four times as likely to leave as those who liked their bosses.

Some old-economy companies are training managers in the art of benevolence. Macy's West, a division of Federated Department Stores in San Francisco, recently began a pilot program of assigning mentors to new managers and telling all management that up to 35 percent of their compensation would be linked to how well they retained the people under them. Consequently, the policy has encouraged managers to be more accommodating to employees' needs. Other companies are also pushing their managers to be friendlier. An International Paper plant in Moss Point, Mississippi, holds morning training sessions on positive reinforcement. As a result, one manager who used to hover and watch for mistakes and as a compliment would offer a pat on the back or a curt "good job," has cut back on the criticism and become more effusive in his praise. He even writes an occasional thank-you note to an employee for an exceptional performance. He also chats with workers more than he used to.

We think being nice should be expected in the workplace; unfortunately, however, many managers have long forgotten how to treat employees warmly and need to be reminded. Trust us on this one, being nice pays big dividends.

Evidence demonstrates that employees are loyal to caring companies. Show your people that you care about them, and they'll respond by caring about you.

Consumers Are Reluctant to Pay Full Retail Price

Years ago, if your Uncle Jack owned a store, you had it made. That's because when you needed a new mattress or a dishwasher, you could get it wholesale from Uncle Jack! He was such a good guy, he'd give your friends and even their friends the same deal. Never mind the high overhead; Uncle Jack claimed he was giving it to them at cost. How did he do it?

"I lose money on every sale, but I make it up on volume," Uncle Jack explained.

For better or worse, the Uncle Jacks of this world have disappeared. They wouldn't have a chance in today's marketplace. True, they survived the full-line department stores, but those little hole-in-the-wall storefronts would be no match for today's discounters. With the discounts that even traditional department stores now offer, Uncle Jack would be left in the dust.

Those of you who had an Uncle Jack can probably still hear him moaning, "How can they sell it below what I pay and still make money?"

The truth is, back in the old days, it was such a hassle to buy from Uncle Jack that many of us were willing to pay full retail price. That's because Uncle Jack rarely had the right color or size. He didn't deliver, so you had to borrow someone's station wagon or truck to pick it up. And if something went wrong, you were stuck. Uncle Jack always said up front, "If you have a problem, I don't want to hear about it."

The good news is that you don't need an Uncle Jack any more. Today, you can just head to a discount store, an off-price department store, or an outlet mall. Or, for that matter, you can see what's on sale at your downtown department store. Practically any week of the year, there's a sale going on!

The Demise of the Department Store

As we discussed in Trend 3, the grand department stores dominated their respective marketplaces for years until they lost their competitive edge. These majestic stores possessed three major advantages over other retailers. First, with several hundred thousand square feet of floor space, they were the original big-box stores. They were located in the center of the city, most often on a prime downtown site. In such a big box, a store could offer many products. Second, these stores were perceived as trendsetters, particularly in apparel. A certain amount of prestige was associated with wearing a Bobbie Brooks outfit from Bloomingdale's. Third, each store had its own charge card, ensuring a loyal customer base. The charge card was—and still is—a powerful sales tool. In some product categories, our research shows that when a person has a store credit card in hand, 90 percent of the time that store will be the first one shopped. Once in the store, 80 percent of store-credit-card-holding shoppers will buy something if they can find their size.

The downtown department store still occupies the biggest box in town, but modern-day big-box stores have considerably more floor space per category.

Specialty stores such as Victoria's Secret, The Gap, and Old Navy have stolen the edge from department stores. They can copy and deliver the latest styles overnight—at lower prices. Thanks to MasterCard, Visa, and American Express and their frequent-buyer programs, the shopper no longer needs a local department store charge card. Some department stores had begun to offer perks to their cardholders, but by then it was too late—their best customers were gone.

Our July 1999 survey asked American consumers: Do you shop at department stores, where you'll pay a higher price? Only 40 percent answered yes. In the early 1980s, practically everyone did.

Who Shops for Discounts?

Our 1999 research showed that more than 85 percent of all consumers in America shop for merchandise on sale. Over the past ten years, this number has increased by 36 percent, up from 62.5 percent.

When we asked those who pay full retail why they do, 44 percent said they didn't have time to shop. Their second reason was that they couldn't find a specific product on sale. Generally, these were high-end electronics not carried by mass merchandisers. These shoppers represented 29 percent of those who paid full price. In a distant third place, 15 percent said they shopped at full-price stores out of loyalty to the merchant. And finally, in fourth place at 10 percent, were those consumers who thought discounted merchandise was of inferior quality.

What we found so interesting about this research is how it relates to Trend 1, Americans' lack of discretionary time. This shows that many consumers feel their time is more valuable than the money they'd save shopping for bargains. They're willing to trade money for time—to them, time is money! Interestingly, their second reason—not finding a specific product on sale—gave them no choice. If they wanted a particular product, they had to buy it at a store that didn't offer a discount. It was a matter of "take it or leave it." For instance, a bride-to-be might register Waterford crystal as a wedding gift, and her friends *have* to pay full retail. In some respects, a person who doesn't have time to shop is in a similar position. She can buy it now at full price or not buy it at all.

The Luxury of Time

Time seems to be a significant factor in so many different areas of our lives today. Our survey asked consumers how much additional time they were willing to spend shopping in order to save $50. They responded as follows:

15–29 minutes	35%
30–44 minutes	24%
Less than 15 minutes	18%
45–59 minutes	11%
1–2 hours	9%
More than 2 hours	3%

Thus, 59 percent said they'd spend fifteen to forty-four minutes of their time to save $50. After a certain point, people don't think the time is worth the savings. Or you can look at the 53 percent of Americans who will take only up to twenty-nine minutes of their time to save $50, but no longer. Then we asked what was more important: saving time by shopping closer to home or saving money by driving further? Fifty-eight percent answered that saving money came first; 42 percent said saving time. We concluded that more people would shop around to get a discount if they had the time.

According to our survey, 64 percent of consumers think paying full retail price is a waste of hard-earned money. Likewise, 43 percent said that finding an item on sale is like "finding money." Evidently, they agree with Ben Franklin that "a penny saved is a penny earned."

When we asked if they shop less at discount stores during a better economy, 89 percent answered that good times didn't alter their shopping habits. Eighty-five percent informed us that they become even bigger bargain hunters during lean times.

These responses indicate that American consumers want to make their lives easier. They are not making frivolous buying decisions; they are carefully thinking things through before they spend their money. This is reinforced by the fact that half said they've stopped shopping earlier for Christmas gifts, even though they will face larger crowds later on. Fifty-seven percent of those who wait until closer to Christmas do so because they know the retailers offer greater discounts as the holiday approaches. In years past, department store sales always took place several days or even weeks after the first of the year. Now some stores begin their sale the Friday after Thanksgiving, and as Christmas approaches, prices keep dropping. American consumers have watched this pattern for years, and they are willing to wait in order to realize bigger savings.

Why Consumers Buy on Sale and Where They Shop

The number one reason Americans dislike paying full retail price is that they think prices are too high. Fifty-seven percent of discount shoppers expressed this opinion. In addition:

- 82 percent said they knew the item would be on sale some-day.

- 82 percent also said that somebody always has it on sale.

- 79 percent said they normally wait for sales because they don't need an item right away.

- 46 percent felt that quality has suffered.

- 34 percent said that service has declined.

Unlike consumers in the 1980s, today's shoppers are not so impatient to take immediate possession. They're more willing to wait until an item is on sale.

Next, we wanted to know where consumers shop to avoid paying full price. According to our survey, they patronize the following:

Discount stores such as Wal-Mart	83%
Flea markets or garage sales	52%
Membership warehouse clubs	50%
Brand outlet stores	46%
Consignment stores	41%
Thrift stores	34%

The definition of a discount store has changed over the past twenty years, and today's consumers have a whole new frame of reference. Wal-Mart and Target shoppers don't consider these stores discounters because they offer low prices every day. For most Americans under thirty, Wal-Mart and Target are full-line department stores. To them, Macy's, Bloomingdale's, and Dillard's are apparel stores—discount apparel stores, at that. In the 1970s, these stores established the retail price of goods. Any store that undersold them was selling at a discount.

We were amazed to discover that 52 percent of Americans shop at flea markets and garage sales and 41 percent shop at consignment stores. This clearly reveals that today's consumers are determined to spend their hard-earned money wisely.

Retailers typically extend a 10 to 15 percent discount on store merchandise to employees and their immediate families. Another finding that surprised us was that 27 percent of Americans take advantage of these employee discounts. This figure is so high that it tells us that employees are making discounted purchases for family members and friends who shouldn't be receiving a discount. In an ongoing battle to meet comparable store sales, most retailers are making little effort to police their employee discount programs.

What Consumers Think About Discount Stores

Does shopping in a discount store carry a stigma? We asked, "Do you avoid buying gifts at discount stores because you don't want people to think you're cheap?" Ninety-three percent answered no. Apparently, discount stores are now mainstream.

When we surveyed consumers in the 1980s, most were embarrassed to let friends know they shopped at discount stores. People were more materialistic then and more likely to boast about how much they had paid for an item and where they had bought it. Today's consumers are more likely to brag about how much they saved and at which discount store. It's as if they are saying "Look how smart I am because I was able to make a smart buy."

Our research revealed that 48 percent of American consumers now shop at stores that sell imperfect merchandise, or seconds. In the 1970s and 1980s, surveys showed that a vast majority of shoppers would not shop at a store that sold seconds. Their reason: "I don't know how to recognize imperfect merchandise, and I don't want to end up buying damaged goods."

Today's consumers believe they can tell the difference. Now consumers say, "I don't have a problem with a store that sells seconds because I'm smart enough to find the imperfection."

This attitude explains why nearly half of all Americans shop at stores that sell seconds. This suggests that today's shoppers are savvy, or at least think they are.

Our research shows that only 27 percent of Americans think there is a limited selection at discount stores. "I don't feel I'm giving up much," consumer after consumer told us. With 73 percent of all consumers thinking they can find most items at better prices at discount stores, it's no wonder they are heading that way to save money.

The Consumer Paradox

It's difficult to read today's consumers because they aren't consistent. To many retailers, this makes them unpredictable. Why are consumers so full of contradictions when it comes to spending? Why will they pay full price for a $500 leather jacket but wait for a $50 sweater to go on sale? Why buy a top-of-the-line sports utility vehicle and then go to Costco for tires? Why do people eagerly pay $3.50 for a cup of coffee but think a $1.29 hamburger is too expensive?

These inconsistencies confuse the retail industry, which fails to recognize that consumers want quality *and* value. It's not unusual to see a high-income, upscale customer shopping at Target. Consumers have figured out that they don't need to pay full retail price for certain types of merchandise. Selective shopping at discount stores also frees up discretionary dollars to spend elsewhere.

Many retailers view this as being cheap. Our response is that they mistake the consumers' demand for value as cheapness. These retailers are not admitting that they have failed to meet the expectations of their customers, who are saying: (1) This is how much money I want to spend. (2) This is how much time I want to spend. (3) These are the brands I will consider.

These are reasonable demands that have nothing to do with being cheap. Retailers who refuse to cater to these expectations are digging a hole that could become their grave.

Today's consumers cherish time and want convenience, but don't be misled: although they view themselves as bargain shoppers, they are, in fact, value shoppers. They know when a product or service or store is worth their time and money—and when it isn't. This is evidenced by a 1998 market research survey by the Dohring Company. Given a choice between a $15,000 new car and an identically priced three-year-old used car that had cost substantially more when new, 62 percent chose the used car. Not surprisingly, sales of small cars selling for $15,000 or less are plunging.

The intrinsic quality that drives today's consumers is value, which is determined as follows: Does the store have the selection I want every time? Does it consistently fulfill my needs? Is my shopping time well invested? Is this store or its brand indispensable to me? Do I get what I pay for? How a retailer answers these questions determines the loyalty of its customers. If the value is not there, if the brand or outlet is not indispensable, not differentiated, customers will move on.

The 85 percent of Americans who don't pay full retail price for all their purchases are willing to shell out full price for certain items, but only when the items meet their expectation levels. It's a matter of giving customers their money's worth, which isn't necessarily measured in dollars. All of this reinforces the notion that it's harder than ever to sell at full retail price.

How Retailers Can Survive

Today's customers face constant change. They may have five or six jobs during their lifetimes. Voting a straight party ticket is a thing of the past. So is buying the same make of automobile when it's time for a new car. The disappearance of the friendly, familiar store clerk cost department stores many customers. A retailer competing head-on with category killers and big discount stores must hire personnel carefully. To win back customers willing to pay a premium for service, a retailer's sales force needs not only excellent product knowledge but also effective selling skills. This requires an investment of both time and money. Can you afford not to do it? As discussed in Trend 1, people with little discretionary time are willing to pay more for excellent service. Our research reveals that a good salesperson influences the customer in:

- 80 percent of furniture purchases

- 60 percent of mattress and box spring purchases

- 75 percent of area rug purchases

- 60 percent of electronics purchases

- 80 percent of audio purchases

- 90 percent of car audio purchases

In the travel industry, an agent sways 40 percent of all customers on their choice of airline.

Since salespeople can exert such a strong influence, it makes good sense to recruit and train a top-notch force. In big-ticket retail, research studies estimate that it costs $18,000 to train each salesperson. Obviously, personnel turnover is very costly. A high turnover of salespeople is also costly in terms of customer loyalty. Top salespeople have their own clientele. When these salespeople leave, their customers desert the store.

Salespeople are more likely to stay if they are provided with a pleasant work environment: good lighting, attractive decor, clean restrooms, a comfortable break area, and so on. Research shows that this adds to the bottom line. Customers can sense when employees are content—and customers' perception of morale directly influences their buying decisions.

A retail store should also carry certain products that aren't available at Wal-Mart or Kmart. A customer simply won't find Bose speakers at a discount store—nor will he find an employee with extensive information about receivers or speakers. Hiring and training a superior sales force will give a store a strong competitive edge. What retailing analyst Paco Underhill said is worth repeating: "The more shopper-employee contacts that take place, the greater the average sale."

The best customers, who are also the most profitable customers, should also be rewarded creatively. United Airlines recently announced a $30 million plan to reconfigure the interiors of about 450 domestic jetliners. A new section in the front of coach will provide five to six extra inches of legroom. The new class, Economy Plus, will be open to elite frequent-flyer customers, as well as to passengers who pay full coach.

United hopes to win the loyalty of business travelers, who make up 9 percent of its passengers but account for 36 percent of its sales and who may be paying six times as much for an economy ticket as the vacationer in the next seat. United surveyed hundreds of frequent flyers and found that what they wanted most was more legroom. The "seat pitch," an airline term that refers to the distance between two rows, will measure thirty-five to thirty-six inches in Economy Plus, nearly matching the thirty-eight inches in first class. The width of the seat will remain unchanged.

We applaud United, and we recommend that you also look for ways to reward your best customers. United is spending millions of dollars to do so, but customers can be given VIP treatment without spending millions to do it. Small, personal gestures can go a long way. This is especially true for owners of small businesses. Here are three characteristics that owner-operators have going for them:

1. **People come to them for advice.** The owner and perhaps her employees are highly knowledgeable in a particular area of expertise. This is not easily accomplished by a mass marketer.

2. **The customer is likely to be acknowledged personally.** People feel important when they are recognized. This recognition doesn't exist at big-box stores.

3. **There is an ongoing relationship.** A follow-up call, a note, or another form of contact after the sale makes customers feel they are special.

Our research shows that when a business owner is directly involved with a customer, there is an 83 percent chance of repeat business. This compares to a mere 16 to 38 percent at a mass marketer's store.

Surveys have shown that customers feel that in a shopping experience there is no greater honor than to be waited on by the owner. It doesn't matter if customers are in a fine restaurant, a clothing store, or an automobile dealership—when the owner serves them, no other retail experience can provide that special feeling.

Three things happen. First, the owner is, in fact, the business. So when he comes over to say hello, it accords the customer a certain status. Second, if the owner shampoos a customer himself, throws in a car wash with an oil change, or simply remembers a customer's name, it reflects on the entire company. The owner can do whatever he wants. He's the ultimate rule breaker. He pays for the inventory; he has the power and authority to negotiate a special deal or service. He can even choose to lose money to keep a customer's business!

The third thing an owner can do better than anybody else is say thank you. Gratitude expressed by the proprietor tells a customer that her business was appreciated by the entire company. The customer is pleased, feels appreciated, and determines to give the company more of her business.

One group of independents that's faring well against discount stores is fine jewelry stores. Chains have economies of scale in their favor, but in high-end jewelry each piece is unique. Few buyers know how to appraise a diamond, and since no two are identical, price comparison is hard to do. Oftentimes, the tiebreaker is a matter of who can be trusted. Confidence in the merchant is the key. According to James Porte, president of the Jewelry Marketing Institute, "That's more important than buying something at a good price and then finding out it's not what you thought you bought."

Even with a national reputation, it's hard for a big jewelry chain to compete with a locally owned, reputable jewelry store, especially if the local store has been family owned and operated for a generation or more. Some jewelers are high-profile community leaders with "celebrity status" in their area. They also have personal relationships with the most affluent residents. This gives them an edge in providing personal service.

A local jeweler might call a longtime customer to say, "I have something that you'll absolutely die for. When can you stop in? Would you prefer that I bring it by on my way home tonight?"

We heard about one jeweler in the Midwest who flew to Aspen to show a million-dollar necklace to a customer. This jeweler also offers his customers warm face towels and beverages.

If your company is second, third, or fourth generation, don't be shy about promoting that fact. Be proud that your father or great-grandfather founded the company. You don't have to be in the jewelry business. You, too, can pamper your customers. You can call your customers to say you just installed a tanning booth and you're giving them three free sessions. If you own a bike shop, why not score a few points by dropping off a bicycle you repaired on your way home? We're not suggesting you drive miles out of your way, but a few extra blocks won't inconvenience you—and your customer will love it. You'll build such loyalty, nobody will ever be able to take your customers away. Practically any retail business—a dry cleaner, a computer store, and so on—can provide the same kind of service.

Of course, this takes commitment and creativity. You need to set yourself apart from discount retailers. They may have lower prices, and you can't compete against certain economies of scale. However, you can win customers through exceptional service, combined with a personal touch. You'll be competing with them on your turf, where you'll have the advantage.

Be sure to go that extra mile for your most important customers. This means making sure your private customer sales give extra value to your customers. Today, we estimate it takes an extra 10 to 15 percent discount to make your private sales successful, but we think it's well worth the extra effort to assure these customers remain loyal.

Based on the influence a top-notch salesperson has on a customer and the special relationship that exists between the two, it's imperative to make sure your salespeople are happy and well paid. This means that when you have a good salesperson on the floor, you don't want to lose him. Look at such an individual as a valuable asset. Consider him a profit center—and place a value on his personal following. Because if you lose him, you're likely to lose some customers too.

One final note: remember that people value time, and so proximity sometimes wins over everything else. Customers shop at stores that are convenient. If you're a small, independent retailer, don't situate yourself where no one can find you. And pay particular attention to the outside appearance of your store. One of our surveys showed that 53 percent of all Americans base their perception of a retail store's selection on its exterior appearance. So the bigger your store appears outside, the better the consumer will perceive your selection inside to be. Consider hiring a good architect or designer who can create a large facade that will make your store seem bigger than it actually is.

More Americans Are Caring for Their Aging Parents

As American demographics change, so does consumer behavior, which creates as well as impacts business trends. One major demographic shift is the dramatic increase in life expectancy.

In the 1950s, sixty-five years was considered a full life. Now if somebody passes away at age sixty-five, we say, "He died prematurely." The bar has been raised, with eighty-five being the official beginning age for what gerontologists call the oldest-old. Those sixty-five to eighty-four are classified as the young-old.

There are an estimated 72,000 centenarians in the United States today, up from about 15,000 in 1980. Each week, 12 Americans are wished a happy one hundredth birthday by Willard Scott on the *Today* show; about ninety new centenarians don't get mentioned. The U.S. Bureau of the Census, National Center for Health Statistics, projects the number of persons one hundred years or older to reach 101,000 in 2005, 214,000 in 2020, and 834,000 in 2050.

With so many Americans living longer, a rising number of adult children are taking care of their elderly parents—a trend that will run well into the twenty-first century. Our focus on this trend is how it will affect consumer behavior because it will surely alter lifestyles and spending habits across America dramatically. Many astute businesses will cash in on this trend, while others are certain to lose out.

It's an Emotional Thing

For the first time in history, Americans want to have the same standard of living during retirement as they had at the peak of their careers. They not only *want* to maintain this quality, they *expect* it. It's not an unreasonable expectation, in spite of over half of all working Americans having neither a private pension plan nor financial assets worth six months' wages. There's no logic here—it's an emotional thing!

It's not simply the aging who think this way. Their adult children also don't want them to diminish their lifestyle. No matter that they lack substantial financial resources. It's not about what they have, it's about what they wish!

This trend is driven by emotions. There is a tremendous psychological stimulus that compels adult children to care for their parents. They are people we love. They loved us and cared for us when we were incapable of taking care of ourselves. Now it is our turn to sacrifice and care for them.

Consequently, millions of Americans are willing to do without to give their elderly parents better care. These adult children spend long hours giving this care: cleaning their homes, running errands, shopping, bathing them, changing their diapers, doing all kinds of chores. They give up well-deserved and much-needed vacations. They forgo weekend golf and bridge games.

They cut down spending on wardrobes and cosmetics and dining out. Our research reveals that America's caregivers spend 10 to 12 percent less on themselves than consumers without caregiving responsibilities. In addition, the total spending of caregivers' immediate families is 6 to 7 percent less. In other words, caregivers' families tighten their belts, but the primary caregiver's is pulled tightest. More time and money go to Mom and Pop. Of course, some caregivers are driven by guilt. They cannot enjoy comfort and luxury when they know that their parents have less. But this is compassion. It comes from the heart.

The "Sandwich Generation"

A study we conducted in 1997 revealed that 25 percent of the U.S. wage and salaried labor force provided elder care during the preceding year. One in five working parents is now part of the "sandwich generation," Americans who are caring for both children and elderly relatives.

This doesn't include millions of Americans who spend their hard-earned money for their children's education and, once the college loans are paid off, assume the burden of parent care. The situation gets tougher. For the first time in history, a married couple is likely to spend more time caring for parents than for children. This is because kids generally require care for twenty years or so and then they're on their own. With aging parents, caregiving could last thirty years or longer. And with the baby boomers' trend to delay having children, some couples in their forties and fifties are caring for a parent while rearing their own offspring.

Dr. Joyce Brothers tells about a friend who describes her "sandwich" status vividly: "Well, that's how I feel, like a piece of taffy, being pulled on all sides."

Dr. Brothers elaborates, "My friend is 51 and the mother of three children. The older two are getting married in the next six months—happy news—but it means my friend has to juggle wedding plans with her responsibilities as an office manager of her husband's accounting firm. At the same time, my friend's 80-year-old mother, who lives alone some distance away, is suffering from medical problems.

"'Last week, Mom slipped and fell on the stairs,' she told me. 'I'm trying to talk her into moving to an assisted-living facility before something serious happens, but she wants to stay where she is. I know how she feels—after all, she's lived in that house for 25 years—but I'm worried to death, and pressured too. I go from one meeting with my daughter's caterer to one with my mother's doctor. Sometimes I don't know where I am.'"

Sandwiching can also mean caring for both an elderly parent

and a spouse. When Martha Jan Thompson's husband was diagnosed with probable Alzheimer's disease thirteen years ago, she cut
her spending and devoted much of her salary as a nurse assistant to
paying off their house. When his care needs forced her to quit work
four years ago, she cut expenses to the bone so they could live on
Social Security. Now, she cares for both her husband, sixty-nine,
and her mother, eighty-one. Mrs. Thompson's mother has chronic
health problems and moved in with her two years ago. Mrs.
Thompson has dwindled to ninety pounds under the stress of caregiving.

Caregiving. It's an endearing term. But it can also be another
way of saying "living hell." Another devoted adult daughter caught
in the sandwich generation is Linda Stumm, an elementary school
teacher and forty-six-year-old mother of two teenage sons.

Linda's mother, Lena Pimpinnella, seventy-eight, has Alzheimer's
disease, diagnosed thirteen years ago. Unable to speak, eat, or move
without help, she spends her days on a hospital bed in the living
room of Linda's row house in South Philadelphia. Linda goes home
every day at lunchtime to change her mother's diapers.

Linda does not consider a nursing home an acceptable option
for her mother, but she says she does not know how much longer
her energy will hold.

"There are times when I'm so tired I could just cry," she said one
afternoon as she spoon-fed yogurt to her mother. "Child care eventually evolves to less and less. There's no end to this. You know
you're going to be changing diapers all the time. It's always the
same. It just gets worse."

Having witnessed their parents' struggle, it's no wonder that
adult children are concerned and planning ahead. Most Americans
are anxious about aging, with 64 percent worried about living for
years in a nursing home because of a physical frailty or long-term
illness and 56 percent worried about developing Alzheimer's disease.

The Tip of the Iceberg

The number of Americans aged eighty-five or older is skyrocketing. The total jumped 51 percent from 1980 to 1996 and will climb an additional 32 percent by 2005. This swelling of this oldest-old age group means more aging parents relying on their families for care. The sixty-five-and-older population is projected to reach 39 million—a 15 percent increase—by 2010. The number of Americans over age sixty-five will increase by 50 percent in the next twenty years. The number over eighty-five will soar by 80 percent, to more than 6.5 million by the year 2020. There's no doubt about it: the country is aging.

A 1998 survey by the Conference Board forecast that by the year 2005, 37 percent of U.S. workers will be more concerned with caring for a parent than for a child. This represents a major shift; we anticipate that employees will demand benefits to reflect this change. We're starting to witness it already. The Health Insurance Industry Association reports that more workers are buying long-term care insurance through their employers. Planning is especially critical when you consider that two of three caregivers have a full-time job. Policy makers fear an overwhelming demand for services from families who are now caring for elderly relatives at no cost to the government.

Once again, middle-class America is being squeezed. The wealthy can afford care for their aging parents; the poor can qualify for welfare. Medicare, the nation's health program for people over sixty-five, allows a total maximum of one hundred days of nursing home care or rehabilitation. As people live longer, it's not nearly sufficient.

As America ages, its caregiving problems will multiply. Peter Uhlenberg at the University of North Carolina has calculated that in 1900 only 7 percent of sixty-year-olds had a living parent, and only 13 percent in 1940. But by the year 2000, 44 percent of all sixty-year-olds will have at least one surviving parent.

The Families and Work Institute's 1997 National Study of the

Changing Workforce reported that a startling 42 percent of employees expect to assume elder care duties within five years. And according to an Alliance for Caregiving study, caregivers are more likely today to say their duties have a negative effect on their work than ten years ago.

We've seen only the tip of the iceberg.

Thoughtful People

They might not complain too loudly. Caregivers, especially those in the sandwich generation, have had their share of bad times. They've done without, and it was no bed of roses. And they don't want their children to suffer the same deprivation.

So, even though they are hard pressed, they've become conscientious savers as well as investors in mutual funds. In other words, they're putting their house in order to avoid imposing on their own children. Retirement plans and long-term health care insurance rank high on their list of priorities.

They are also watching their children start their own families later in life. Investment and insurance industries will benefit from this trend. Contrary to public opinion, investment and insurance purchases are generally emotional rather than rational. We did a 1998 study that revealed that more than 44 percent of adult children who have assumed care for an elderly parent are saving more than ever. Likewise, 38 percent had expanded their health care insurance. The same study that surveyed these individuals shows that half are now prioritizing retirement saving.

A Matter of Time

If you think you're busy these days, imagine factoring in time for elder care! These responsibilities average nearly eleven hours per week. Men and women spend equal amounts of time on elder care. More than one third have reduced their work hours or taken time off to provide that care. Smaller families, single-parent families, and two-career couples have substantially reduced the pool of able-bodied unemployed adults available to provide elder care, just as the demand for care is rising. For working individuals who assume the full burden without family or outside help, an immense time commitment is required.

Just imagine what it would be like. Dave, a fifty-eight-year-old divorcé, works in the accounting department of a small manufacturing company. After paying alimony, Dave can't afford much outside help. His two sisters and his only son live out of town. Dave's eighty-three-year-old mother resides about fifteen minutes from Dave's house. She has a small apartment and lives month to month on Social Security. Except for arthritis, Mom was in reasonably good health until she fell and broke her hip. Ever since, Dave's life has revolved around her.

Dave used to arrive at the office at 8:30 each morning and work until 6:00. Now he goes in at 9:00 because he stops at his mother's apartment first. He helps her wash herself and dress. He prepares breakfast, and they eat together. With the extra driving time, Dave figures his morning visits require an hour.

"It means less sleep," he says, "and arriving at the office a half hour later. I make up the time by brown-bagging it. I fix both our lunches at her place in the evenings."

Unable to get away during work, he hired a high school girl for two hours after school. The girl assists Dave's mother to the bathroom, does light housekeeping, and, depending on the weather, takes her for wheelchair rides. This is Dave's helper. Dave used to work past six on some nights, but no longer. Now he leaves to have dinner with his mother, which he either cooks or brings in. He stays with her until ten, catches up on his reading, and watches television. After helping her bathe, he puts her to bed and heads home. His weekends and vacations center around her needs. He does the shopping, laundry, and some housekeeping. It's a dreary life, leaving Dave with practically no leisure time. His social life is nonexistent.

"Somebody has to do it," he explains, "and there's nobody in this world to care for her but me. She's my mother, and I love her. What choice is there?"

When asked why they don't live together, he says, "I need my own space, but if need be, that's always an option."

There are millions of Daves in America, caring for their elderly parents and cutting back on other activities. Millions of people are burning up billions of hours they would otherwise spend dining out, going to movies and plays, bowling, playing golf, vacationing, shopping—the list goes on and on. This group of consumers—otherwise a prime target for many products and services—is being removed from the marketplace. In some ways, their absence is fiscal: they're spending money on their parents that could have been spent on themselves. Their absence is also physical: there simply aren't enough hours in the day to do everything.

Elder care givers have become part of the growing consumer group that is less tolerant of people who waste their time, as mentioned in Trend 1. They become angry when an advertised product is unavailable in their preferred color, size, model, or style. They're impatient when salespeople aren't well informed, and they're short-fused when the checkout line moves at a snail's pace.

Pity the poor caregiver who rushes to the supermarket after work, then goes home to prepare meals for both parent and family. These caregivers complain that long checkout lines are "the biggest waste of time of their entire day." Supermarkets must expand their ten-item express checkout service as well as having other lanes for twenty items or fewer.

If you're in the service industry, you'd better not disappoint these customers. If you say you'll be at their house between nine and eleven, be there. They don't have time to wait around for you.

Our 1998 research shows that nearly 10 percent of caregivers openly admit that they are so busy that they plan shopping trips around one store. More than 36 percent said they do it to save time. Nearly 27 percent have so little time that they shop only for essentials. About the same percentage said they spend less because they have less time to spend money.

These consumers can't watch their favorite television programs as they once did, rarely read magazines, and at best only skim the daily newspaper. For this reason, many companies are changing their advertising campaigns. Retailers get the most bang for their buck with targeted direct mail and with Sunday newspaper inserts that communicate their store's selection in many varied categories. This allows the overworked, overburdened adult caregiver to shop more thoroughly and quickly at his or her convenience, a luxury for many.

How They Are Cutting Back

America's caregivers responded in a 1998 ARG study in these percentages:

- 19.8 have less money to spend on their immediate family.

- 36.1 pay some of their parents' bills.

- 24.4 eat out less with their family.

- 46.5 have become more savings-conscious.

- 44.2 save today because they spend less.

- 26.7 spend less because they don't know how long they will have to take care of their parents.

- 51.2 now only shop for the lowest price.

- 38.4 say buying for themselves is not important—their parents come first.

How This Trend Will Impact American Business

As America ages, certain businesses will be forced to change to accommodate those who require care. Changes will be required to serve the elderly as well as those with caregiving responsibilities. Companies that cater to both senior citizens and caregivers will profit from this trend.

Note that as today's caregivers shop for home care and nursing home care policies, their children are also prime candidates for such products.

The food industry must adjust to this trend. Because caregivers are hard pressed for time, restaurants, supermarkets, and gourmet grocery stores that offer ready-to-combine ingredients or complete meals will prosper. We're already seeing prepackaged salads in the produce section and "fixings" such as grated carrot, chopped celery, and so on.

People of all age groups will become even more health-conscious. The expression "If I'd known I was going to live this long, I would have taken better care of myself" will no longer be a joke. Hence, the number of "health nuts" will increase. Health product companies selling minerals and vitamins will prosper if they emphasize how their products reduce fatigue. Physical fitness and health food businesses will also be big winners. And we can expect to see drugstores and supermarkets expand their nutritional supplement departments.

Consumer-related businesses will have no alternative but to offer improved service to their customers. Caregivers will continue to demand prompt and efficient service. Businesses that excel in this area will realize more market share. Eventually retailers will extend store hours to accommodate their customers' hectic schedules. We'll see more retailers offer free valet parking, not only to save time and to make after-dark shoppers feel safe, but also to allow feeble but still mobile shoppers to shop for themselves as long as possible.

Department stores will need to revive home delivery to accommodate their aging customer base as well as caregivers who are pressed for time. Personal shopping services will be in great demand, and an increasing number of consumers will shop by appointment in exclusive stores.

Also, to accommodate harried shoppers, retailers will run sales on weekdays, when they're not normally busy with customers. For example, a department store may begin its sales in the middle of the week so the time-conscious can avoid weekend crowds. Our studies have determined that private sales offering true savings of 10 to 15 percent will be extremely effective, especially when both husband and wife can make a buying decision during a single store visit.

To accommodate new-car shoppers, dealers will dispatch their salespeople to the consumer's home for a test drive. Interestingly, car dealers in Japan have been successfully selling cars this way for decades. The dealers that will benefit most from this trend will be those that offer the best service after the sale, that is, pickup and delivery of a car that needs service. Of course, this will drive up the sticker price, but surveys indicate that Americans would welcome this—if all dealers did it.

Clothing salespeople will sell directly to customers at their homes or offices. A salesperson will make a house call at a time convenient to the customer. This upscale couturier will sell everything from a single item to complete ensembles by showing fabric swatches and photographs. A customer's measurements will be taken and kept on file for future phone orders. The goods ordered will be delivered personally. The good news is that the cost of goods will not increase because merchants can save on overhead.

Retailers will conduct on-site seminars on the subjects of aging and caregiving to attract caregivers and perhaps even their elderly parents. Naturally, these seminars won't be limited to retailers; companies ranging from real estate agencies to securities firms will conduct them to attract prospective clients. You can also expect to see a lot of this kind of information being communicated via the Internet.

Although it is true that few senior citizens today regularly "cruise the Net," in time the Internet will become important to them. Why? Because the Internet can provide so many opportunities to those who have time to sit at a computer but don't get around very well. It can also be a great source of entertainment.

"But old people don't use computers," you may say.

For the most part, that is true. But as technology becomes less expensive and more accessible, more senior citizens will participate.

Many people in their fifties already use the Internet. It won't be long before they're retired and surfing the Web. Just think about what they'll do: communicate with relatives and friends all over the world; research and read about their favorite interests; and buy everything from toys for their grandchildren to discount drugs. The Internet literally puts the entire world on their desktop. The hours these senior citizens spend at home will make this a favorite pastime and a real bargain, considering its cost of less than a dollar a day.

Many new businesses will cater to the senior citizen on-line, offering training, education, and a host of services. Caregivers will be the biggest advocates, encouraging their elderly parents to use the Net, where they'll spend a lot of time—and a lot less of their children's. They'll see their parents stay informed and alert, which is well worth whatever the cost.

Direct-sales organizations such as Mary Kay Cosmetics, Avon, and Amway will fare well as a result of this trend because they offer shop-at-home convenience. Accordingly, there will be an increase in multilevel selling across America. More people will be attracted to work in multilevel selling because they can work flexible hours, which will permit them to schedule their jobs around their caregiving responsibilities. And look for more multilevel sales organizations selling to the elderly and caregivers. Their product lines will include blood pressure cuffs, kits for testing cholesterol and blood sugar, special beds, chairs, walkers, canes, and so on.

Real estate brokers will also tailor their sales presentations to the specific needs of these customers. They'll conduct detailed "fact-finding" telephone interviews with prospective home buyers, followed up by extensive computer searches. This will enable them to eliminate homes unlikely to meet the customer's needs, speeding up the otherwise lengthy buying process of a home.

Home-building contractors will automatically plan garage apartments or "mother-in-law wings" equipped with ramps and lifts in primary residences. Homes without steps or stairs will be in greater demand. Professional remodelers will be hired to enlarge rooms, install handrails, eliminate narrow corridors, and make better use of floor space. Adding a first-floor bedroom or a bathroom with a two-person shower will be necessary for many caregivers. Likewise, astute realtors will sell homes based on future caregiving needs. Instead of suggesting, "This is a perfect room to convert into a solarium," the real estate broker will say, "This will be the ideal space for your mother when she comes to live with you!"

Likewise, customers with deep pockets will patronize companies offering "adult baby-sitting." This new service is certain to have a more commercial name—we won't attempt to predict what it will be. Also, a slew of home health care consulting services will sweep the country. There are already such services that cater to those who live far from their aging parents. Although these people wouldn't think of contacting a social services program, they are willing to hire a caregiving consultant, much as they'd hire an attorney or accountant. As one said, "It sure beats having to take time off from work or the expense of flying in from out of town." From the aging parent's point of view, this permits continued autonomy and provides the security of nearby reliable help.

Another product that will become popular is a personal emergency response system that summons the rescue squad at the touch of a button. Several companies, including hospitals and the Red Cross, lease these small devices, worn on a chain around the neck or wrist.

We're starting to see a major change in the life insurance industry because of elder care. For years, investment companies have been buying policies from people with AIDS and other terminal diseases. Now we can expect elderly people to sell their policies to commercial insurers at discounted prices while they are relatively healthy. These prices can vary greatly. For a $100,000 policy, for example, a terminally ill person with a life expectancy of six months might receive $80,000. But people in their sixties and seventies with another, say, ten to twelve years to live, by actuarial estimates, might receive much less—perhaps $5,000 to $20,000. Depending on the situation, it makes good sense to sell the insurable interest. This way, an elderly parent can minimize the burden on his adult children by helping defray medical bills and reduce taxes on his or her estate. Policy trading is on the rise. Viaticus, a unit of CNA Insurance Companies, one of the biggest commercial insurers, is a leader in this realm and bought an estimated $300 million in policies in 1998, up from $75 million in 1997. The life insurance industry estimates that the face amount of policies purchased from individuals by investment companies rose from about $200 million in 1990 to $600 million in 1997.

Another consideration is whether to buy extended care insurance for parents. Closely related to this subject is the need for a "living will." A host of legal decisions must be made, requiring the services of attorneys and accountants who specialize in estate planning. One important decision, for example, is who should have power of attorney over a parent's affairs. And someone must have the legal right to make medical decisions for parents who are incapacitated.

The travel industry will be affected by this trend, with caregivers scaling back on long vacations abroad to take three-day weekend trips to nearby destinations. And because caregivers will be more conscientious about their own health, many will go to health spas during these brief getaways.

To assist employees with their caregiving concerns, more companies will offer health insurance covering three generations. What's more, health insurance policies will be transferable from one company to another—or, at the very least, be vested if employment is terminated. This is an interesting change, since health coverage was originally offered to employees without vesting so they would be penalized for changing jobs.

Furthermore, to accommodate the caregiving worker, flextime will permit employees to care for an adult parent. Likewise, accrued vacation time will increasingly be used as personal leave. Some forward-thinking managers will evaluate their employees' productivity based on performance rather than the number of hours spent doing a particular job.

To attract and retain good people, companies will run cafeterias that will offer nutritious meals to health-conscious employees. Workplace food service will enable caregivers to take shorter lunch breaks, balanced between the time clock and caring for their parents.

Corporate America has good reason for concern about its employees who are devoted caregivers, as it loses more than $17 billion per year in productivity to elder care. This figure is based on a productivity loss estimate of $2,500 a year for each worker with elder care responsibilities.

Investment Tips

Investors who understand this trend are privy to information that should benefit their portfolios. Companies that carry trusted brand names such as Procter & Gamble, Tiffany, and Nike will prosper because shoppers will be too busy to shop nonbrand products. Likewise, companies such as Nordstrom will benefit by offering such services as raising hemlines on demand and shipping merchandise cross-country. Retailers with fast-moving checkout service and broad inventory will attract more shoppers than their competition.

Publicly owned direct sellers such as Avon, Amway, and Tupperware will also be winners. So will catalog companies such as Lillian Vernon and L.L. Bean. And as more busy consumers shop the Internet, companies such as America Online and Amazon.com will prosper.

Retailers with exceptional distribution capabilities will fare well. Most notable is Wal-Mart, a mass marketing retailer that excels in its just-in-time distribution system. Getting merchandise to stores on a timely basis so shelves are always well stocked will be critical. As noted earlier, caregivers seek out retailers that are well stocked in the merchandise they advertise. Wise investors will look into companies that manufacture technology for state-of-the-art distribution systems.

Caregivers will realize that, like their elderly parents, they too will live longer and will someday require care. This will make them more aggressive investors, and well into their late sixties they will attempt to accumulate enough wealth so they do not burden their children. Depending on how the stock market performs, coupled with the timing of their retirements, investment strategies of this nature will benefit some and hurt others.

Companies selling health care products or services will benefit from this trend, especially those that serve an increasingly aging population, such as Schering-Plough, Abbott Laboratories, and Pfizer.

The investor who considers this caregiving trend when choosing stocks can assemble a portfolio that is likely to outperform the market.

The Number of "Paper Millionaires" Is Mushrooming

Back in the 1970s and '80s, double-digit inflation had some people believing we'd all soon be millionaires. To most of us, a million dollars is still a lot of money, but in fact it no longer qualifies someone as filthy rich.

For a while, prices kept going up and up, especially real estate prices. In the 1970s, people moved to places such as Beverly Hills, bought a home for $100,000, and sold it fifteen years later for $1 million to $2 million. One man from Pittsburgh moved to Beverly Hills for a job in middle management that paid around $60,000 a year. When he moved back twenty years later, his net worth was more than $2 million—nearly all of it the profit he made on his house! Eventually, he bought a home in Pensacola, Florida, for $300,000 and retired. However, he's earning more in retirement than he did during his career. He's an avid day trader on the Internet. All that money he made on his Beverly Hills home is now in equities, and in the past three years, his portfolio has more than doubled. Stock prices increasing at 30 percent annually have taken him, along with millions of other Americans, on a joyride.

For decades, our biggest asset was our home. Skyrocketing real estate prices once provided reassurance to the middle class. Now, soaring stock portfolios are doing the same. Historically, gains on stocks have averaged 8 percent a year. That means every nine years an investor's money doubles (if it is in a tax-free account). With the market's recent annual 30 percent increase, however, an investor's money doubles in only three years! At that rate, a $200,000 retirement fund will be worth $800,000 in six years and $1.6 million in nine years!

A *New York Times* analysis of Federal Reserve data revealed that in 1990 the average household's stock investment was 12 percent of its wealth. Seven years later, it was 28 percent. In 1990, real estate represented 33 percent of the average household's wealth. By 1997, it had dropped to 27 percent. This is not because real estate values declined; the shift of cash to equities and increasing stock prices account for these changes.

A strong stock market combined with a low inflation rate is encouraging Americans to continue investing in equities. As wealth grows, more people are being attracted to the action. Because so many investors are in equities and because so much personal wealth is created by their holdings, this trend is having a tremendous impact on consumer behavior in America.

To report on this trend, we conducted a national survey in May 1999. Every interviewee owned stocks or equity mutual funds. Seventy percent were male.

"How Are We Doing Today?"

Once upon a time, when one coworker asked another, "How are we doing today?" it was nothing more than a friendly, passing greeting.

Not anymore. Today, it's an inquiry: How did our company's stock do today?

To attract and retain good people in a tight job market, more and more companies are offering better retirement packages, including stock options. As a result, more people are tuning in to the stock market, paying particular attention to the current price of their employer's stock. Never before have so many people watched their own company's market activities. In 1999, 52 percent of the people we surveyed who have a retirement account or a pension program stated their ownership in the company as the reason they follow its market price.

This contrasts sharply with a survey in the 1980s that asked, "What do you think is the dollar range that your company's stock has been trading at this year?" Two thirds of Americans could make only a wild guess. Today, a majority of people review their company's stock price an average of 2.2 times a week. When you ask that question today, you'll find that not only can people tell you the price, they can also tell you the price-earnings ratio.

People have never been more investment-aware. Our research shows that 78 percent of the investors we surveyed are reading the business section of the newspaper more often today. An astonishing 47 percent read the business section first. As we discussed in Trend 1 on discretionary time, most people are so rushed they can barely find time to read the newspaper; consequently, they are selective about what they do read. Evidently, Congress and the Yankees don't interest these readers as much as their portfolios do.

People care about their company's performance on Wall Street because they have a vested interest. Their retirement depends on company stock, so they have ownership in the company. The company represents their future. When people consider themselves investors in their own company, they have a far different attitude as employees. They are more motivated. "This is *my* company," many boast. Some come to work earlier and go home later. They become angry when another employee slacks off. The pride they have in their company is reflected in their productivity. They know high productivity will boost the price of the company's stock. Employees' interest in the stock market has made it more difficult for unions to penetrate nonunion companies. Unions are also less likely to strike because employees with ownership understand that prolonged strikes drive down share prices.

Today's Investors Make Better-Informed Decisions

Our 1999 national survey disclosed that 54 percent of investors read or subscribe to *The Wall Street Journal;* 28.7 percent read or subscribe to *Investor's Business Daily;* 29 percent read or subscribe to a major business magazine; and 44 percent read or subscribe to at least one specialty magazine. Seventy-three percent watch financial networks such as CNN-FN or CNBC, and 54 percent watch financial programs on PBS. Twenty-nine percent have attended an investment seminar in the past ten years.

It's interesting to see who's getting what information from these sources. Even though 78 percent of active investors read the business section, 32 percent of investors under thirty-five, and 29 percent of investors over sixty-five, do not. This means it's the new investors between thirty-five and sixty-four who are most likely to read the business news. The people in this age group are the most productive and highest paid in America's workforce. They are also the busiest, with the least amount of time. Yet they still find time to read the business section.

Likewise, while 73 percent of American investors watch financial networks, 41 percent of those between twenty-five and thirty-five do not. In all other age groups, nonwatchers were in the mid–20 percent range.

As of June 1999, 40 percent of investors used the Internet to track their investments, while 31 percent didn't have Internet access. Of those investors who are on-line, 58.5 percent track their investments. As more Americans gain access to the Internet, and as users tell nonusers of the benefits, the number of these investors will increase dramatically.

It's probable that a high percentage of investors under age thirty-five who aren't reading the news or watching financial networks are getting their information on-line. As this group matures, the Internet will remain their primary source of information. The present over-sixty-five age group of computer illiterates will be replaced by a new generation of Web-surfing senior citizens.

High Expectations

The portfolio of the average investor polled in our 1999 survey had grown by 29.5 percent during the past four years. With results like this, it's no wonder investors have such a Pollyanna outlook. Watching their money grow, they believe that they can manage their own portfolios. Many ask, "Why go to a broker and have to pay high fees?"

In the late 1990s, even people using the dartboard approach prospered. Yet when we asked investors how luck had affected their success, only 13 percent answered, "Very much." Fifty-seven percent admitted that luck had had something to do with their success, while 30 percent said that "luck had little or nothing to do" with how well they had done managing their investments. In other words, a vast majority felt pretty smart, perhaps downright cocky.

Investing in the Internet Itself

The Internet as information source will continue to impact investment decisions strongly. As more investors have become increasingly familiar with the Internet, they have begun to speculate on technology and Internet companies. A Gallup survey for Paine-Webber earlier in 1999 showed that 44 percent of on-line traders have invested in Internet stocks, compared with 15 percent of all investors.

Meanwhile, those who have invested in high technology have reaped rewards that outpaced the market as a whole. The Standard & Poor's High Technology Index increased fivefold from June 1994 through May 1999, while the broader S&P 500 stock index tripled.

Thousands of people have become fabulously rich from their stake in start-up technology and Internet companies. "Microsoft millionaire" has become a familiar term. We wanted to find out what investors thought about America's "overnight billionaires." We asked, "Do you admire the people who have made enormous wealth from the Internet companies they own and run?" More than half—53.3 percent—answered that they do. The percentage of investors under thirty-five answering yes was higher, at 63 percent. Only 47 percent of investors over sixty-four responded affirmatively. As a group, senior citizens didn't think people who got rich fast because of Internet companies deserved their wealth. They said people should have to work harder for their money.

Meanwhile, our research reveals that younger investors have some new role models: business tycoons such as Bill Gates, Michael Dell, and Steven Jobs. Granted, these individuals founded computer and software companies, but they also ushered in the Internet era. Gates, Dell, and Jobs represent a new brand of business in America. They have replaced icons such as Ross Perot and General Electric's Jack Welch.

Young people's admiration for many of the nation's two hundred or so billionaires affirms that the American Dream is alive and well.

Paper Millionaires' Spending Habits

Our 1999 survey revealed that 48.2 percent of investors making a substantial profit in the stock market neither rewarded themselves nor reinvested in a risky venture. Nearly 52 percent responded that they held on to their money. Because the percentages are so close, we can say that people have a fairly even chance of going either way with their profits.

Let's focus on what the 48.2 percent did with their windfall: 20.5 percent bought something; 20.4 percent reinvested their profit; and 7.3 percent did both. This is how they spent their windfalls:

Automobile	20.86%
Vacation/travel	15.83%
Major appliance	10.07%
Home	9.71%
Furniture	7.91%
Electronics	7.55%
Boat	6.83%

Vacation home	6.47%
Jewelry	3.60%
Education	3.24%
New wardrobe	2.16%
Real estate	0.72%
Recreational vehicle	0.72%
Livestock	0.36%
Collectibles	0.36%
Home improvements	0.36%
Miscellaneous	3.24%

Knowing they already owned cars and took vacations, we questioned them about their choice of cars and vacations after their windfall. They said they were "upgrading" to more expensive cars than they already owned and to more luxurious vacations. Interestingly, when it came to purchasing air travel, they remained in coach. They wanted nicer vacations, but the difference between coach and first-class prices was so substantial that they balked at spending the extra money.

One person may have summed it up for the entire group: "For the three hours it takes to fly to our destination, the first-class tickets cost several times more. My wife and I didn't think it warranted spending so much more money."

Cruise travelers were willing to upgrade their cabins, however. This is being seen throughout the cruise industry: cruise lines have difficulty selling low-end cabins compared to better cabins and staterooms. The travel and vacation industries also benefit from people upgrading the cars they rent, staying at better hotels, and buying into time-share condominiums.

Of the one in five investors who had splurged, we asked if they had made a second purchase with their windfall. Here's how they responded:

None	50.72%
Furniture	8.27%
Major appliance	7.91%

New wardrobe	6.47%
Vacation/travel	6.12%
Electronics	3.96%
Education	3.60%
Jewelry	2.52%
Vacation home	2.52%
Home	2.16%
Automobile	1.80%
Boat	1.80%
Home improvements	0.36%
Livestock	0.36%
Real estate	0.36%
Miscellaneous	0.36%
Don't know	0.36%

For starters, we see that a slight majority (50.72 percent) never made a second purchase. Those who did bought items such as furniture, major appliances, clothes, and, again, vacations and travel. No single item dominated this list.

When asked if they had made a third purchase, 81.4 percent answered that they had not. A scant number (3.9 percent) spent their money on vacations and travel, which were high on all three lists. Other third purchases were electronics (2.6 percent), major appliances (2.6 percent), and education (2.16 percent).

Since the survey was taken in June 1999, we asked, "If your investments continue to perform well, do you plan to purchase something significant before year-end?" Twenty-three percent said they planned to spend more. This percentage included both those who had already made a significant purchase and those who had not. Note that 23 percent approximates the 20.5 percent who had made purchases between January and June. Here's what they plan to buy:

Vacation/travel	30.37%
Automobile	14.66%
Boat	8.90%
Education	6.81%

Home	5.76%
Jewelry	5.24%
Furniture	4.71%
Electronics	4.19%
Vacation home	4.19%
Major appliance	3.14%
Real estate	1.05%
Carpet	0.52%
Home improvements	0.52%
Collectibles	0.52%
New wardrobe	0.52%
Livestock	0.52%
Miscellaneous	2.09%
Don't know	6.28%

Here, too, vacations and travel ranked with automobiles as their top choices. Spending money on a boat jumped to third place, as might be expected in June. When asked if they might buy something they could do without, 64.2 percent said they wouldn't, while 19.1 percent said yes and the remaining 16.7 percent didn't know.

We concluded that, across the board, today's investors are conservative with their stock market earnings and plan to remain this way in a continuing bull market. This conservatism must certainly have something to do with their response to another question: "Do you think it's possible that a sudden bear market could wipe out your gains?" Fifty-eight percent answered yes; 39.3 percent answered no. Fewer than 3 percent said they didn't know what to think.

When asked about what precautions they've taken to prepare for a possible falling market, their comments were:

"I have a balanced portfolio."	53.8%
"I check my portfolio more frequently."	31.6%
"I am taking a strong cash position."	12.4%
"I haven't done anything."	1.9%
Miscellaneous	0.7%

Again we see a more conservative investor than we might expect in a prolonged bull market.

Our next set of questions revealed that in the face of a projected bull market, investors are concerned that it could change anytime. Nearly 45 percent believed it could take a nosedive within the next three years. And 35 percent of today's investors claim that if the market were to take a big hit, they'd have difficulty sleeping at night. Furthermore, 20 percent stated that they'd stop making major purchases if they expected the market to drop.

When asked what they might cut back on, most mentioned items such as jewelry. One man said that instead of buying his wife a birthday present such as a $500 gold necklace, "I'd take her to dinner and pick up a dozen roses."

Later, we asked those who had reinvested their profits in other stocks if they had ever been tempted to spend the money on consumer products instead. While 56.5 percent admitted they had, as the numbers attest, only 27 percent had actually done so. At the same time, 32 percent of reinvestors said they would reduce their spending immediately if they expected the market to go down seriously in the next thirty days.

There is a large group of Americans who are very stable in their spending habits, with only about one fourth opening their purses as a reaction to their market successes.

How to Cash In On This Trend

With so much attention focused on today's bull market, today's investor is showing more interest in his portfolio. Witness the attention the business section of the newspaper receives today. That's where smart advertisers should be buying space. Currently, the business section attracts mainly those selling financial services.

Knowing that many investors are spending their profits on such purchases as upscale car models and better cabins on cruise liners, luxury companies can capitalize on this trend when placing advertising space in financial publications and business sections of newspapers. If you happen to own a Lexus dealership, for instance, you should take notice. Most car dealers have traditionally placed ads in the sports section, thinking that men are the ones who buy most cars. How archaic! The same goes for luxury travel agencies and deluxe hotels targeting upscale customers. They should be placing ads in the travel *and* financial sections. All companies that sell products and services to affluent customers should follow this advice. This includes jewelers, upscale clothing companies, and high-end acoustics and home entertainment manufacturers.

Today, more than 70 percent of investors watch the financial programming on CNN-FN, CNBC, and more than 50 percent watch the financial programming on PBS, with this in mind, advertisers catering to the wealthy consumer might want to reconsider their TV advertising. Instead of placing commercials on network sitcoms, upscale companies should consider advertising on the programs that investors are watching. This audience has cash to spend.

These companies should also consider sponsoring programs such as CNN's *Pinnacle,* an Emmy Award–winning program that profiles achievers of the American Dream. Feature profiles have included contemporary business successes such as Alan "Ace" Greenberg, chairman of Bear Stearns & Co., and Donna Karan, founder of the Donna Karan Company.

Local companies can sponsor shows featuring local high-profile business leaders. If you are a television producer, you might consider producing a show of this nature in your hometown.

There is another major advantage of sponsoring programs on cable TV channels such as CNBC or CNN-FN: our studies show that a high percentage of their viewers are interested only in business news, so they are less likely to flip channels during commercial breaks. Many have their TVs on at their offices, so they have no interest in watching other programs. So while these cable channels don't attract large audiences (and thus technically their ratings are lower), a higher percentage of their audience stays tuned in during commercials, giving sponsors more bang for their buck.

You might also consider placing two-minute commercials on

cable television, where airtime is cheaper than on the networks, rather than traditional half-minute or one-minute commercials. A commercial running for two minutes (or, more precisely, 117 seconds) gives a sponsor adequate time to tell a detailed story that will captivate the audience. A cruise liner can highlight its staterooms, casinos, and elegant dining rooms—effectively transporting the weary, news-watching business executive from his or her office to one of its exotic destination ports. Try doing *that* in twenty-eight seconds!

Stockbrokers are in for a rough time ahead. As long as today's investor can realize significant gains by trading on-line, the number of investors unwilling to pay large commissions to full-service brokerage firms will continue to increase. No one can predict how long the bull market will continue. But as long as it remains intact, more investors will be researching and trading on-line. Discount brokers may suffer most; investors either will pay full price for lots of service or will want no service at all and very cheap trading fees. Either way, the discount broker will lose.

It remains to be seen how young investors will react in an extended bear market. It's certain, however, that they will be in for a rude awakening. Meanwhile, they are going on-line for both information and trading. They have different habits when it comes to reading newspapers and watching television. Marketers who want to reach this youthful group of investors must consider more nontraditional advertising.

Another overlooked place to reach what we consider a captive market is a company's own shareholders. We think there are many opportunities to make special offers to one's own shareholders, yet few companies ever solicit or give attractive discounts to their investors. For the most part, these are people who believe in the company, and their continued support is essential. A restaurant chain, for example, could include money-off coupons in the annual statement it sends to its shareholders; a bank could waive its ATM fees for its shareholders; a retailer could offer discount cards.

Retailers will continue to profit from those investors who convert their market profits into purchases—in particular, car dealerships with top-of-the-line models, cruise liners, high-priced vacation destinations, and, to a lesser extent, sellers of furniture, major appliances, and expensive clothing. But if there's a downturn in the market, they, too, can expect a decline in business.

Annual retail sales are now at an all-time high. At the same time, people realizing record high profits in the stock market continue to accumulate wealth through conservative spending. Finally, there is no place today to invest other than the stock market that yields such a high return. Americans no longer see real estate as a great investment. Today, a new home is just a nice place to live in; it's not an investment.

As more Americans become paper millionaires, Johnny-come-latelies attracted to the stock market will think, "Better late than never." And who knows? It's been a long ride, and the prosperity could very well continue for several more years. While the stock market has been the right place to invest your money during the past decade, don't be misled by thinking it's a sure thing. By its very nature, investing in equities is speculative and involves risk-taking.

On a final note to those stockbrokers who are seeing an increasing number of their clients trade on-line—don't despair. The last five years are not the norm. The returns we are witnessing have been far above historical returns, and we can't expect this prosperity to continue indefinitely. While it's true that investors are becoming more self-educated as a result of all the data available to them via the Internet, the trick during a bear market will be distilling that information so they can profit by it. That is a time-consuming process. We think it's unlikely that investors will continue to make their own investment decisions during periods when their portfolios take some major hits.

Furthermore, these investors need more than just advice on specific stocks—what's needed is a solid long-term investment strategy. This means that buying stocks must be done in the context of a bigger, diversified effort to acquire wealth—with the guidance of an experienced professional financial advisor.

Dual-Income Families Are Becoming Single-Income Families

For the past fifty years or so, the number of women in the U.S. labor force has been increasing faster than the number of men. Before World War II, about 30 percent of America's women were employed outside the home. Today, 60 percent of all adult women are gainfully employed, and they represent about 46 percent of the entire U.S. labor force.

Of course, many social and economic changes during the second half of the twentieth century contributed to the rising number of working women. Fifty years ago, the average working woman did not have a high school diploma. Today, fewer than 9 percent are dropouts, and about 60 percent have some college. Also, couples now marry and have children at a later age. The women's movement of the 1970s removed many barriers to job advancement, and legislation now prohibits discrimination in the workplace. Consequently, today's young women may embrace careers historically dominated by males.

In spite of these favorable conditions, we detect several major signs of a reversal in this fifty-year-old trend. Indeed, it will have significant impact on America's business environment. Imagine large numbers of women leaving the workforce. This would not only create a shortage of personnel, it would significantly change

America's spending habits. Unquestionably, our economy is geared to run full speed ahead with the support of both genders. If the number of women in the workforce declines, a chain reaction will occur.

Worn-out Working Moms

Once again, we cite Trend 1 on discretionary time: in a 1997 *Ladies' Home Journal* survey of working women, 66 percent said they long for more time for themselves. Sixty-five percent wish they could carve out a few minutes for exercise, and a fatigued 48 percent could use some extra sleep.

More and more working parents complain about the effort required to hold down jobs and raise their children; it seems there is never enough time to do both well.

It's no wonder they're feeling such a time crunch. Despite holding full-time jobs, employed moms tell us they do nearly as much around the house as women who stay home. Seventy-two percent say they are primarily responsible for the laundry (compared to 79 percent of their at-home counterparts), 70 percent say they do the cooking (versus 74 percent), 66 percent shop for groceries (compared to 69 percent), and 46 percent are primary child care providers: changing diapers, preparing meals, and missing work to manage doctor's appointments (versus 48 percent). Working women are unhappy with this unfair distribution of family chores. Forty-eight percent say they are "bothered a great deal" by the fact that men have fewer household responsibilities; just 36 percent of nonemployed women feel this way. Many working women—mothers in particular—feel trapped and are having second thoughts about what's realistic.

Reconsidering the Dual-Income Family

In a 1998 survey conducted by *The Atlanta Journal-Constitution/ WBS-TV*, seven out of ten working parents said they would be "very likely" or "somewhat likely" to quit their jobs if they could afford it. When fathers were asked whether they would prefer to have their working wives stay home with the kids if it were financially feasible, more than 70 percent said yes.

In the metropolitan Atlanta area, more than 80 percent of parents with children under eighteen work outside the home. Of mothers with children younger than six, 52 percent reported working full-time.

These Atlanta demographics reflect the attitudes of working parents across America. As one parent said, "I think if a mother doesn't have to work, we owe it to our kids to give them those years. It's better for them, and in the end it will be better for us. All of us."

Now let's talk about reality. Working parents' beliefs and behaviors don't match. It's one thing for people to say what they would prefer to do, quite another to do it. However, what people think ultimately influences what they do. In our survey of late 1999, 40 percent of parents who both worked full-time said they were considering quitting or working part-time. Significantly, this figure was only 18 percent just three years ago. ARG research has shown that 25 percent of the people must be considering a trend before it gets the momentum to initiate. Since we're already in the 40 percent range with this issue, it may well turn into a trend. When it takes off, look out!

Remember, the two-income family allowed Americans to buy big homes, second and third cars, lots of appliances, and so on. If 40 percent of families go back to having a single income, our nation's economic engine could lose steam.

Most often, it's the woman who elects to stay at home with the kids. As reported in a 1997 Bureau of Labor Statistics report, only 4 percent of families had a working mom and a stay-at-home dad.

Most people say they work because they feel they must, to pay off household bills and personal debt and to build a nest egg. Family incomes, adjusted for inflation, have increased by more than 25 percent since 1969, and according to the Census Bureau that increase is almost entirely because of working wives. If women's contributions are removed, household income rose just 1.5 percent. However, the cost of living has climbed steadily.

Based on these figures, most dual-income families are in no financial position to give up one paycheck unless they can manage to reduce their standard of living. Interestingly, some couples are willing to exchange their spending power for a better quality of life. Stay-at-home parents enjoy the luxury of time with their children. They are willing to sacrifice material possessions, accepting a lower-priced car, a smaller house, a leaner wardrobe, a smaller investment portfolio, and so on. In return they hope to gain a more closely knit family with children who are more likely to be stronger and healthier physically, mentally, and spiritually.

When One plus One Doesn't Equal Two

Do you ever feel that even though you have two paychecks in the family, you're not getting ahead? Your suspicion is correct. Recent studies show that more than half of a second paycheck may go to expenses incurred to earn it: child care, transportation, clothes, meals, taxes, and other work-related expenses.

There is some truth to the expression "It takes money to make money." Dual-income couples are starting to figure out how much it costs for both to work—and, most important, how much they actually net. According to the U.S. Labor Department, the average dual-income family loses up to two thirds of its second paycheck because of work-related expenses. This means that one spouse who earns $30,000 a year and works fifty to sixty hours a week (including commuting time) may actually be taking home only $10,000 after taxes. Is it worth neglecting the kids for $10,000 a year? Is it worth exhaustion? Stress on your marriage? For less than $5 an hour after taxes and expenses, why sell out your life?

People who do not go out to work have more time to buy and prepare food intelligently, stockpile supplies when prices are right, research major purchases, fix what's broken (without calling a plumber), make and enforce a budget. They also save money by cutting their own grass and doing odd jobs around the house. When these are included in the equation, that $10,000 mentioned above keeps shrinking, doesn't it?

As dual-income families study these numbers, they may ask themselves, "Why am I working?" This is an excellent question for all the working parents who said they would quit if they could afford it. Apparently, many can who didn't think they could!

Some dual-income couples eventually conclude that they'd be better off with a single family breadwinner. They are aware that the trade-off is more time for their children. It really boils down to priorities. Tough issues must be weighed. Couples may want to ask themselves: Can we adjust to reducing our lifestyle? Will we miss what we previously could afford? Do I plan to resume work when our preschoolers start school? Will dropping out of the workforce for a few years reduce my opportunities for advancement? Will I miss the excitement and challenges of the workplace? Will our family have adequate health insurance?

The "Columbine" Factor

What happened in Littleton, Colorado, on the morning of April 20, 1999, will be deeply ingrained in our memories, much like the John F. Kennedy assassination or the *Challenger* space shuttle explosion. At 11:21 A.M., two students entered Columbine High School and began a shooting spree. By noon, a nation watched in shock on national television. Few of us will ever forget the images of frightened boys and girls running past dead classmates, hands on their heads to show they were unarmed. The final tally: fifteen dead and twenty-two wounded.

School violence occurred often enough in the 1990s, but the Columbine massacre was by far the worst in American history. It was also the most vivid for millions of American parents, who realize that a Columbine can erupt in any community. It already has in Paducah, Kentucky; Conyers, Georgia; Jonesboro, Arkansas; Pearl, Mississippi; Granada Hills, California—no community is exempt.

"The places you used to think were safe have been violated by these random acts of violence," said Kathy Thomas, a mother of three from Thousand Oaks, California. "I certainly don't want my kids to live in fear."

Since Columbine, the near-universal response has been to beef up school security. Metal detectors and surveillance cameras have become nearly as common as trophy cases and sports banners.

How concerned are parents? In our August 1999 survey, 59 percent were very worried about the safety of their children at school, and 37 percent said they were somewhat worried. Only 5 percent didn't let it get to them. In the same survey, 70 percent of parents thought the danger in the schools would increase, while the remaining 30 percent were optimistic that safety in the schools would improve.

While Columbine and similar incidents are blamed on everything from peer pressure to the proliferation of guns, 73 percent of parents we surveyed said that both parents' working is also a factor; only 13 percent said it wasn't. Fourteen percent didn't know. With nearly three fourths of parents seeing the need for better supervision of children, we conclude that the dual-income family is on the decline.

Based on the above results, we asked if homeschooling was a plausible solution. To our surprise, 37 percent replied yes. Prior to Columbine, the interest in homeschooling simply reflected dissatisfaction with formal education in the United States. Homeschooling is defined as the "education of school-aged children at home rather than at school." Homeschoolers believe that students who receive instruction simultaneously from the home and the community at large will be culturally more sophisticated than those whose learning is mostly confined to a school.

How does homeschooling match up with conventional schooling? Available data show that not only do homeschooled children test above average, they closely match the performance of children in private schools. Brian D. Ray, president of the National Home Education Research Institute, notes that regardless of income, race, sex, or parents' level of education, homeschooled children consistently score between the eighty-second and eighty-third percentiles on achievement tests.

Today's informed parents are well aware of the educational advantages of homeschooling. Add in dissatisfaction with the public school environment (safety, drugs, peer pressure) and the idea of educating one's child at home is compelling. As homeschooling becomes a viable alternative to public schooling, working mothers are likely to drop out of the workforce to educate their offspring. A common characteristic shared by homeschooling parents is their confidence in their ability to educate their children competently with minimum institutional support. We suspect that many working mothers who assume this responsibility will come from professional and management ranks.

Working parents are not only worried about children in school. Our 1999 survey reveals that 97 percent feel strongly about having a parent at home for the kids after school. For obvious reasons, they are especially concerned about young children, but they worry about their kids' whereabouts whatever their age. Too well do they understand that bad influences can have bad consequences.

In a 1999 *Newsweek* poll, 64 percent of parents of children under eighteen were somewhat or very concerned that their children might get hurt or into trouble while visiting the homes of friends who own guns. "I lived in New York City for fourteen years and felt safer there because nobody had a gun in the house, but here people have rifles," said Debra Leonard, a physician who lives in rural Bethel Township, Pennsylvania. "I tell my kids nobody can protect themselves from a gun if it's not locked up in a cabinet, so they should leave the [friend's] house and call me to pick them up if anyone ever handles a gun."

Traditionally, working mothers have left their jobs to care for small children from diapers to schoolbags. Once the kids entered first grade, they resumed employment. But parents are starting to realize that older kids, who are volatile and hormone-driven, are the most likely to rebel and succumb to temptation. Here's where strong moral guidance is needed. Here's where close parental supervision should be applied. Here's where a parent is needed at home after school. In many ways, these are the critical, formative years.

Other Alternatives

Many dual-income families are unable to make ends meet on a single income. Having one parent drop out of the workforce is not always an option.

There are, however, other alternatives: part-time work, split shifts, telecommuting, and home-operated businesses all provide additional income and can indeed be scheduled around family. They also enable one parent to be home for the kids after school.

As long as a couple can manage on one and a half salaries, part-time employment can be a winning solution. It enables one parent to prioritize child care ahead of work. When one parent works a split shift, it enables parenting partners to take turns as child care providers. In a five-year study just released by the National Institute of Mental Health on first-time parents and the effects of working different shifts, one third of couples interviewed say they work different shifts to avoid having to pay for child care. Thus they maintain two incomes but must cope with the stress of having so little time together as a family. It definitely strains the marital relationship when husband and wife sleep different shifts. Telecommuting and home businesses are also good alternatives that enable a parent to stay home and still make money. But some people have difficulty being productive at home amid so many distractions. Another disadvantage is that home-based employees are never away from their work—and although they're physically there for the kids, mentally they're really not!

How You Can Benefit from This Trend

As the number of dual-income families dwindles, major economic consequences can be anticipated. The reduction in the number of qualified workers might increase the cost of labor; this effect, however, might be offset by decreases in the demand for goods. Single-income families will spend less on discretionary items. This will affect the consumption of expensive cars, high-priced houses, personal travel and vacations, restaurant meals, and so on. Business wardrobes will disappear from closets; dry cleaning and grooming budgets will shrink. Traditionally, cutbacks of this nature have caused economic havoc. But at present, we believe the economy is strong enough to withstand a downturn of this nature. Furthermore, efficiencies that result from Internet technology should offset expected labor shrinkage.

As a businessperson or investor, there are many ways you can cash in on this trend. One way is by involvement in the temporary employment business. Temp agencies are thriving and, we believe, are sound investments. As families learn to fix things themselves, home improvement centers such as Home Depot and Lowe's Home Improvement Warehouse will continue to prosper, as will fabric stores, craft stores, and garden centers.

Businesses that sell products for use in the home will also be big winners. Expect an increase in book, audio, and video sales, as well as sales of TVs, sound systems, and computer equipment.

Single-income families are more likely to shop at discount stores. Why? Because they will have more time on their hands and also be more value-driven. Retailers that mail out discount offers may find a more receptive audience. Likewise, these consumers will be more responsive to inserts and circulars offering brand coupons in the Sunday newspaper.

These consumers will also have more time for comparison shopping. Not only will they scrutinize ads to compare prices, they will read more labels at the supermarket. Since they will want quality, they will continue to purchase brand-name products.

Parents who have more time for their family will be able to participate in more school activities. Local businesses that sponsor school organizations will make a favorable impression and win new customers. Those same parents may now be able to watch more daytime TV. Companies that want to reach these women should plan their advertising programs accordingly. Likewise, these consumers will be free to shop on weekdays. Retailers should make note of this and be sufficiently well staffed to serve them. It should also be pointed out that upscale women are more demanding about receiving good service.

The real estate industry will also be affected by this trend. Some families may be able to afford only less expensive homes. Ironically, they will have more time to enjoy a nicer home, but sacrifices and compromises are necessary. However, because schools in suburban areas that are financially well supported by their communities are perceived as safer, real estate in the suburbs should continue to hold its value.

Experts say that quality time is the best recipe for creating healthy children. As parents spend more time with their children, hotels, theaters, restaurants, museums, galleries, shopping centers, and amusement parks that program activities for all ages will do well. Manufacturers of toys, games, bicycles, skates, and similar paraphernalia should also expect an increase in sales. Companies that sell casual clothing will benefit at the expense of those that sell business attire.

In conclusion, businesses that focus on the family will benefit.

Frequent-Buyer Programs Have Come to Govern Consumer Spending Habits

In 1981, American Airlines launched the first frequent-flyer program, American AAdvantage. Little did anyone suspect that its long-term impact would be felt around the world. Our 1999 research shows that 63 percent of all American households now participate in a frequent-buyer program. These programs go beyond air travel premiums; today, purchase points can be racked up on everything from flowers to charitable contributions. Program members can even double-dip, getting frequent-flyer miles as well as earning points on their credit card when purchasing a ticket!

InsideFlyer newsletter reports that no fewer than 3.6 trillion miles are sitting in people's accounts. Nearly half of these miles have come from credit card purchases, mutual fund investments, long-distance calls, and similar transactions.

"The whole pace of travel activity has intensified," says Rolfe Shellenberger, who developed American AAdvantage and is now a consultant for Runzheimer, a travel management research firm. "As a result, travelers are rich with miles, and there's more competition for whatever space there is."

According to Randy Petersen, editor of *InsideFlyer* newsletter and WebFlyer.com, this represents a major shift in the way airlines give away seats. By selling miles to corporate entities that use them to market their own products, the airlines essentially profit on unsold, full-price seats, fueling expectations that those seats will be available as freebies.

When American AAdvantage began in 1981, it was compared to Green Stamps, a popular supermarket bonus program dating back to the 1950s. Merchants gave stamps for money spent at their stores. Customers glued the stamps into small paperback books, which could be redeemed at Green Stamps outlets for merchandise. The tiny stamps were cumbersome to collect; they had to be licked or moistened before being glued onto a page, and dozens of books of stamps were needed to redeem even a small item such as a toaster. Rising costs and waning consumer interest led to the eventual demise of Green Stamps. Under the new programs, toasters were replaced by a far more desirable reward: free air travel.

As other airlines came out with similar programs and the competition heated up, other perks were added to complete the travel package: hotel rooms, car rentals, and cruise line cabins. Eventually, to attract consumers who rarely flew, lower levels of awards were created, so that customers could redeem points for less expensive items—perhaps even a toaster.

The Loyalty Factor

Many companies have aggressive marketing programs that focus mainly on getting new business and pay relatively little attention to maintaining their existing customers. They sometimes work so hard at making new sales, they neglect their loyal customers, who consequently switch companies. Imagine the reaction of a company that lost 5 percent of its inventory every quarter. Management would panic, bring in outside consultants, downsize, and perhaps even shut down warehouses until it solved the problem. Yet many companies lose much larger chunks of their customer base and ignore it altogether.

Frequent-buyer programs are designed to ensure customer retention. This isn't a brand-new concept. Rewarding good customers is one of the oldest practices in commerce. Good restaurateurs do this automatically, greeting their best customers by name, offering them choice tables, plying them with free drinks and desserts, and so on. Successful merchants do likewise: a boutique owner, for instance, may call a frequent customer to tell her that an outfit in her size and color just came in or that a particular dress just went on sale.

Frequent-buyer programs are different only because they are executed on a mass scale. Loyal customers equal repeat business, which over time builds a customer base.

When American Airlines began to award points for miles flown on its airline, customers were persuaded to fly American rather than other airlines. In theory, the more times customers flew American, the more likely they'd book future flights with the airline to keep accumulating points. American became *their* airline, as long as they were treated right. Consumers who are treated right don't shop around elsewhere. They become loyal customers, and they keep going back to "their beauty shop," "their dentist," "their clothing store." An airline that treats its customers well becomes "their airline."

In any business, there's a onetime acquisition cost for each new customer. A novice stockbroker, for example, spends a significant amount of time making cold calls to generate new accounts. But as he gathers clients over the years, he has to make fewer and fewer cold calls because his satisfied, loyal customers place repeat orders with him. If he fails to provide them with exceptional service and counsel, he'll have to continue making cold calls, which, like advertising, is an ongoing drain on time, if not money. Likewise, a retailer may advertise, run promotions, and even develop incentives to encourage customers to send friends to his store. Repeat business is better business because there's no acquisition cost. If enough customers keep coming back, a business can reduce or eliminate its advertising costs and fatten its bottom line.

It doesn't take a genius to realize that a company's most loyal customers are also its most profitable customers. The airlines have the right idea. Our 1999 research shows that 69 percent of frequent flyers are more loyal to the airline that gives them points. Considering that competing airlines offer a similar product at almost identical prices, this confirms that frequent-flyer programs have been a success.

Of course, there are degrees of loyalty. Twenty-two percent of the frequent-flyer members we surveyed admitted that they've paid more for a ticket rather than travel on a competing airline that wouldn't give them points. Likewise, 21 percent admitted to booking connecting flights with later arrival times just for the points. True, nearly 80 percent of those surveyed wouldn't pay more or accept inconvenience—but more than one in five would!

It's not that the other four out of five customers are disloyal. It's a matter of selecting another carrier when their airline of choice cannot offer comparable service. The loyalty factor of frequent flyers extends to making the hotel, or the car rental company their preferred choice.

Several credit card and long-distance companies give new customers 5,000 to 10,000 bonus points toward airline tickets and other rewards. That initial bonus puts customers well on their way to earning a trip, so the offer is quite valuable. Yet nothing prevents customers from signing up, redeeming their points, and then defecting. AT&T calls these customers "spinners" because they switch carriers back and forth—some as many as three times a year—always looking for the best deal. Such customers have no loyalty to any long-distance carrier, and they're not worth the cost of acquisition because they stay with the company for only a short time. Who needs business like this? This is not a smart way to win customers because it's only a matter of time until you lose them!

In the early 1990s, Pan American Airways advertised a three-week deal that offered 5,000 bonus miles for each flight between Boston and New York or vice versa. The round-trip cost of the flight then was $149. That meant that for two round trips costing $298, you'd get 20,000 bonus miles. A trip to Hawaii cost about $800, so some couples would fly to New York or Boston for a day of business or pleasure and got tickets to Hawaii in exchange. Did Pan Am think it was making customers more loyal? Or was it simply attracting customers in search of a great bargain? Frankly, we think offers like this have little to do with building brand loyalty and at best build loyalty only to the program itself. Had another airline come along with a better deal, those Pan Am customers would have happily walked to the competition's ticket counter.

There has to be a better way to win customers' loyalty than simply offering them wonderful deals. Pan Am only encouraged travelers to milk the system. Friends or colleagues boast, "So-and-so airlines paid me triple miles for flying in February, plus I received quadruple miles for connecting through St. Louis, plus extra points for my car rental because it was in the middle of the week."

Meanwhile, Pan Am has gone belly-up. The airlines have realized that bonus miles may work as a marketing tool in the short term, but they don't necessarily build brand loyalty.

What Do the Points Cost Businesses?

With 3.6 trillion points already awarded and more on the way, airlines seem to be acquiring an immense future debt. How much is a point worth, anyway?

One way to figure it out is to cash in your points and see what you get. This will vary from one program to another, and from one award to another. You'll have to compare the going rate of a hotel room, a car rental, a round-trip ticket from Kansas City to Paris, and so on. Since these prices fluctuate based on many different variables, you'll end up comparing apples with oranges. At best, you'll have a "guesstimate."

Our research shows that nonairline companies that work with airlines pay about one and a half cents per mile for their customers' frequent-flyer miles. Keep in mind that the airlines have a built-in profit on this cent-and-a-half charge, so it probably costs the airlines less than a penny a point. Also, some people are given points but never redeem them. In 1999, the nineteenth year of frequent-flyer programs, our research revealed that 27 percent of all members had not redeemed a single point.

What Consumers Think

Our 1999 survey asked, "When you turn in frequent-buyer points, do you feel you're getting something for nothing?" Forty-eight percent of Americans answered yes, slightly outnumbering the 46 percent who said no; 6 percent were undecided. The fact that most people believe they are getting a free gift leads us to believe that these programs are highly successful.

When asked if they would rather pay less for products and forgo the rewards, 74 percent said they would, while 26 percent said they would actually spend more in order to receive the rewards. Fifty-six percent think airlines that have reward programs must have to charge higher fares. However, most people would be insulted if they knew how little the airlines are actually giving them. In fact, the cost of giving awards is so insignificant that if the programs were discontinued, fares probably wouldn't drop.

What's so amazing about these numbers is that one in four consumers is actually willing to spend more to receive the points. When more than a quarter of their customers feel this way—considering what the programs actually cost—sponsors are getting a lot of bang for their buck. Where else can you give customers a 1 to 2 percent discount in exchange for their gratitude and loyalty?

We asked consumers who had turned in points during the previous twelve months how much they thought the points were worth. One third thought their free awards were worth more than $400. We also asked consumers to guess what 50,000 points were worth, and 45 percent thought more than $400. Our conclusion is that they have some vague ideas about what points are worth, but they haven't seriously thought it through. Consequently, they overestimate their actual value.

Seventy-three percent of the people belonging to a frequent-flyer program have converted their points to awards. Of those who did redeem points, 51 percent used them for travel. The most popular award was a coach class domestic ticket, followed by a domestic hotel room, a first-class international ticket, and a free car rental.

Forty-one percent of the people who have redeemed points said that they were able to take a vacation they otherwise wouldn't have taken. Since 63 percent of households belong to a frequent-flyer program, that means just under 20 percent of all Americans have taken at least one vacation as a direct result of an airline's frequent-flyer program. Furthermore, 94 percent of customers who used points for these vacations told us that the programs had helped them tremendously. This gives us an idea of the huge impact these programs have had on the U.S. travel industry.

Rumors abound that airlines don't actually want customers using their accumulated points, so they make it difficult. For instance, they might limit the available seating so members can't book flights on the dates they want to travel. When we surveyed people who had actually redeemed points, we found that these rumors were untrue. Seventy-six percent said the companies had made it easy to redeem their points. Only 10 percent disagreed, and the remaining 14 percent didn't have an opinion. Of the general public, only 14 percent thought companies did not want them to use frequent-buyer points.

With so many frequent-buyer programs in the marketplace, one might assume that they have steadily lost their impact. Our survey contradicts this, however. Ninety percent of the consumers we contacted said that although they have accumulated many points, their enthusiasm for the programs is as high as ever.

Then we asked consumers if companies should have the right to terminate unused points after a reasonable time. The response was equally split. We were surprised to see that half of all frequent-flyer members support this prerogative. Just the same, we would caution companies to be flexible in this practice as no company can afford to alienate 50 percent of its customer base. Accumulated frequent-buyer points should be viewed as a long-term debt—one that eventually must be paid. Considering that the points are worth only 1 to 2 percent of revenues, it's a small price to pay for loyal customers!

Whose Points Are They, Anyway?

Business travelers are often unable to purchase tickets at a discount because they don't know their plans in advance. They are also less likely to schedule Saturday-night layovers. Consequently, companies whose employees travel already incur significantly higher costs per ticket than nonbusiness travelers do. As a result, a new issue has surfaced: Should the traveling employee get the points, or should they go to the employer who paid for his ticket? Facing high fares, corporate America can make a strong case in favor of deserving the points. They can be applied to subsequent tickets, reducing the company's business travel expenditures.

No matter how reasonable it seems for a company to take points away from its employees, 69 percent of American employees believe the points should go to the individual who did the traveling. Only 14 percent thought the points belonged to the company, and the other 17 percent didn't have an opinion. We suspect that those who sided with the employer were not required to travel on company time. Thirteen percent of the employees who responded to this question added that if their points were taken away, they would quit immediately or start looking for a new job. It's mind-boggling to think that 13 percent of Americans are so strongly opposed to losing frequent-flyer miles that they would quit their jobs if they were taken from them!

Finally, 52 percent of employees who keep their points are grateful to their employer. But 28 percent aren't—they see the points as their due. The remaining 20 percent didn't care—again, we suspect that they don't travel on company time. Evidently, employees whose jobs take them away from their families feel entitled to the rewards as a form of compensation. It's certain that many travelers were opposed to losing their points, although not enough to quit.

Based on our studies, we recommend that frequent-flyer points should always go to the business traveler. We also believe that companies would be wise to promote this as a fringe benefit, thus generating employee appreciation. Companies could also have incentives based on performance whereby they cover other family vacation expenses when employees' points are redeemed. For example, a company could pick up part or all of their lodging costs or reimburse the cost of tickets to museums, sports events, and theme parks. These types of gestures that will be long remembered by employees and their families.

Regardless of who picks up the tab, 85 percent of Americans oppose any sort of government tax on the monetary value of redeemed points. They believe that there are already so many taxes on travel, including on airline tickets and hotels, as well as certain tourism taxes, that the government already gets its fair share of travel-related taxes.

Ingredients of a Successful Frequent-Buyer Program

Frequent-buyer programs have worked so well for the airlines that they're being offered by other services, from charges on credit cards to long-distance telephone calls. To consumers, these programs represent "something for nothing" because consumers are spending money they would have spent anyhow. Points induce a customer to buy from one company consistently. This increases customer loyalty.

We were interested in knowing what makes these programs so successful, especially when they only cost about 1 percent of total revenues. A 1 percent incentive is truly amazing, considering that today's consumers won't cross the street to shop at a 10 percent discount sale! Compared to the discounts a retailer must offer to entice today's shoppers, a successful frequent-buyer program is indeed a terrific bargain for its provider. Just the same, some work better than others. To enhance customer loyalty, a program should incorporate the following six objectives:

1. Value. Simply offering premiums and awards isn't enough—customers must perceive value. Four Seasons customers, for example, aren't going to stay at Days Inn just because they can get a better price with frequent-buyer points.

2. Choice. More and more programs now offer more selection. Airlines, for example, no longer limit their awards to airline tickets. They now offer hotel rooms, car rentals, club memberships, and even nontravel awards such as computers and clothing.

3. Aspirational value. Rewards should be something special, something the customer is excited to receive. The AT&T True Rewards program sputtered because the customers got only more long-distance calls. Americans don't aspire to win free phone calls. They're simply not a big deal to them. Today, AT&T offers frequent-flyer miles.

4. Relevance. This has two parts: Are consumers offered something that they really want, and can they reasonably earn rewards? This may take some customer research to find out what a company's customers want. And if the number of points required is set so high that customers think they're unattainable, they'll either give up or just lose interest. Rewards might be set at various levels. For instance, 10,000 points might be redeemable for a weekend stay at a hotel, 5,000 points for a dinner for two, and so on. Once customers start reaping rewards, they'll be hooked.

5. Convenience. A fatal flaw in a frequent-buyer program is difficulty redeeming points. Companies should make it easy, or they'll risk losing their customers.

6. Communication. Members should be informed of exactly what they can win and how they can do so. A newsletter distributed with frequent-buyer correspondence is a wonderful way to circulate other news about a company.

These six criteria were covered in a landmark article by Louise O'Brien and Charles Jones, "Do Rewards Really Create Loyalty?" in the May–June 1995 issue of *Harvard Business Review.* Our 1999 research confirms much of what they said. For instance, 35 percent of consumers said they would stay in a more expensive hotel and rent a higher-priced car to rack up frequent-buyer points. A business traveler who stays at fifty hotels a year could certainly moderate his expenses and save enough to purchase something more valuable than what he ends up with in a frequent-buyer program. But the nicer travel and accommodations *plus* the points are evidently worth more to him.

No frequent-buyer program can overlook aspirational value or the dream factor. Consumers love to dream about owning and doing things that seem grand and extravagant and that are not realistically within reach. Now, with frequent-buyer points, some of their dreams can be fulfilled. Here's how the consumers we surveyed plan to redeem their frequent-buyer points:

First-class international airline ticket	16%
Domestic hotel	14%
Coach class domestic ticket	12%
Cruise	10%
Coach class international ticket	7%
Free car rental	6%
First-class domestic airline ticket	4%
Electronic equipment	3%
Clothing	3%
Savings bond	3%
International hotel room	2%
Car rental discount	2%
Gift certificate of $500 or more	2%
Jewelry	2%
Luggage	2%
Recreational equipment	2%
Long-distance telephone calls	2%
Gift certificate up to $250	1%
Local phone service	1%
Gift certificate from $250 to $499	1%
Don't know	5%

We asked frequent-buyer members what they thought would enhance their programs. Right behind more points, they wanted a wider selection of merchandise requiring fewer points. Not everyone wants a big, exotic prize that's practically unattainable. We found that frequent flyers are in fact most likely to cash in their points for car rentals, domestic hotel rooms, coach class domestic airline tickets, and first-class domestic airline tickets. What's surprising is that free flights for coach and first-class flights were in third and fourth places. Note that the rewards people actually settled for were not the same as the aspirations listed above when they planned to redeem points for coach domestic tickets (third place) and first-class domestic tickets (seventh place).

This confirms the O'Brien-Jones findings that many customers lose interest if it takes too long to be rewarded or if the "big prize" requires too many points. When less expensive gifts such as magazine subscriptions or small electronics are offered, more consumers can participate, which broadens a company's customer base.

The downside of offering low-level awards is that companies end up rewarding all of their customers instead of just their best ones. On the surface, this seems equitable. But a company's best customers are its most profitable customers, so they are more deserving. For example, when a "big prize" such as a trip to Australia is offered, customers have a long-term incentive to stick around. And the more they keep coming back, the more they think of you as their company.

Still, more and more frequent-buyer programs are offering smaller awards. Is this good business? Eighty percent of the people surveyed said that frequent-buyer programs in general have improved during the past five to ten years. Forty percent of that group were impressed that programs are now offering more points, and 20 percent said that a larger selection of merchandise requiring fewer points was what they liked most. Based on this, we're inclined to recommend offering lower-level awards.

Our research reveals that 49 percent of people have less loyalty to a company that makes it inconvenient to cash in points. Forty-seven percent said that this doesn't sway their loyalty, and the rest had no opinion. This tells us that customers like rewards, but if the carrot is dangled too far ahead of them for too long, they get upset and their loyalty diminishes. The lesson here is: don't make them angry, or your program will backfire. The wrong program might do more harm than good.

In "Making Loyalty Programs More Rewarding," in the March 1999 issue of *Direct Marketing,* Kurt Johnson stated that he uses a six-month "attainability rule." In other words, the average member should get some kind of reward within six months. For example, if a company's average customer spends $2,000 annually, he should be eligible to earn a first-level reward after spending a maximum of $1,000. According to Johnson, a good rule of thumb is that a program should deliver on average at least $30 to $40 in perceived retail value per year.

Perceived value is an important consideration. The objective is for customers to perceive that the value of their rewards is greater than what the company pays for them. How does this work? If the reward is cash, the perceived value of one dollar is one dollar. When customers redeem points for merchandise, travel, or partnership rewards, however, a company gets more bang for its buck. Ultimately, what they receive seems as if it's worth more than what it actually cost the company. In other words, for each dollar the company spends on an award, customers should feel that what they get is worth two to three dollars. Tangible rewards of this kind always outperform cash.

Sheraton Hotels and Resorts' frequent-buyer program offers members cash instead of rewards. We think the hotel chain should offer privileges that would appear more valuable than cash.

It's difficult for customers to assess the value of frequent-flyer points. That's because so many variables make one ticket more valuable than another. The cost depends upon when the ticket is purchased, when the flight takes place, travel restrictions, and so on. If you don't believe this, ask five strangers on your next flight what their tickets cost. Chances are that each will quote a different fare!

The Critical Difference

Every company strives for a competitive advantage over its competition, which becomes the critical difference in getting market share. In many industries, the airlines being a prime example, consumers have difficulty differentiating among companies. A well-executed frequent-buyer program can become the tiebreaker. Industries offering products and services that have value consumers cannot easily assess get good results from frequent-buyer programs.

Our 1999 research revealed that 39 percent of all Americans had changed credit card companies to earn frequent-buyer points. In the same study, we learned that 25 percent had changed their long-distance service for the same reason. These high numbers show that a company neck-and-neck with its competition will lose a large amount of market share if its competition has a frequent-buyer program and it doesn't.

In today's competitive marketplace, there is no longer a choice "to have or not to have" a frequent-buyer program. All major credit card companies and long-distance carriers now offer them. And we're now seeing more frequent-buyer programs in other industries. Actually, simply having a program is not enough. A company has to go one better. A credit card company, for example, may offer its card and a frequent-flyer program and charge no annual fee, as well. Or it may offer a six-month interest-free period after the card is issued. Its frequent-buyer program may offer a 5,000- to 10,000-point bonus for signing up. Another company may outstrip the competition by advertising alluring prizes for fewer points.

Here are seven ways of injecting some excitement into your company's frequent-buyer program:

1. If your competition has a rewards program, go one better with a sweepstakes. Depending on your budget, it could be a chance to win a new car, a vacation of a lifetime, or a large cash prize. But anything under a minimum of a $5,000 cash prize for even a local contest won't get customers' attention.

2. Consider a "buy one, get one free" promotion.

3. An interest-free promotion is effective on big-ticket items that cost $500 or more.

4. Short-term reward programs are effective. For example, you might offer a set of fine china over an eight-week period (e.g., making all five pieces of a table setting available to program members with a minimum purchase of $75 plus $9.95). Remember to make the award something special that consumers would love to own.

5. Create a sense of urgency by having a reward program special that runs for a limited time, which encourages your customers to respond *now*. You can offer double points for a certain period or a special discount for a specified number of days. This will stimulate customers who normally shop at your store only during its big sale to act now.

6. A program should have customer rewards that don't take "forever" to earn something. Make sure your program offers some rewards for a relatively small number of points.

7. Make sure your customers know all the rules, and make them easy to understand. Customers become discouraged when they're confused about a frequent-buyer program. Remember that your objective is to create customer loyalty, not confusion.

A Rosy Future

We asked, "Do you think more companies should offer frequent-buyer programs?" Seventy-five percent of our respondents answered yes, while only 20 percent said no.

We followed up with the question "If you owned a company, would you create a frequent-buyer program?" Twenty-eight percent said they would not, and 16 percent didn't know—but 58 percent said they would. Seventy-three percent of the people who would start a program said they'd do it even if it meant giving up profits.

These numbers tell us that Americans believe in frequent-buyer programs and are willing to put money behind their opinions.

A Frequent Bettor Program

One of the most effective and unusual programs we came across is conducted by Harrah's Entertainment, Inc. The gaming company, which currently has 19 million customers in its database, is still growing. To reach these numbers, Harrah's has invested more than $100 million in computers and software to develop what is widely regarded as the industry's most sophisticated "frequent bettor" program. Like airline frequent-flyer plans, Harrah's "Total Rewards" program awards participant perks—for instance, rooms, meals, and other benefits—and bombards them with promotional mail. In 1997, Harrah's started its rewards program. Here's how it works: customers are issued a card to insert into slot machines to track their gambling activity. The more that customers play the slots, the more points they accumulate. At blackjack, craps, and other gaming tables, pit bosses and casino managers record customers' play. With its technology in place, the company gathers personal information about its customers, which could include their superstitions, entertainment preferences, and how frequently they visit a casino. This information is then used to encourage them to spend more time at Harrah's. For example, knowing that many of its loyal customers from around the country like to gamble periodically in venue-rich Las Vegas, Harrah's sends them discount vouchers and other enticements to play at Harrah's rather than at competing casinos. Furthermore, a customer who hasn't visited for a while is likely to receive a call offering an incentive to come back soon.

Las Vegas, the mecca of gambling, is home to the most expensive hotels in the world. Other casinos have invested huge sums in bricks and mortar. Bellagio, the most expensive hotel in the world, is said to have cost $1.6 billion. Bellagio also invested an estimated $300 million in its world-class art collection, plus another $100 million in its theatrical production of "O," reportedly the most expensive show ever, anywhere. Then there are the "theme" hotels in Vegas—the pyramid-shaped Luxor; New York, New York, with its replicas of the Big Apple's famed skyline; and Treasure Island, featuring two life-size pirate ships that battle nightly. Keep in mind, all Vegas casinos offer the same products—slot machines and gaming tables—so it's not the product that brings customers through the front door. Harrah's has put its money into technology to learn about its customers, communicate with them, and reward them for their loyalty through its Total Rewards program. In the long run, we think this kind of investment beats the facades its competitors have constructed. That's why we bet on Harrah's with its current twenty-one casinos to be the long-term winner in the gaming industry.

More than 80 percent of Harrah's revenues—an estimated $3 billion—comes from the most loyal 20 percent of its customers. The company's chief operating officer, Gary Loveman, architect of the Total Rewards program, insists the only way to grow without building new casinos is to entice the most loyal customers to keep coming back. Loveman's ultimate goal is to make customers so faithful to Harrah's that they won't stray to competing casinos. Right now, he figures Harrah's gets only 26 percent of what its customers spend in casinos overall. "We don't have to get customers to play any more than they already do," he says. "We just have to get 40 cents out of their dollar instead of 26."

Come Fly with the Trend

Based on our surveys and on the fact that 63 percent of Americans belong to frequent-buyer programs, we believe these programs have become part of Americana and are here to stay for a long, long time. If your company has one, we hope we have shown you how to improve yours. If you don't have one, let's discuss how you can start one.

You don't have to own or operate an airline, hotel chain, or long-distance service to participate. For example, Neiman-Marcus has InCircle Rewards and Saks Fifth Avenue has SaksFirst. Both offer rebates and rewards as incentives to use their own credit cards. There are many opportunities for big and small companies to start a program.

Ultimately, these programs are based on the principle of offering customers a baker's dozen: a customer buys twelve cookies, doughnuts, or rolls and gets a thirteenth free. A dry cleaner, for instance, can punch a customer's card for every $20 spent, and after twelve punches the customer gets a free dry cleaning. This approach can work with businesses ranging from shoe stores to amusement parks: "Buy twelve pairs, and get your thirteenth pair free." "Visit ten times, and the eleventh visit is free." Programs of this nature are elementary; just the same, they generate repeat business. We've heard about such programs working for bus companies, pizza shops, packaged goods companies, and casinos.

It's important that your employees be enthusiastic about your rewards program. If they're nonchalant, your customers' enthusiasm will be diminished. Your employees must reinforce the value of the rewards.

Our studies show that for a frequent-buyer program to truly excite people, the reward has to be something that's "out of the ordinary" or "on the exotic side." So a supermarket that offers a dollar's worth of food for 99 cents isn't going to turn too many customers on. The same supermarket, however, might partner with an airline to reward customers with international trips. Just imagine the excitement of a working-class family that has always dreamed of visiting Tahiti and suddenly finds it a possibility.

Partnering with an existing frequent-buyer program is an ideal way to be a player. Even medium-sized companies can buy points from an airline or hotel chain at a slight premium. But the cost will be less than 3 percent of your revenues, which isn't prohibitive considering the repeat business you'll generate.

If your company does business only locally, you might consider forming an association with other local merchants. Points could be redeemed for prizes at other members' stores within the group.

Before you start your program, make sure it's practical. It's a big decision and requires a long-term commitment, with obligations that will arise several years down the road.

One last thing: loyalty is a two-way street. Ask yourself these questions:

- Would customers switch to a competitor to save money?

- Would they switch for a new product or better service?

- Would they switch simply because a competitor asked them to switch? This may sound frivolous, but remember, AT&T customers sometimes switch to MCI or Sprint just because they're asked!

Then ask yourself these questions:

- Do I give preferential treatment to existing customers?

- Do I communicate with them regularly to see whether they're satisfied?

- Do I let them know I appreciate their business?

- Do I make them feel I care about them?

- Do I know their needs and cater to them?

Today's Consumer Wants Brand-Name Products

What do athletic shoes, chicken, mattresses, and ketchup have in common? They, like most products, sell far better when they have established brand names.

Branding is a hot topic in boardrooms because most CEOs recognize that a strong brand is a powerful driver of shareholder value. Indeed, McKinsey & Company analysis suggests that about half the market value of the *Fortune* 250 is tied into intangible assets. For some of the world's best-known companies, the figure is even higher.

In 1999 McKinsey researched the connection between brand strength and corporate performance at 130 consumer companies. It suggests that strong brands generate, on average, total returns to shareholders that are 1.9 percent above the industry average, while weaker brands lag behind the average by 3.1 percent. With numbers like these, it's no wonder marketing executives plead with the bean counters for extra bucks to develop their brand names.

We discovered something very interesting about this trend: every ten years, there is a two-and-a-half-year period when brands are less important to American consumers. During these periods, consumers become extremely price-conscious and are willing to buy Brand X rather than a national brand. America's Research Group has studied

consumer buying habits over the past twenty years, and this historical trend has remained constant. The last two-and-a-half-year period
ended in 1995, so we can anticipate the current demand for brand-
name products to continue until 2002.

Pushing private labels while brands are hot can be calamitous.
In 1994, Montgomery Ward decided to discontinue major brands
and sell its own private-label merchandise. The giant retailer in-
tended to capture a bigger markup, and for a period, its profit margins were impressive. But when the brand cycle kicked in again,
Montgomery Ward's sales took a nosedive and the company went
into bankruptcy. Such is the peril of going against the grain of a
major trend.

Over time, consumers resent paying for so-called premium
products and quit buying them. It's as if they wise up and realize
they're not getting the added value for the higher price. Then, after
a couple of years or so, they begin buying them again.

Why Consumers Buy Brand-Name Products

Let's start with why brands aren't always the first choice of all sellers
and buyers. First, retailers don't make as much on brand-name
products as they do with generic or private-label products. Second,
consumers usually pay a higher price for a brand name. So why the
big fuss over brands, especially when sellers make less and buyers
pay more?

Our 1999 survey showed that 60 percent of American consumers will pay a higher price to buy a brand-name product. Only
two years ago, a similar ARG study indicated that 51 percent were
willing to spend more. This time we asked consumers why:

1. **I believe I will get better quality.** For years, the public perception
has been that a brand known by name, reputation, and so on is better than an unknown brand.

2. **I feel I can trust the company.** Consumers believe that a familiar
company will stand behind its brand; they're not so sure about an
unknown one.

3. I know what I am getting. Consumers feel that they know who they are doing business with when they buy a company brand and there won't be any surprises later on.

4. I believe I can rely more on the company and its product. Again, consumers rely on the company's reputation and believe it will be around if there's a problem down the road. An unknown company might close down or pull out in the middle of the night.

5. I think it will be worth more to me. Consumers will pay more because they think a known brand is worth more. Why? For all of the reasons above, and then some.

More than 80 percent said the five reasons above somewhat or definitely apply to why they buy brands. After careful analysis we concluded that each of the above five answers was actually directly or indirectly related to saving time. This is clearly an example of how one trend co-exists with another.

Let's say you're at a supermarket in the orange juice section. The choices are Minute Maid and the store brand. Even though the private-label product costs 20 percent less, Minute Maid goes into your cart. Sure, you can read the nutrition facts on each carton to make a choice, but that's time-consuming. Not many people are willing to read the package of every food they consider buying. So they assume that the brand-name product is probably better. Although it costs more, you believe you'll get your money's worth.

You do the same thing when you choose Smucker's jam over Mary Jane's, and Vlasic pickles over Peter's. It doesn't matter that you spend more money; it's quicker. Besides, you know and trust these brands, and you don't want to take any chances on a generic product.

Trust is particularly important when it comes to buying baby formula. After all, your baby's health is no place to cut corners. This is why Similac and Enfamil command 86 percent of the American market, according to ACNielsen. Even when educated mothers read the labels of generic products and find that the ingredients are identical, they tend to stick with Similac and Enfamil.

Your next stop is the liquor store. With products you buy less frequently, you're even more brand-conscious. That's why you're likely to buy Smirnoff or Absolut vodka over other brands half the price. In fact, if you mix the vodka with orange juice or tonic, the difference in taste is so negligible that you might as well have purchased the cheap vodka.

On your way home, you drive by several cut-rate gasoline stations and pull into a Shell station to fill up your tank. Do you really think there's a difference in the quality of gas that warrants paying an extra ten cents a gallon? The truth is, you don't know. You probably do the same thing with oil, tires, and so on. Chances are you even decided which car to buy based on its brand name.

Our research confirms that the American consumer thinks the product with the most familiar name offers the best quality in its category. This is why consumers are willing to pay a premium for such products. It's important to realize that this is what they think, their perception. It's not necessarily reality.

The World's Most Famous Brand-Name Product

It's not possible to bring up the subject of brands without discussing Coca-Cola, the world's most recognized product.

When pharmacist John Stith Pemberton first concocted Coca-Cola in 1886, he had no idea that someday it would be sold in more than two hundred countries around the world. Today, Coca-Cola is the most recognized brand name in the world. The company's market capitalization is in the $150 billion range, making it one of the richest corporations in the world. More than anything else, this market value is based on its brand, which analysts concur is worth more than its tangible assets. And for good reason: it is indeed consumers' perception that causes them to crave a "Coke" to quench their thirst, even though dozens of imitators have knocked the product off and some have succeeded in manufacturing a product that is nearly indistinguishable from Coca-Cola.

In the early 1900s, figuring out the exact formula was no easy matter. Today, however, sophisticated laboratories have the capacity to break it down, analyze it, and come up with a beverage to challenge the "real thing." But try to get a Coke fan to settle for a Pepsi and see how unhappy he becomes. Granted, taste is important. But we know what's really important is the Coca-Cola name.

Brand Loyalty

In general, a consumer must save at least 25 percent, ideally 33 to 40 percent, to switch from his or her preferred brand to a private-label product.

We asked 1,002 adults nationwide to rate products to which they are very loyal. The highest-rated products were:

1. Soft drinks	33.9%
2. Insurance	32.6%
3. Bath soap	30.9%
4. Hair products	30.6%
5. Health and beauty aids	29.9%
6. Automobiles and trucks	29.0%
7. Coffee	28.9%
8. Mayonnaise	28.1%
9. Laundry products	26.4%
10. Over-the-counter medicines and pain relievers	26.4%
11. Toilet paper	26.0%

When it comes to products that they consume on a daily basis, such as beverages, cleaners, and so on, Americans know what they like. But insurance? It ranked number two on the list. We concluded that clients are loyal to an agent who gives them personal service and because auto insurance is sometimes difficult or expensive to obtain, people feel compelled to stay with the company that is willing to insure them—as long as the premium seems fair.

Building a Strong Brand Name

With the exception of women's apparel, brand names are rarely established in a short period of time. They're built either through extensive advertising or over extended time by word of mouth. Electrolux is a good example of a strong brand name that was established through word of mouth. The manufacturer of vacuum cleaners and floor polishers consistently provided a product of both high quality and superior service.

Rich Luisi, executive VP of sales, explained that Electrolux customers have seen their mothers and grandmothers use them for years. "Our reputation precedes us," he said. "Sure, we can show a pile of endorsement letters during a presentation, but nothing is as convincing as having products stand the test of time in their own families."

With so many women in the workforce, direct-sales organizations without established brand names are on tough ground. Because today's women are so pressed for time, they are reluctant to open their doors to salespeople representing an unknown company. They are also afraid to allow a stranger to enter their house—but are more willing when the salesperson or serviceperson represents a well-known company.

This prompted us to ask Luisi, "In today's business environment, how could someone successfully sell a nonbrand floor care product?"

"It would be five times more difficult," Luisi replied. "Electrolux stands for quality and great service. That name opens doors for us that would otherwise be closed."

Luisi, a living legend among Electrolux salespeople, holds many national sales records. So we asked him, "What does Electrolux do to convince prospects to listen to a sales presentation? How do their salespeople close sales? Is the Electrolux brand a major factor?"

"We've been in this business for over seventy-five years," Luisi said, "and have sold over fifty million vacuum cleaners. We have over six hundred service locations throughout North America that handle our products, so there are many customers who need repairs and supplies. They think their friends and relatives would like our product, too, and they refer them to us. By having a terrific product, a great service department and strong brand identity, our company is way ahead of the curve."

Nike is a prime example of an athletic sporting goods company that built a brand reputation through strong marketing. It signed basketball hero Michael Jordan to promote his own line of shoes. The Air Jordan brand name became synonymous with gotta-have athletic footwear and headed the top of Christmas lists all over America. Through subsequent advertising with Charles Barkley, Brett Favre, Ronaldo, Ken Griffey, Jr., Venus Williams, Andre Agassi, and Tiger Woods, Nike captured nearly 50 percent of the U.S. athletic footwear market. Whether Nike products are better than Reebok, Fila, or Converse is irrelevant; consumers think they are, and that's what counts because perception is what sells a product.

The Value of a Reputation

It's estimated that the franchising industry accounts for one third of all retail sales in America. This includes everything from fast food to automobiles. And franchising succeeds because of a brand loyalty acquired through consistent levels of product and service. This consistency is what established McDonald's reputation for quality. You go to McDonald's because you know exactly what you'll get—there are no surprises. A Big Mac tastes the same in Manhattan as in Omaha. When you pull off the interstate, you'll choose McDonald's over Fred's because you know exactly what to expect. You trust the food to be fresh, well prepared, and safe to eat. Franchisees invest in McDonald's because consumers recognize the golden arches wherever they go. And the company's annual advertising budget to promote its brand name exceeds $1 billion.

Likewise, customers have definite expectations of certain hotels. For example, they expect cleanliness at a Holiday Inn, as the chain has historically provided a level of quality that represents a good value. They expect Four Seasons or Ritz-Carlton to provide more than just cleanliness. They pay more, but they receive value for their money. Unlike many independently owned hotels, the large chains can rely on the reputation of their name.

Grocery shoppers are willing to pay extra when they buy a brand that is consistent—that has the same taste, tenderness, and quality every time. The poultry industry can provide this because big poultry companies generally own everything in the production chain, including feed mills and egg operations, and nearly all chicken and turkey sold at supermarkets today carries a brand name. Much of the branding is tied to the processor, but some poultry products are marketed under the retailer's brand. According to the National Broiler Council, branded chicken typically sells for at least ten cents a pound more than nonbranded birds.

Brand names go beyond consumer products and services. The number of applications to famous-name colleges is on the rise. Many suburban schools send 70 to 80 percent of their students to college, and as globalization of the economy continues, vocational education is dwindling, down nearly 50 percent from its peak. In 1999, the number of students enrolled in four-year institutions of higher education set a new record: 14.8 million, up from the record 14.6 million in fall 1998. All this creates pressure on young people. They're as concerned today about attending the right school as their predecessors worried about having a good résumé on leaving college. Ivy League schools and top-tier universities such as Northwestern, Duke, and Stanford are receiving a record number of applications from top students across the country.

Graduating seniors from top colleges want to land jobs with prestigious corporations. Recruiters from such companies that visit college campuses generally have the most students signing up for interviews. Why? Perhaps it's the "success breeds success" syndrome. But more likely, well-known companies, like well-known products and colleges, stand for quality in people's minds.

Salespeople, too, are eager to represent brand-name companies. Think about it: Wouldn't you be more likely to accept a phone call from a friend with Merrill Lynch than from one with a brokerage firm you'd never heard of? And wouldn't you be more inclined to buy a vacuum sweeper from an Electrolux salesman than one with Company X? There's no question that a salesperson representing a company with a good reputation has a significant advantage over the competition, and—from a recruiting point of view—we suspect he earns more commissions, too.

In an ARG study in early 2000, we measured the value of brand names appearing in advertising. Our survey made comparisons of a retailer's ad featuring a Maytag washer, which is a 40 percent brand, with a White/Westinghouse washer, which is a brand that influences 7 percent of shoppers. Based on the results, we concluded that a Maytag ad featuring a $499 washer will drive more customers than a White/Westinghouse washer at $399. Maytag's 4:1 brand impact leadership demands that White/Westinghouse must run an ad price point from under $299 to reach the same number of shoppers.

As expected, strong brand names and a strong retailer combination attract more traffic than a strong brand product with a weak store image or a strong store combined with a weak brand product combination. When a retailer with a strong brand name places an ad that offers a strong brand product at low price points, watch out! This is the winning ticket to drive customers into a store.

In the eyes of shoppers, a $249 La-Z-Boy brand recliner is more attractive than a $229 Berkline recliner. Even selling at $20 lower Berkline loses, because the La-Z-Boy brand name rates a premium higher than 10 percent over Berkline. La-Z-Boy would have to be priced over $100 in order for Berkline to be able to create the same traffic in an advertisement.

Never lose sight of the fact that when strong brand names exist, many brands have as many loyal users as the store has loyal customers. Further analysis of the most effective ads often reveals shopping response was divided between customers who wanted to buy from that store and customers who wanted to buy that brand.

People feel more comfortable spending on the brands they know. So brands can help make or break a newspaper ad—the "right" entry-level price point coupled with the "right" brands offered by the "right" store is a winning combination. More than 59 percent of buyers look first for brands in ads. When they see "their" brand, people say, "That speaks to me."

Perception Sells

Obviously, the biggest thing a strong brand has going for it is that it's perceived as the best. Consumers believe that a brand they know has to be better than a brand they don't know. They think that if another product was better, they would know it. It doesn't matter that Hitachi may make a better TV than Sony. The perception in America is that Sony is the best, and so it outsells Hitachi by a wide margin. Similarly, most Americans would choose Broyhill furniture over Thomasville. Broyhill isn't better, but it's perceived as better, so it outsells Thomasville.

One of our favorite success stories is how Heinz Foods, founded in 1876, has been making America's number-one-selling ketchup for more than thirty years. Found in 97 percent of households, ketchup is the king of condiments; Heinz's market share is in excess of 50 percent. What we find so spectacular about Heinz ketchup is that it monopolizes the restaurant industry. It's rare to find a restaurant that serves another brand. Heinz ketchup is perceived as the best by a majority of Americans, and no restaurateur worth his salt wants his patrons to think he's cutting corners by serving an unknown brand.

Brand-name products sell better when the nontraditional shopper does the buying. When a wife, for example, sends her husband to the supermarket, he's much more likely to buy a bottle of ketchup with the Heinz label on it because it's the only brand he recognizes. To illustrate our point, let's say she gave him a "generic" shopping list instructing him to pick up the following five items: "box of tissues, salt, chocolate syrup, frozen peas, and mayonnaise."

Chances are his shopping bag would contain the following brand products: Kleenex, Morton's, Hershey's, Birds Eye, and Hellmann's. Why do we think a husband would be likely to buy the above brands? Our logic is based on the theory that when shopping for someone else and in doubt about what product to purchase, people tend to buy the most familiar brand names. They buy brand names because it reduces the risk of buying the wrong thing. As more husbands and wives shop for each other to reduce their combined time spent shopping, sellers of brand-name products will reap the benefits.

Private Labels

With all the reasons why consumers buy brand names, there's still a case to be made for private labels. Many retailers favor the use of a private label to enhance profits, stimulate customer loyalty, and offer their product at a lower price to their customer. With the middleman eliminated, margins are greater—even at a 25 percent lower price, savings can be passed on to the customer.

One prime example of a strong private label is Brooks Brothers. Founded in 1847, America's oldest clothier has a brand more recognized than other clothing manufacturers' brands, which makes it quite valuable. Loyal customers are proud to wear Brooks Brothers clothing, which can't be purchased anywhere but in a Brooks Brothers store. Its golden fleece trademark stands for quality and exclusivity—as well as a well-deserved higher markup.

Federated Department Stores, the largest such operator in the United States—over four hundred department stores and one hundred fifty specialty shops—currently promotes Macy's own brand Charter Club, a line of apparel and home accessories. Other Macy's private brands include Alfani, Arnold Palmer, Club Room, I.N.C., The Cellar, and Tools of the Trade. Before merging with Macy's, Federated had an estimated thirty-five people working in its private-brand sector, which accounted for less than 5 percent of total sales. Today, that group of thirty-five has grown to four hundred, pushing toward 15 percent of total sales. While established vendors may not like Federated's trend, they aren't contesting the giant retailer. Consumers who comparison shop will find Federated private-label merchandise somewhat cheaper than branded goods. Federated wisely maintains a balanced mix of brand names and private labels to satisfy its customers and vendors.

Grocery chains also take advantage of private labeling. For example, Byerly's, the large grocery chain, has its own Chef's Market brand meat products. Cub Foods, another giant grocer, promotes its Smokehouse line. Why? After soft drinks, meat is the next largest dollar-producing category in overall grocery store sales. So there's extra profit to be made by selling it under a private label.

When it comes to selling brand names, perhaps nobody gets more excited than do drug outlets. Drugstores mark up the price of some generics by more than 1,000 percent, for example, $34 for ulcer medication that can cost a store less than $3.

Markups on some generics are extraordinarily high, as revealed by market researcher PMSI Scott-Levin. For example, stores charge an average of $18.08 for the generic equivalent of the antipsychotic drug Haldol, 2,800 percent more than the 62 cents paid to the manufacturer. A prescription for the generic version of Zovirax, an antiviral drug, sells at pharmacies for about $61.64, more than eight times the manufacturer's price of $7.22. Generic "Xanax" sells for $15.56, while pharmacies can buy it for about 78 cents. Markups on the branded versions of these drugs, by comparison, generally range from 10 percent to 30 percent.

Of course, a precious gem is a blind item, meaning price comparisons are difficult because no two stones are identical. So in the jewelry industry, consumers buy stones such as diamonds and rubies based on the reputation of the jeweler. Nationally, while firms such as Tiffany and Cartier have long been recognized as brands, many local jewelers in cities across the country have also established their stores as the place to shop locally for fine jewelry. Such merchants attach and receive large markups.

On the other hand, the name of a major publisher seems to

have relatively little effect on the purchase of a book. Consumers typically buy books based on the subject or the author's reputation. Thus, established authors can be considered brand names. Fans of Stephen King and John Grisham will buy their latest book, regardless of its title or theme. And writers Mark Hansen and Jack Canfield have built a career with their *Chicken Soup for the Soul* series.

Just how well brand names sell varies from one industry to another. In our 1999 survey, we asked consumers if they would be more or less likely to buy a brand name product, and here's how they responded:

Kind of Product	More Likely	Same	Less Likely
Major appliance	57%	24%	19%
Women's apparel	45%	30%	25%
Men's apparel	45%	28%	27%

In the same study, when we asked them whether they'd buy a brand over a generic or private-label product, 49 percent answered they'd be more likely, 23 percent said it didn't matter, and 28 percent said they'd be less likely. When asked about electronic products, 53 percent said they would be more likely to buy Sony or RCA than Sharp or Hitachi.

Brand-Name People

As mentioned, even some people are brand names. Ralph Lauren, Donna Karan, and Ann Taylor come to mind. All started companies that they named after themselves, which through exceptional marketing became household names.

Oprah Winfrey is also a brand name. She is a phenomenon because she started as a talk-show host and became an icon. According to John Grace, executive director of New York–based Interbrand Group, "Oprah stands for a certain set of very specific American values that very few of her celebrity competitors can claim, like honesty, loyalty, and frankness. It's a value set that is rare in business institutions and celebrities. If you ask people if they trust celebrities—even the ones they like—the answer is probably no. If you ask any consumer or viewer about Oprah, they will say yes. That's because she has established a fundamental trust in an era of skepticism. That's why she resonates so well."

Charlotte Beers, chairwoman of J. Walter Thompson, believes that Winfrey has succeeded in separating herself from other talk shows by "informing, inspiring, and teaching in a way that is classified as entertainment. That's what you call a neat trick."

Another successful personality who sells products is Martha Stewart, whose publicly owned Martha Stewart Living Omnimedia is based on her commercial image. The high priestess of gracious living split from Time Warner in 1997 to form her own media conglomerate of books, magazines, TV, radio, newspapers, and catalogs. Like Oprah, Martha has a following and, like other company founders who become brand names, presents a risk. A corporation is legally perpetual. Human beings are not, something a long-term investor should consider.

Karyl Innis, a Dallas career management consultant, said, "The company needs to change from an individual to a brand image—much like Betty Crocker." Innis thinks the company "has to figure out how to replicate in a brand, in a product, the subjective aspects of what she is."

"But history suggests that not many people have been able to do that—particularly around something as subjective as taste," adds Kenneth Roberts, chairman of Lippincott & Margulies, a brand-consulting firm in Manhattan. For every Chanel—hardly remembered by today's generation as Coco's signature—there is a Laura Ashley, the British fabric designer. Her death in 1985 plunged the company into a mire of difficulties from which it is still struggling to recover.

Davia Temin, president of Temin & Company, a New York marketing and brand-consulting firm, stated, "If you are basing your entire public image on that one name, you have to question how you can broaden it so that the whole company does not suffer if the head person gets hit by a bus—or by a scandal."

Think about this before you invest in a celebrity-driven company. Celebrities are notoriously perishable, like shooting stars. Those who do endure, such as Bill Cosby, Lauren Bacall, and Dick Clark, are rare.

A special brand-name category is that of well-known entertainers. These superstars earn tens of millions of dollars because of their public appeal. Filmmakers know that Meryl Streep and Harrison Ford will do well at the box office because they're talented actors and have many fans. Whether the movie is action, drama, or high comedy, certain performers are always a pleasure to watch. They have a reputation built on past success. Similarly, nearly all brand names that endure have a reputation for quality.

America's Brand-Name Mentality

We were waiting for a delayed flight and talking about this book when we got into a conversation with Jeff, twentysomething.

"I don't buy brands anymore," Jeff insisted. "I don't think people are into it these days."

"Then why did you buy those Nikes instead of a generic brand for twenty percent less?"

"I know this product," he answered.

"Aren't those Polo pants?" one of us asked. "And that's a Bobby Jones collection golf shirt, isn't it? What kind of car do you drive?"

He beamed when he told us he didn't own a BMW. "I drive a Lexus," he said with pride. "I'm not buying status, I'm buying reliability."

Of course, a Lexus is as much a status symbol today as a BMW was in the 1980s. And if it's reliability Jeff wanted, he could have bought a Ford.

Jeff insisted he wasn't a yuppie. But no matter how much he denied being influenced by brand-name products, there was overwhelming evidence to the contrary. He was writing with a Montblanc pen, but we didn't make an issue of it. Jeff was no different from many people who claim they're not influenced by brand names but really are.

Today we're seeing a lot of frayed, ripped, beat-up, and down-right dirty jeans. Their wearers imply that they're protesting status fashions. Don't be fooled; grunge is hardly a newcomer to fashion circles. The flower children of the 1960s may think they sparked the trend toward discarded clothing—bleach-splattered jeans and faded T-shirts—but one need only watch a rerun of *The Many Loves of Dobie Gillis* to see that such a look reaches back to the Beat Generation of the 1950s.

Designer Calvin Klein made a splash during the September 1999 New York fashion shows by announcing that "dirty denim"—greasy-looking jeans that could have been discarded by a mechanic—would play a major role in his spring line. Now manufacturers and retailers such as Levi Strauss & Company are gearing up with their own variations of dirty denim.

"We have a major thrust planned for 2000—we're talking millions of units," says Kent Pech, vice president of consumer marketing at VF Corporations' Lee unit. Lee's Busted, a heavily worn denim, has started selling in stores such as J. C. Penney. Its grimy-looking Metro Denim was launched during the first quarter of 2000.

Manufacturers are betting that consumers will pay a premium for jeans the Salvation Army would reject. Calvin Klein's dirty jeans sell for up to $78 retail, $20 higher than classic Calvins.

Bart Sights, president of Sights Denim Systems in Henderson, Kentucky, is paid by the nation's largest jeans manufacturers to take perfectly good pants and beat them up. Of the 150,000 pieces of clothing Sights processes weekly, about 90,000 of them are permanently dirtied or frayed in some way. The company is something of an industry legend. Twenty years ago, nobody dreamed there'd be a company that specialized in destroying denim.

As a result of heavy advertising aimed at young consumers by fashion-forward chains such as Old Navy and designers such as Donna Karan, kids begin brand seeking by the time they start school. They make the purchase decisions at nine or ten; Mom and Dad simply provide the money. Children have always known peer pressure in fashion, from Buster Browns to Birkenstocks. Their desire to dress like their older siblings and even adults is increasing.

Selling Brands on the Internet

While there's a buzz among customers about finding great deals on-line, selling brands on the Internet is a huge factor in moving merchandise. To entice people to buy products they can't see and touch, credibility is the key to success.

If consumers truly spent their time surfing for the best deals, prices would be nearly uniform across the Web. Yet that is far from true. MIT's Sloan School of Management studied the period from February 1998 to May 1999 and found that the prices of particular CDs varied by an average of $4.95; for books, the price range averaged $5.98. Surprisingly, the study suggested that on-line shoppers attach relatively low importance to finding the lowest price.

At Amazon.com, for example, prices were far from the lowest on the Web in 98 percent of comparisons. Bn.com, run by Cendant, averaged $1.60 less than the same books at Amazon. Yet Bns.com had only 2 percent of the on-line book market. Why? Branding, awareness, and trust, the researchers suggest. "Customers don't really know if they're going to get the products, so they will want to go with a company that they trust," one of them said.

Customers go to sites they know, suggesting that Web retailers are correct to pour money into getting their names before the public. This tells us that on-line selling depends on brand names—a Web site's name as well as a product's.

Old Brands Never Die, They Just Fade Away

Burma Shave, Brylcreem, Pepsodent, Ovaltine, Lectric Shave, RC Cola, Barbasol, Hai Karate, Black Jack Gum. At one point, these brands were widely recognized and frequently purchased. Many have now faded or become ghosts of their former selves. In 1993, Nabisco reported twenty-nine ghost brands, Schering-Plough seventeen, and SmithKline fourteen, according to Stuart Elliott of *The New York Times.*

Some brands die because of shifting consumer needs, heavy competition, or waning awareness, while others suffer from marketing malpractice. Many well-trained brand managers believe that brands, like people, follow predictable, irreversible life cycles: they grow, they mature, they decline, they die. When the sales of a brand fall, companies respond by cutting back on their marketing activities of that brand and reallocating funds to new brands.

An ongoing investment of effort and money is required to keep a brand name strong. Without advertising, the consumer's awareness fades, and new brands replace old brands. When one manufacturer fails to promote its product, another manufacturer captures its market share. Having the best-quality product isn't essential but marketing strategy is, and in today's marketplace, this means advertising. A company that cuts back on advertising is doomed.

Some brands get stuck in the past. For instance, Bay Rum might remind a twenty-year-old of his feeble grandfather. Mentholatum and Aspergum are perceived as relic remedies; cold sufferers assume that modern medicine has better answers. Yet the underlying reason for rejecting mature brands is simply attitude. A common comment heard about older brands is that they have lost their appeal, lost their identity, and been overshadowed by competing brands.

Unilever recently reduced the number of its brand-name products from 1,600 to 400. The manufacturer of Lipton Tea, Dove cleansers, Magnum ice cream, Birds Eye vegetables, and Elizabeth Arden cosmetics said that its top 400 brands accounted for almost 90 percent of the company's $44 billion revenue in 1998. A spokesperson explained, "We want to put all our resources behind the 400 brands with worldwide reach, and the others will simply fall away."

Unilever said that redirecting marketing spending would lead to growth rates of 6 to 8 percent annually for the 400 brands, compared with current targets of 4 percent. Pruning the brands would save $1.6 billion within three years. We applaud this marketing strategy.

Expanding the Branding

Unilever is one company where having fewer products means making higher profits. This strategy allows it to focus on its best brands, backing proven winners with its advertising dollars. As a variant, a company can apply some leverage by using a strong brand to sell other products. Care must be exercised, however, not to prostitute a popular brand. For example, in the 1980s, through multiple licensing agreements, Gucci labeled as many as 22,000 different items. The name lost its air of exclusivity, elegance, and high quality. Consequently, the company's revenues plummeted. It took years to restore the brand, which Gucci managed to do by (1) not renewing licensing agreements, (2) increasing prices, (3) tightening controls over quality, and (4) increasing advertising.

Conversely, FAO Schwarz, the upscale toy retailer, is expanding its brand. After several quarters of operating losses, the company decided to move beyond toys. As this book goes to press, the company is introducing a line of children's "lifestyle" products, including clothing, furniture, and eyewear. Licensing deals are in the works for a slew of new products that will pit the company against producers of children's goods by fashion designers Ralph Lauren, Tommy Hilfiger, and Calvin Klein.

But how far can FAO Schwarz go beyond its high-end toy stores from Fifth Avenue in Manhattan to Union Square in San Francisco? Mike Toth, founder of Toth Brand Marketing, said that FAO Schwarz has a much tougher task than companies such as Ralph Lauren and Tommy Hilfiger, which are established lifestyle brands.

"If it's just another pair of glasses and just another outfit, just another set of dresser drawers, then there's nothing unique or special," Toth said. "They have to be very careful about capturing and delivering something that is true to the brand as they do this."

BIC is another company that pursued a leveraged strategy. After successfully marketing a nineteen-cent ballpoint pen, the company tried branding products from fragrances to panty hose. The American consumer, however, didn't see the connection, and the strategy bombed.

There's nothing wrong with expanding branding. Product diversity is smart. But you can't put your good name on too many different products and expect them all to sell. You must ask yourself what it takes to persuade consumers that Product X is as dependable as Product Y because it's made by the same company. The fact that BIC made a great cheap ballpoint pen didn't mean it could knit fine panty hose. On the other hand, if BIC had marketed stationery or desk accessories, customers might have given them a try.

Johnston & Murphy has been making handmade shoes since 1850 and is now selling a lambskin bomber jacket. This is a good product fit. Ivory Soap is another company that stayed close to its star product when it moved into shampoos. Likewise, Colgate put its name on toothbrushes, and Nike sells socks as well as athletic garments.

Interestingly, in 1998, PepsiCo bought Tropicana, America's number one juice maker, from the Seagram Company. Should the company be mixing its drinks? Why not? Coca-Cola has owned Minute Maid, juice maker number two, for more than thirty-five years.

Both PepsiCo and Coca-Cola are trying to convince consumers that like their cola brands, their orange juices also have consistency. Minute Maid juice concentrates are distributed to all points of the globe. On the other hand, Tropicana packages juice straight from the orange. Its premium brand is promoted as freshly squeezed— and commands ten cents a quart over other brands. Take your pick, Tropicana or Minute Maid—no matter where you go, your juice will taste the same, just as Pepsi and Coca-Cola do.

According to Richard Cooper, Minute Maid's president, "One of the hallmarks of a brand is consistency. What we are trying to do with Minute Maid is make the taste the same everywhere. That was a conscious decision we made related to the brand building we're doing."

Of course, there are other factors to consider when a company takes on a new product line, everything from channels of distribution to financing.

Competing with a Big-Brand Company

In our 1997 book, *Predatory Marketing*, we advocated the following:

> In the world of marketing, a true predator always attacks the other guy at his strengths. Interestingly, this strategy contradicts offensive tactics taught on more conventional playing fields. In the world of sports, a boxer must attack his opponent's vulnerability, jabbing away at a bruised rib or perhaps an eye laceration; a football team repeatedly runs the ball through the weak side of the defensive line, or it may launch an aerial attack on a rookie cornerback; a tennis player pounds away at an opposing player's weak backhand. The great generals of the world engage in this same brand of offensive strategy on the battlefield—assaulting the enemy wherever he is weak and unprotected.

We believe this same strategy must be implemented when you're the little guy up against a giant brand-name company. You attack the big guy's strengths, not his weaknesses. You won't steal many customers by fighting on ground that's not worth taking. Customers aren't drawn to the big guy by its weaknesses. They shop the competition because of its strengths. This means you have to give them a better reason to do business with you instead of your competition.

This is what Polly's Gourmet Coffee did. For twenty years, the Second Avenue coffee shop in Long Beach, California, had virtually no competition within twenty miles and dominated the affluent Belmont Shores area. However, like many small shopkeepers in America whose businesses suffered brutal beatings due to "category killer" chains, Polly's found itself going head-to-head with one of the most formidable mass retailers of the 1990s. In 1994, Starbucks opened a store just a few blocks away from Polly's, whose sales fell by 10 to 15 percent. Then, in 1998, another Starbucks opened— only seventy-eight yards away.

"We were getting despondent," owner Michael Sheldrake said. "We were just trying to hang on. We had a chain problem and didn't know what to do."

It's been said that no phenomenon more profoundly transformed America's Main Streets in the 1990s than the "chain problem." From tony Annapolis, Maryland, to Hollywood's Melrose district to bohemian Harvard Square in Cambridge, Massachusetts, retail streetscapes have been steadily homogenized as heavily marketed national chains have outgunned and displaced locally owned rivals, whose resources and organization generally pale in comparison to the likes of the chains'.

When the second Starbucks opened, Sheldrake didn't roll over. Instead, he launched a predatory marketing strategy. He decided to take aim at Starbucks in two ways: by beating the chain at its own game by operating even more efficiently and by exploiting the inherent vulnerability of many chains.

"The problem with a chain is that it's like a mall; it's all mechanical, and there's no relationship with the customers," said Bob Phibbs, a consultant Sheldrake hired to fight off Starbucks. Phibbs believes people are tiring of megastores. "People are disaffected," he explains.

On Phibbs's advice, Polly's adopted the chain's best organizational and management ideas, ending a plethora of special arrangements between employees and longtime customers for free or cut-rate services and tightening cash management procedures. Employees attended mandatory classes to improve their sales skills.

"The advantages of the chains are their procedures and administration," Phibbs emphasized. "If an independent doesn't learn how to be just as efficient, they're going to be dead."

In addition to attacking its competition at its strengths, Polly's played up its competitive advantage over Starbucks. It advertised that the store roasted its own coffee on-site, which isn't practical for a mammoth chain such as Starbucks. Polly's also promoted its wider selection of coffees. Starbucks, considered trendy by many customers, was derided in Polly's local advertising as a purveyor of "ordinary" coffee.

As big chains expand in pursuit of growth, they risk losing a consistently high-quality product and strong customer service. This opens the field to entrepreneurs such as Michael Sheldrake, whose survival depends on holding his own against the big boys. Small enterprises such as Polly's will always enjoy the advantage of having the owner available to serve the customer personally. This is something no chain operation can provide.

Cashing In on Brand Names

It takes time and money to establish a brand name. Generally, it takes a lot of both. Brooks Brothers and Johnston & Murphy sold their products to our great-great-grandparents. That's a long time for a brand to endure. Still, longevity isn't insurance. Once-prominent companies such as Eastern Airlines, Railway Express, and Gimbel's are ancient history. Others remain that have lost their luster. Companies that stick with the same old formula lose with the fickle American consumer. Jeans didn't go out of style, but the Levi's brand did as competitors such as Diesel pitched to hip young consumers. No company today can afford to rest on its laurels.

Companies that relax their marketing efforts lose out to competitors who try harder. Leaders such as Coca-Cola, McDonald's, and Procter & Gamble are relentless in marketing their brands. What's more, they're constantly seeking innovative marketing approaches to gain still more market share.

We realize that not every business can afford to spend millions of dollars on advertising. Still, a small company can develop its brand in the local media. As it prospers, it can expand to nearby communities and eventually statewide, then into adjoining states. Study the *Fortune* 500 companies, and you'll discover that many had humble beginnings.

Entrepreneurs who are committed to quality products, excellent value, and exceptional service will earn well-deserved reputations. Every city across America has restaurants known for haute cuisine that take reservations weeks in advance. Building contractors, decorators, and architects with impeccable reputations find customers lining up for their services. The same is true of attorneys, dentists, and physicians: successful practices are built on solid reputations, which must be earned and never taken for granted. (A reputation can be lost overnight.) It's easy to spot the top real estate company in a community. It's whichever has the most "for sale" and "sold" signs. As one real estate broker told us, "Service, service, service, kill your customers with service. Give them so much service they'll feel guilty even thinking about doing business with somebody else."

In local communities, reputations and branding go hand in hand. Retailers that stand behind what they sell are the same ones that get repeat business. We're talking about thirty- and sixty-day returns—no questions asked, handled with a smile and a "thank you for your business." We're also talking about companies that honor a twenty-four-month warranty a week or so after the expiration. Regardless of your product, you've got to go that extra mile for your customer. In the long run, this is what builds strong brand identity.

Nine Tips on Brand Names for Retailers

If you're in retailing, the following are ways you can enhance your profits by carrying brand-name products:

1. Display brand-name products prominently in your store.

2. Brand names stand for quality, and they must be displayed accordingly. Poor displays detract from the quality of the product.

3. Use brand logos in your advertising, but don't overdo them.

4. Too often, brand-name products are used only to draw traffic into a store. Be sure to mix in your assortment of other merchandise with the brand names. This way some of your higher-margin goods will benefit from customers who were initially attracted to the brand names.

5. Be sure to have a sufficient inventory of advertised brand names in your store. At the same time, have an adequate inventory of your other merchandise at high price points to take advantage of the draw of your brand names.

6. Send private mailings to your customers to sell brand names. With established customers, the reputation of a particular brand will reinforce your company's reputation. Consumers assume you sell better-quality merchandise when you carry brand names they know.

7. Since 73 percent of Americans consider television an educational vehicle, brand-name manufacturers should, as a matter of course, provide their retailers with first-rate production footage of their products to seize a quality advantage.

8. Train your store employees always to mention your brand names to customers who inquire about a specific product category. If a store salesperson forgets, ignores, or doesn't like a brand, the customer will mimic his or her attitude. Such a salesperson's attitude is in conflict with your store's merchandising strategy.

9. Top brands usually generate smaller margins; nonetheless, they draw customers into your store. Build a relationship with those customers, and they will buy other merchandise too.

Locally, brand names are also built by professionals who take an active role in the community. They are recognized as caring, thoughtful individuals—qualities that stand for integrity and honesty. Their good deeds are reflected in their companies.

How would you really know the best surgeon or attorney in your community? Even if you had a front-row seat in the operating room or the courtroom, how could you know she was doing a good job? You can only go on reputation.

One way to acquire a brand immediately is to buy a franchise. Putting up a sign that says "McDonald's" or "H & R Block" gives you instant credibility in your locale. If you buy a franchise, you'll also pay an ongoing fee. However, with the right franchiser, it will be worth the money. In return, you'll get the advantages of national advertising and brand recognition.

As an independent retailer, you can stock a brand and ride on its shirttails as the "exclusive" dealer in your area. A jewelry store might tout itself as "the largest Rolex dealer in the tristate area." A furniture store can do the same with Sealy and a stereo dealer with Bose.

Ever wonder how big pharmaceutical companies get physicians to prescribe new drugs? The free samples that salespeople hand out to doctors are passed along to patients. Compassionate doctors ease the expense of health care by occasionally handing out free drugs, and patients are grateful for them. By the time the freebies run out, patients are comfortable with the drug and may continue taking it for the rest of their lives. Likewise, baby formula makers have nurtured intense brand loyalty through aggressive giveaways to parents and pediatricians, along with big rebates to state welfare programs. Their message is simple if vague, and it can be found in doctors' offices everywhere. A leaflet distributed by Ross Laboratories promoting Similac says, "All infant formulas are not the same."

Iams Company, a Dayton, Ohio, premium pet food maker, applied a similar marketing strategy. For nearly thirty years, Iams was a small and obscure regional supplier of high-protein dog and cat food. With little money for advertising and marketing, company owner Clay Mathile and his wife and family hand-packed samples of Iams dog food in the family basement. Mathile spent nearly every weekend visiting kennels, dog shows, and breeders, asking them to try his product. He also called on pet shops and pet supply outlets. One customer at a time, he built strong relationships. Iams is now a $600 million international enterprise, the seventh largest pet food company in the world. It continues to focus its efforts on close customer contact rather than mass advertising.

You can do the same with your small company. If you are a distributor of cosmetics, for example, you can leave samples with beauticians and hairdressers in your area, along with literature that customers can read while getting their hair done. In time, your products will be known as the ones used by professionals.

Graeter's, a well-known ice cream shop in Cincinnati, also has several shops in Columbus, Ohio. Some of the area's best restaurants include the Graeter name on their menus. "If Morton's of Chicago Steakhouse serves Graeter's ice cream, it must be high quality," patrons conclude.

Some companies build a strong brand identity by appealing to tourists, who spread their reputations across the country. Coors was such a strong local brand in Colorado that travelers bought cases of Coors to take home. Coors was known all over the country long before it was sold on a national level. So if your game plan is to start a new business and take it cross-country, make your debut in a hot tourist spot.

As you can see, branding adds incalculable value to a company. When confronted with dozens of choices of toothpaste, consumers find it easier to buy Crest. And a senior manager can rest assured that installing IBM mainframes is a reliable option. No senior manager is likely to question a subordinate's decision to go with IBM. In short, brands sell products. And when a non-brand product is up against a brand-name product, odds heavily favor the brand to break the tie.

Remember, too, that size is a strong competitive advantage. Merck, for example, the largest drugmaker in the United States, spends about $2 billion on research, something its smaller rivals can't do. Likewise, FDX Corporation, parent of Federal Express, has a distribution system so entrenched that a start-up company would encounter insurmountable odds for success. These companies have created big barriers to entry, making them highly successful and attractive to investors. Remember that 60 percent of U.S. consumers are willing to pay extra for a brand name. The same is true of investors. Therefore, we advise maintaining a diversified portfolio with top brand companies.

Gaming Casinos and Lotteries Have Joined America's Mainstream

Until the late 1980s, if you wanted to gamble in a U.S. casino, you had to go to either Nevada or New Jersey. Today, you can make some kind of legal wager in every state except Utah, Hawaii, and Tennessee. There are many ways to gamble: casinos, state lotteries, horse- and dog-racing tracks, video poker, and other electronic games, including charity-run bingo. There are casinos or casino-style gambling in thirty-one states, with lotteries in thirty-seven states and the District of Columbia.

Going on vacation to gamble has become so prevalent that Las Vegas has become America's number-two tourist destination, second only to Orlando. In 1999, 33 million tourists visited Vegas, compared to 50 million-plus who went to Disney World and other theme parks in Central Florida. Of course, visiting Orlando is a family vacation involving Mom, Dad, and the kids. Vegas only gets the folks. So while Orlando is America's favorite playground, Vegas is unquestionably America's favorite "adult" playground.

The National Gambling Impact Study Commission conducted a two-year study into the social and economic impact of the gambling boom. In 1998, Americans bet $630 billion through legal gambling, up 1,600 percent since 1976, and lost $50 billion. By comparison, they spent $7 billion on movie tickets, $26 billion on books, and $450 billion on groceries.

It's even possible to gamble on the Internet. The number of Internet gamblers doubled from 1997 to 1998, with 14.5 million of them wagering $645 million. If legislation does not prohibit on-line gaming, the forecast is that it will hit $2 billion by 2001.

America survived as a nation because our founding fathers were risk takers. Early settlers took enormous risks when they crossed the ocean to a faraway land and ventured into the wilderness. Americans probably embraced gambling because life itself—getting out of the mills and mines, getting through Comanche territory in one piece— was a gamble. The American Dream is still based on taking risks and striking it rich. This is the premise of our free enterprise system.

Gambling is as American as the gold rush, the boom in Internet stocks, and other quests for immediate wealth. In 1612, the first lottery in America raised £29,000 for the Virginia Company. George Washington, who deplored the rampant gambling at Valley Forge, supported a lottery to help build the city that bears his name. Lotteries helped build General Washington's army and were also responsible for funding several early buildings on the campuses of Harvard, Princeton, and Dartmouth.

With the explosion of the stock market in the last few years, the number of lotteries and legal casinos has soared across America. Like everything else, betting is socially stratified. Stock shares are for the prosperous, lotteries are for the poor, and casinos are for those in the middle. The more money you have to gamble with, the better your odds of coming out ahead. In the stock market, the dealer's cut is only a small commission or a management fee. In state lotteries, operators skim as much as 40 percent.

The religious Right preaches that gambling generates nothing of value and does nothing productive for a community; it simply siphons money from some people and transfers it to the pockets of others. Others complain that it fosters crime and perpetuates the myth that one can get something for nothing. Then, of course, there is the insidious risk of addiction.

Gambling's advocates, on the other hand, are quick to point out that gambling creates jobs within communities and also raises revenues for local and state governments.

It is not our intention to debate the pros or cons of gaming, nor do we intend to discuss moral issues. Our interest is in the growing popularity of gambling in America and the impact this trend has on business. As you read on, be aware that you're in for a surprise. Our research took us into unpredictable areas that on the surface seem unrelated to gambling. This sometimes happens with trends, and it's what we think makes them so interesting.

A Nation of Gamblers

Our research shows that 58 percent of Americans purchased lottery tickets or visited a casino in 1999. This figure is up from 35 percent in 1985. One reason for the hefty increase is that so many lotteries and casinos simply didn't exist fifteen years ago. But this increase can also be attributed to supply and demand.

We asked those who had gone to a casino in 1999 if they go more or less often than they did five years ago. Forty-two percent said they go more often, 32 percent that they go at the same frequency, and 26 percent that they go less often. With almost twice as many gamblers increasing their visits to casinos, this is clearly a trend.

Gambling is quickly becoming one of the nation's favorite pastimes, involving nearly 60 percent of Americans. Of course, casinos are in business to make money, so the odds are in their favor. We wanted to find out how winning and losing affect spending habits. In the case of those who walk away with winnings, our study reveals that 56 percent spend more money immediately. The remaining 44 percent save it for another day. Interestingly, all of the people we interviewed had an immediate answer to this question. Evidently, they know from past experience exactly what they will do if they win.

Casino visitors are likely to dine at a restaurant: 62 percent said they patronize a local establishment; 37 percent remain at the casino or find food nearby.

Other than spending on meals, three main areas where gamblers spend their money are show tickets (35 percent), souvenirs

(35 percent), and alcohol (21 percent). Shopping for clothes was a distant fourth at 5 percent.

With more losers than winners, we wanted to know how people's spending habits change when they lose. Forty-one percent said they spend less immediately; 59 percent said that losing doesn't curtail their spending. This is how losers cut back:

Go to fewer restaurants	55%
Buy fewer clothes	14%
Spend less on vacations	11%
Go to fewer sporting activities	11%

We were surprised to find that 68 percent of gamblers stick to their budgets; they have the discipline to walk away after losing a predetermined amount of money. Seventeen percent don't and exceed their budgets; 12 percent said they walk sometimes, but not always. Only 8 percent said that they've lost sleep due to gambling losses.

The Urge to Escape

We asked, "What do you enjoy most about gambling?" The responses were:

The chance to win	45%
Excitement	21%
Winning	20%
Social aspects	8%
Free accommodations/drinks	4%
Other	2%

In a follow-up survey, we asked, "Do you see gambling as a challenge or casual recreation?" Sixty-six percent enjoy it as casual recreation; 34 percent view it as a serious challenge. To many Americans, having fun and being competitive are closely tied.

As mentioned, 59 percent don't cut back on their spending when they lose. Evidently, most casino visitors don't lose so badly that it hurts them financially. This is evidenced by the fact that 79 percent said they write off their losses as money spent on recreation.

With casinos popping up on Indian reservations and riverboats, the urge to gamble no longer requires a junket to Las Vegas or Atlantic City. Driving time to a casino for most Americans is forty-five minutes to an hour. As a result, people are taking weekend vacations at casinos to add a little excitement to their lives. In this respect, visiting a casino is a "replacement activity." For instance, some people may take several minivacations a year to visit nearby casinos to gamble instead of taking a one- or two-week vacation. Couples may drive to a casino for a date rather than dining and dancing in town. Still others go gambling in lieu of fishing, football, and so on.

We wanted to know if, win or lose, just going to a casino changed people's spending habits. Seventeen percent of the respondents said they spend less on clothing, 15 percent take fewer vacations, 15 percent postpone replacing a car or truck, and 10.5 percent postpone home improvements.

At first blush, these numbers appear to confirm the worst suspicions of those who claim casinos take money away from local businesses. But the big fear that certain enterprises would suffer badly because of gambling has passed. Remember that 42 percent of Americans don't go to casinos, which substantially reduces these numbers. So while an 8 percent reduction in purchases at local hardware stores and haberdashers may be significant, it is not as bad as doomsayers predicted. Furthermore, when people postpone clothing, vehicle, or home improvement spending, the key word is "postpone." This is because a two- or three-day getaway occupies time that would have been used in another activity. The other activity isn't replaced by gambling, it's simply postponed.

The real losers are local restaurant owners and nearby resorts that lose traffic. Even faraway resort areas may feel a slight squeeze because a couple of minivacations sometimes replace the annual "big" vacation.

Of course, there are bound to be some people who take big hits at the tables. Some do lose so badly they can't afford a new car or an addition to the house. Certainly, this happens with some frequency—but according to our study, it doesn't impact business significantly. Not at present, that is. If American gambling continues to increase as it has in the past decade, larger numbers could impact certain industries.

Why are casinos so popular? What's the big attraction? Excitement! It's a lot more fun than painting a hallway or pruning shrubs! Remember that lack of discretionary time so many Americans feel? Well, here's a way of squeezing in a quickie vacation: shorter stay, shorter travel, still fun. With a strong economy and overtime pay, Americans have cash to spend frivolously—they feel secure enough to blow some hard-earned money and, at the same time, blow off a little steam.

One interesting aspect of this trend is the mind-set of those who choose a casino as a getaway—not only from work but from their kids as well. It's strictly self-gratification, a break from their tedious routine.

A casino is the ideal venue for escape. In fact, a casino is designed for this purpose. It contains no windows or clocks, so occupants lose track of the time. Its action-packed milieu has been well calculated to prevent anyone from thinking about anything outside its walls. Furthermore, to engage in the fast-paced activity of gambling, one must devote complete attention to it. Games such as craps, blackjack, and keno require total concentration. It's no wonder gambling gives us a buzz—for some it goes beyond a buzz. It can cause a chemical reaction within the brain that can be addictive. Certainly the pleasurable aspects of gambling keep patrons coming back again and again.

Lotteries

State lotteries have the worst odds of any common form of gambling. Most existing lotto games are stacked against the player at odds of millions to one. But they also promise the greatest potential payoff in dollars.

What angers many is that the government is engaged in an activity that is illegal for anyone else to participate in. For years, states prosecuted anyone involved in any form of gambling. Only when state governments contemplated the potential revenues did they pass legislation to open up the lottery business. The first state lottery was introduced in New Hampshire in 1964, and ultimately politicians in thirty-seven states sold their constituents on this "painless taxation" under the auspices of replacing school levies and other tariffs.

To many, a lottery is nothing more than a regressive tax, exploiting people's greed and aspirations toward enormous wealth. It represents the chance of a lifetime to realize an otherwise impossible dream. Perhaps inevitably, lotteries prey on the poor. People who earn modest wages and those who are poorly educated spend a greater percentage of their incomes on the lottery than better-educated, more affluent people, according to 1998 New Jersey State Lottery data.

But the analysis of lottery and household income data found that people in the lowest-income Zip codes spent more than 1 percent of their 1998 income on lottery games, compared to 0.25 percent of income of those in the highest-income Zip codes. *The New York Times* reported that for every $10,000 of annual income in lower-income areas, $108 is paid in income tax, while $111 is spent on the lottery; the wealthy pay $319 in income tax and spend just $25 on the lottery.

To some people the lottery is harmless entertainment, but in truth, lotteries exploit people who are bad at math. A person who spends $20 a year on lottery tickets could put the same twenty bucks into a mutual fund yielding 12 percent for eighteen years, or $1,434. At $4 a week, or $200 annually, she'd end up with $14,340. A grandfather who annually spent $500 on tickets for 18 years could receive $4,289 from that 12 percent mutual fund, which could go toward a grandchild's college education. At $500 a year for eighteen years, there would be $35,860 for a grandchild's education. Twenty-five dollars a week, if invested at a conservative 8 percent per year, would be worth $103,000 in twenty-five years. Keep this in mind when somebody wins a $300 million Powerball lottery: while one individual ends up with a vast fortune, tens of millions of other people are losers.

Incidentally, Massachusetts leads the nation with $505 per capita spent on lottery tickets annually. A Maryland study showed that the most active 20 percent of lottery players with annual incomes below $10,000 spent an average of $128 per month on the Maryland lottery.

A 1999 poll conducted by Luntz Research Companies and Peter D. Hart Research for the American Gaming Association found that 83 percent of Americans think that whether or not to gamble should be an individual decision. The telephone poll of 1,200 people was skewed to include a disproportionately high number of weekly churchgoers. Still, 74 percent of regular churchgoers in the poll backed the individual's right to decide whether to gamble.

Moral issues and negatives aside, our research shows that lotteries have no material impact on business in America.

A Message to American Management

When we analyzed this trend, one message came through loud and clear: the driving force behind the popularity of casinos is the need for so many Americans to escape. Admittedly, this may sound far-fetched, considering that we're writing about the trend to more gambling. But this is how the study of trends often works: you think you're going in one direction, and you end up where you least expected to.

The fact is, more and more people have an urge to get away from the stress and boredom of their everyday lives. This is what attracts millions of people to casinos. And this desire to escape carries over into other aspects of the world of business.

Interestingly, there is a subtle, important lesson to learn that is of benefit to anyone in a managerial position. It goes beyond the lure of rolling a seven or even taking a luxury cruise to a faraway, exotic land. If that were all there was to it, we'd simply advise you to ship your employees off for a good escape. However, in a matter of time the allure would wear off and your employees would be back in a rut. It makes more sense to put some excitement into their jobs. Do this well, and you'll end up with a workforce of energetic, enthusiastic people.

Of course, you can't do this by replacing desks and copiers with roulette wheels and one-armed bandits. Instead, you must get your employees excited about their work. For starters, begin by treating people with respect. Let them know you value their opinions and welcome their input. You really listen to what they tell you. You enlist their help in solving problems. When suggestions are made but not implemented, management explains why—and sincere thanks are given.

Once you get the hang of this style of management, you'll understand why people get bored with their jobs, feel stressed, and crave an escape. Imagine how you'd feel if you knew your opinion never mattered. How long would it be before you were spending long weekends at a casino?

When workers are treated as chattel, they harbor resentment. They may come to work every day, going through the motions, but their hearts and souls aren't in it. Certainly, benefits are appreciated, but they don't replace people's need for respect.

Winning Customers

No, we can't help you pick the winning numbers. But we can tell you how to win customers.

Selling dreams of wealth is nothing new. About a third of all new magazine subscriptions are sold through sweepstakes, which offer contests with multimillion-dollar prizes to persuade people to buy magazines. American Family Publishers and Publishers Clearing House have been doing this for years, with much success. True, consumer advocates have cried foul, claiming they use gimmicks and deception. Who hasn't received "personalized" greetings announcing, "You may have won $10,000,000.00"? Some of these letters are so cunningly crafted that only a lawyer can find the fine print that says your actual chances of winning are one in 80 million.

We're convinced that there are ways of exciting customers without resorting to trickery. A few years back, for example, a successful Coca-Cola campaign had millions of soft drink lovers looking underneath bottle caps for rewards and prizes. From time to time, Burger King or McDonald's has a promotion with instant lottery-type cards that pay out a soft drink or a cheeseburger to winners.

There are many ways to cash in on America's gambling fever. A restaurant or a retailer, for example, could install a miniature roulette wheel at the register—a winning spin yields a discount. Bigger discounts have the highest odds, and not everyone goes home a winner. But it's fun and it creates excitement, if only for a few moments.

Of course, gambling isn't required to create excitement in a retail store. But getting customers excited helps to make their shopping experience a good one—particularly when it's a place where they go to escape. This is why the comfy, warm atmosphere of popular bookstores is compelling. Book lovers can relax with a cappuccino and browse. Even a few minutes of this provide a welcome change of pace from a hectic or monotonous workday. And this is something brick-and-mortar bookstores can do that the Internet cannot!

Speaking of the Internet, the best-produced and -designed Web sites will generate the most hits. Like a casino, they too provide an escape. Successful TV commercial producers recognize this attraction. Some of the most effective commercials are, in effect, thirty- to sixty-second "minimovies." In fact, some are more interesting than the programming. Ford Motor Company, for instance, made advertising history with its two-minute video on November 1, 1999, shown on virtually every network and cable channel around the world. Shot in nine different countries, the commercial paid tribute to Ford customers, contrasting how different cultures say "Hello" and "Good-bye." It subtly showcased Ford's seven automotive brands in a montage of emotional vignettes, suggesting that they fit seamlessly into people's lives around the world. It showed a war veteran riding in a Ford Mustang convertible in a homecoming parade, an Italian couple embracing in front of a Volvo, a well-dressed woman putting her sleek dogs in the back of a Jaguar, and Japanese girls playing in cherry blossoms near a Mazda. The often disconnected images were held together by the song "Just Wave Hello," written expressly for Ford.

According to James C. Schroer, vice president for global marketing, Ford wants the viewers to conclude that the company has "a heart and soul and has the kind of people and products that people will want to get to know better and will trust us."

Warm and inviting is what five-star restaurants and hotels are. They make their customers feel important and comfortable, a winning combination. The experience starts with a warm greeting by name by a mannerly manager who's been notified of your arrival. Oftentimes, the small personal touches are most appealing. The Ritz-Carlton, for instance, might stock a room refrigerator with a customer's favorite brand of whiskey and bottled water. A guest may receive a complimentary pitcher of orange juice because an alert desk clerk notices she has a dreadful cold. A hometown newspaper may be delivered each morning. The Ritz-Carlton pampers you throughout your stay, and you feel like royalty. For a brief interval, you live in luxurious, majestic style, far removed from the doldrums. It might not have the excitement of a casino, but it's a welcome relief and one some people enjoy splurging on every now and then.

Hotels that cater to people in need of a weekend getaway have been a boon to downtown locations traditionally occupied by business travelers during the week. When hotels install health spas, weekend vacancies drop substantially. Resorts that pamper their guests with mud baths and full-body massages are also cashing in on America's growing need to escape.

To retailers, we recommend trying a grand opening for a different kind of excitement. Our research shows that an effective grand opening can get 42 percent of an area's consumers to come in during a store's first ninety days in business. The average locally owned retail operation that's been around for thirty years attracts only 38 percent of the market area's shoppers. This is proof that by stirring things up, you can short-circuit the advantages of an established store, match it, or even exceed it in only ninety days! So take advantage of grand openings and remodeling events whenever opportunities avail. And do them in grand style. Depending on your budget, invite local celebrities such as entertainers or athletes, serve delicious hors d'oeuvres, hire a band to play, create a circus atmosphere. To get things really rolling, give away something extravagant such as a sports car or an exotic vacation for two. It might not compare to winning the lottery, but the odds of winning are a lot better and it will bring heavy traffic into your store.

One ARG client conducted an innovative grand opening by running an unusual contest. A $25,000 winner-take-all competition was offered to the area radio station that could draw the most listeners to the store's grand opening. Compared to the cost of a traditional radio campaign, this was cheap publicity. Five of the area's top radio stations competed, broadcasting live remotes from the store. Half the money went to the winning station's disk jockey. So for the next six months, the winning station announced, "We don't care what the ratings say, when it came down to the real test—the store's grand opening—we proved that we're the area's number one radio station!" So for six months after the grand opening, the store continued to get free advertising.

There's no telling how far you can go with an exhilarating milieu. Jordan's, one of America's most successful furniture stores, is an excellent example of how this works. Its Boston-area store in Avon, Massachusetts, has an unusual attraction that draws large crowds from far away. The 110,000-square-foot store features an IMAX-style movie, technically called Motion Odyssey Movie but known as MOM by well-informed New Englanders. Not coincidentally, MOM made its debut on Mother's Day in 1992. The screen in the forty-eight-seat theater is four stories high; the seats move in eight directions, depending on the movie. With its huge screen and huge sound, viewers experience the bumps and sharp turns of a roller coaster, a dune buggy expedition in the desert, or a whitewater rafting trip down the Grand Canyon's Colorado River.

One of Jordan's four stores, its 130,000-square-foot Natick, Massachusetts, site, also attracts thousands of people of all ages. Since 1998, shoppers inside the main entrance have found themselves on Bourbon Street in New Orleans during Mardi Gras. They walk through full-scale French facades leading to furniture showrooms. Attractions include a riverboat, a nine-minute FX experience, and, on weekends, live Dixieland music. A Streetcar Named Dessert sells fifteen different ice creams. Like the ice cream, MOM isn't free either, at $5 per person. But nobody seems to mind because all proceeds go to charity—in particular, to Mass Adoption Resource Exchange (MARE), one of several civic organizations that owners Barry and Eliot Tatelman support. Note that all monies raised by the two extravaganzas are donated to the charities. We think this is very generous, considering that MOM alone is estimated to have cost $2.5 million.

Like Jordan's, other retailers cater to the consumer's need to escape. Take, for example, Galyan's Trading Company, a sporting goods chain that features a rock-climbing wall. The wall draws such an audience that chairs are lined up in front of it to accommodate spectators. The same concept draws in patrons at theme restaurants such as Hard Rock Cafe, Planet Hollywood, and many sports bars across the country. Some are not doing as well as others because they sometimes forget that they're in the restaurant business. True, excitement draws crowds, but patrons must also enjoy their food or they won't return.

Sure-Fire Tips for Retailers

There's a lot to be learned from America's gambling habits that can be applied to nongaming industries. The following recommendations are mainly for retailers, but they will work for manufacturing and service companies as well:

1. Develop a sweepstakes event(s) with drawings for spectacular gifts that may include cars, foreign vacations with airfare and lodging, large-denomination savings bonds for $5,000 or $10,000, and major sporting events such as the Super Bowl, the NCAA Final Four, or the NBA finals.

2. Small companies can offer an all-expenses-paid night out on the town at a four-star restaurant, plus limo. In order to generate a lot of interest, go first class—all the way!

3. In states where it is legal, minicasinos, complete with real slot machines, can be used for promotions. Prizes can be coupons that can be applied to the purchase of real merchandise at great savings.

4. When you use gambling for a grand opening, do it in grand style. Spice it up with bigger-than-life activities (big-band music, live entertainment, and so on).

5. Buy lottery tickets and give them away during sales and by-invitation-only events. One ARG client gave lottery tickets to customers during a $50 million state lottery. Each shopper received three lottery tickets just for showing up. Boy, did that ever draw people to his store!

6. Consumers who buy lottery tickets are more likely to respond to events and sales with free gift offers or "buy one, get one free" offers. With this in mind, save your lists of these customers for future events of this nature.

7. Give something special to customers with complaints to show them you appreciate their business. One ARG client purchased vacation certificates that were redeemable for two free nights at any one of more than two hundred hotels across the country. Whenever the company failed to meet a customer's expectations, an apology was given—accompanied by a free two-night hotel certificate. One formerly disgruntled customer wrote back, "Thank you for your thoughtfulness. My wife and I enjoyed a won-

derful weekend at the same hotel where we honeymooned 40 years ago. We are now loyal customers of your store, and so are our eleven children and their spouses. They, too, thought your kind response was terrific." This couple might as well have won the lottery!

8. When a thank-you to a customer is appropriate, include with a thank-you note a special discount offer of 10, 15, or 20 percent off, but for a limited time.

Tips for the Investment-Minded Reader

You can be part of the house by investing in one of the many publicly traded gaming resorts. Some of the major players are Harrah's Entertainment, Park Place Entertainment, MGM Grand and Mandalay Resort Group. Of course, there are many chains such as Marriott International and Hilton Hotels that have gambling at some locations. You could also invest in publicly traded nongambling hostelries and resorts that have high occupancy rates because they are great escapes. Similarly, you might want to investigate a cruise line. (Research these companies carefully before investing in them.)

To cash in on the need to escape, consider a company such as Harley-Davidson. The motorcycle company is enjoying annual double-digit growth. It's not just Hell's Angels who are riding big bikes these days; masses of white-collar workers go cruising on their bikes on weekends, hitting the highways to get away from cubicles and corner offices. For the same reason, the wealthy are buying pricey sailboats and yachts, making companies such as Chris-Craft worth considering for your portfolio.

Fly fishing and skiing are two of the fastest-growing outdoor sports in America, both providing excitement and relaxation away from the office. And the ever-popular game of golf gains new devotees every year. Resorts, manufacturers, and publications catering to sports enthusiasts are prospering with this trend.

Although logic suggests that theme restaurants should flourish, we recommend only those eateries that also dish up good food.

Consider also theme parks, movies, plays, and sports events that are avenues for escape. Knowing this, you might want to research companies in these areas.

Finally, in the not-too-distant future there will be companies that offer the ultimate escape—and it will be far out, farther out than you can imagine. On the drawing board is out-of-this-world adventure travel. Once the domain of science fiction, space travel for the masses may be within our reach if Robert Bigelow has anything to do with it. He's investing $500 million to build the first cruise ship to orbit the moon. Bigelow owns Budget Suites of America, a hotel chain worth an estimated $600 million. In 1999, he started Bigelow Aerospace and hired a respected NASA engineer to head the project. The goal is to shuttle paying passengers to a luxury spacecraft permanently docked in Earth's outer orbit. One believer in this space entrepreneur is Buzz Aldrin, the second man on the moon and an advocate of space travel for nonastronauts. Aldrin has hailed Bigelow as a pioneer.

Recent studies indicate that thousands may be willing to pay $1 million each to become the first space tourists. Market research shows that Web sites devoted to the commercial aspects of space exploration are among the fastest growing on the Internet.

Bigelow isn't taking reservations yet. His cruiser is years away from a launch, some fifteen years by Bigelow's estimate. First someone has to come up with a cheaper, more efficient way to lift humans and cargo into space. Already a handful of companies are working on designing reusable rockets to do just that. We predict that commercial space travel will be a hot trend sometime toward the end of the first quarter of the twenty-first century.

People Today Complain
of Feeling Invisible

Does this sound familiar? Did you ever want service in a store, and employees whizzed right by you? Have you ever stood at an airline counter while the ticket agent talked on the telephone and totally ignored you? Or have you ever stood waiting at a bank with no one else in line and tellers at four open windows either shuffling papers or conversing with one another? It's as if they didn't even know you existed!

In such situations, most of us wait patiently; even when pressed for time, we remain cool. But we can take it for only so long. Eventually, we become annoyed and lose our patience.

Frustrating, isn't it? No one likes to be treated as if he or she were invisible.

One man told us a horror story that happened at the Los Angeles airport. After waiting at a boarding area for ten minutes, he approached the counter. "I'm on the 11:30 flight to New York," he told the agent.

"You're too late. The passengers have already boarded."

The man apologized for being late, and, seeing the plane still at the gate, he asked, "Is there any way I could get on that plane?"

"I'll have to put you on the next available flight, buddy."

"When's that?"

"It departs L.A. at 11:55."

"Whew," the man exclaimed. "I'll still have time to make my 8:30 dinner meeting. I don't mind a twenty-five-minute wait."

The agent laughed. "Twenty-five minutes? How about twelve hours and twenty-five minutes? The next flight leaves at 11:55 P.M."

"Then you've got to get me on that flight," the man insisted.

"Nothing I can do."

"Is it possible to talk to the pilot from your phone?"

"Yeah, I could do that."

"Then do it," the man said, "and make sure you tell him who I am."

This got the agent's attention. "Who are you?"

"I'm a goddamn customer, that's who."

The startled agent called the pilot: "We have a customer for you." Moments later, the man boarded the plane.

It's a shame that a customer isn't automatically treated with respect. No one should have to demand proper service.

There Is No Shortage of Rude People

In our 1999 survey, 72 percent of Americans said they feel people are more rude today than in the past. When asked why, they stated that:

People are more stressed.	35%
Families don't stay together.	25%
People care only about themselves.	24%
People have less time to be nice.	9%
People travel and are more transient.	5%

As discussed in other trends, people are more stressed today because they are pressed for time or short of money. With family members increasingly going their separate ways, there's less continuity in our lives. America is a nation of two-income families, with married couples working split shifts and fewer family meals eaten together. Many people are so overwhelmed that they feel it's all they can do to take care of themselves. In other words, anytime they put another person first, they feel it threatens their survival.

In the same survey, we asked where the rudest people were encountered.

On the road	40%
In stores	32%
In restaurants	10%
At work	6%
In public transportation	4%

This confirms that nearly half of us have been the victims of road rage. When stressed-out drivers are encased in a steel vehicle with enormous horsepower behind them, they become aggressive. When time is short, relatively minor lapses of etiquette cause otherwise tolerant people to go berserk. It only takes someone driving too close or too slowly or getting the last empty space in a parking lot—that's the last straw. Tempers flare. Drivers act out by honking, gesturing, yelling, even getting into fights. They may speed after other drivers and actually attempt to run them off the road. The most violent incidents end up in smashed cars, people being beaten up, even shot and killed!

Road rage is not something that happens only to other people; it is a relatively common occurrence. Not too far behind, Americans experience rudeness face-to-face in stores. In a distant third place is restaurants; in fourth and fifth places are the workplace and public transportation. Let's address public transportation with a simple explanation: subways and buses are almost always overcrowded. When people are already rushed and must share their comfort zone with strangers, they feel uncomfortable and may behave rudely.

Rudeness to Customers

Thirty-nine percent of Americans—two out of every five people— think employees at retail outlets and restaurants are ruder today due to the low unemployment rate, which has resulted in less qualified people being hired. How do we react to rude treatment? Fifty-eight percent said they go elsewhere.

Fifty percent said the rise in rude behavior is due to ignorance on the part of clerks or servers. "They simply don't know any better" goes the rationale. The other 50 percent thought these people were purposely rude: "They knew what they were doing—they have an attitude."

Forty-one percent who received offensive treatment in a retail store said it had caused them to postpone a purchase or not make it at all. Those who thought the clerk didn't know any better were more tolerant; only 25 percent either refused or postponed a purchase. This suggests that consumers may forgive people they consider unenlightened or inexperienced.

We asked the same group if they valued being fussed over. Thirty-one percent said it influenced their decision to go back. Only 12 percent said they always or nearly always get special attention at stores and restaurants they frequent regularly.

In restaurants, people expect to be treated fairly by the owner, manager, maitre d', or server. Sixty percent said they resent having to wait when a VIP immediately gets a table. Likewise, 38 percent said they resent airlines giving special perks to first-class passengers, such as faster check-in and priority boarding. This resentment is grounded not in envy but in feeling "second class." Furthermore, 32 percent believe airlines should give empty first-class seats to coach passengers; 52 percent said they should go to whoever paid the highest fares or flew the most.

How important is it to treat customers equally? When asked "If you owned a store, would you treat everyone equally?" 86 percent answered yes. Treating people as you would like to be treated is not only the right thing to do, it's good business.

How People React

If you ever thought you're the only one who feels as if people are looking through you, rest assured you're not alone. It's happening to a lot of us. When we asked: "Have you ever felt 'invisible' because you were ignored?" fifty-five percent of Americans answered yes.

When we asked them where this happens, they responded:

Department store	38%
Grocery store	16%
Government agency	11%
Restaurant	9%
Airport	7%
Gas station	7%
Specialty apparel store	5%

And this is how they reacted to such treatment:

Did nothing	36%
Walked out	25%
Never went back	18%
Asked for a manager	17%
Caused a scene	4%

Thus, a whopping 66 percent of Americans won't tolerate such mistreatment. Frankly, we were surprised to see that only 36 percent did nothing; evidently, these people are either too nice, too shy, or too indecisive.

Imagine 25 percent of these offended customers walking out of a store—individuals whose intention was to shop there or they wouldn't have been there in the first place! And 18 percent who refuse to come back. Note, too, that 17 percent were so upset they asked for a manager—and 4 percent caused a scene. Most people don't like confrontation, so the majority get upset but remain passive. But 21 percent vocalize their displeasure, nearly one fifth of this group in dramatic fashion. If this trend continues, the term "store rage" may become part of the vernacular.

Electronic Invisibility

It doesn't take a genius to recognize that voice mail, while useful, epitomizes how impersonal business has become. This progressive, efficient form of communication is so commonly used today that it is encountered everywhere—from the bank to the doctor's office.

It's understandable why voice mail is so popular. It works twenty-four hours a day, 365 days a year. It's a tremendous money- and timesaving convenience for a business. The catch is that it's not always convenient for customers.

In a 1999 survey, we asked, "Does it bother you to call a company and get voice mail?" Thirty-six percent of Americans reply that they are somewhat bothered and 56 percent are bothered very much. Only 8 percent say it bothers them little or not at all. Incidentally, in 1997 the number who were strongly opposed was 40 percent; in 1992, only 20 percent were strongly against it.

Today we can quantify a customer's irritation level when she is forced by a retail store to navigate a complex voice-mail hierarchy to get service. Companies that treat people like numbers may reduce their operational costs but could find that their customer population is dwindling. This is not good business.

Much voice mail is simply not customer-friendly. It sends the message "We can't deal with problems effectively, so you'll have to be inconvenienced." Perhaps a mix of voice mail with live operators is a solution.

ARG did a study for *US Banker* magazine that revealed that 80 percent of Americans preferred a human teller to an ATM. This confirms what we learned about voice mail: people don't want to be handled by a machine; they'd rather deal with a human being.

Likewise, the increasing use of e-mail has diminished personal contact. We don't propose eliminating e-mail, but we do believe some people use it too much. While it's efficient and inexpensive, it takes away from what Edward M. Hallowell refers to as "the human moment." A Concord, Massachusetts, psychiatrist and instructor at Harvard Medical School, Hallowell defines the human moment as an authentic psychological encounter that can happen only when two people share the same physical space. In the *Harvard Business Review*, January–February 1999, he wrote, "I have given the human moment a name because I believe that it has started to disappear from modern life—and I sense that we all may be about to discover the destructive power of its absence.

"The human moment has two prerequisites: people's physical presence and their emotional and intellectual attention. That's it. Physical presence alone isn't enough; you can ride shoulder-to-shoulder with someone for six hours in an airplane and not have a human moment the entire ride. And attention alone isn't enough either. You can pay attention to someone over the telephone, for instance, but somehow phone conversations lack the power of true human moments.

"... A human moment doesn't have to be emotionally draining or personally revealing. In fact, the human moment can be brisk, businesslike and brief. A five-minute conversation can be a perfectly meaningful human moment."

Hallowell goes on to explain that the lack of human contact is why many people feel lonely, isolated, or confused at work. He stated that when human moments are few and far between, hypersensitivity, self-doubt, even boorishness and abrasive curtness can be observed in the best of people. Productive employees will begin to feel lousy, and that, in turn, will lead them to perform poorly or look elsewhere for work. The irony is that this kind of workplace alienation stems not from lack of communication but from communication of the wrong kind. The remedy is not to get rid of electronics but to restore the human moment where it is needed.

With dwindling discretionary time, communicating on-line is a fast and easy way of staying in touch. But we sometimes find ourselves sending "telegraph" messages, incomplete sentences that sometimes come across as curt, aloof, and demeaning. Consequently, e-mail can foster a breakdown of communication.

Frank receives an e-mail letter from his boss, Stan, that contains one line: "Received your proposal and need further explanation."

Frank doesn't understand Stan's message, and fires back his response: "My proposal is complete. What can't you understand?"

Stan's reply: "Your proposal."

"Be more specific," Frank suggests.

"Redo it," Stan replies.

Frank: "Just tell me what you don't understand."

Stan: "I don't like it. It's not acceptable."

The last message breaks the camel's back—Frank is furious. He feels disenfranchised, and begins to rethink his future with the company. Again and again, we hear horror stories like this one. We blame the problem on poor communication; people are having fewer eyeball-to-eyeball meetings. What's missing is the absence of body language, facial expressions, and tone of voice—all important forms of communication. It's estimated that nonverbal information makes up 90 to 98 percent of what our brains process as communication. The problem is that that information is missing from the Internet.

The Depersonalization of America

"Bigger is better" has long been the American creed. Whether it's an amusement park, a building, or a movie screen, in community after community, you'll see signs proclaiming "The World's Biggest" or "The Nation's Biggest." Today, people take pride in working for the biggest company in an industry, attending the biggest university, joining the biggest union, belonging to the biggest church. They boast about a stay in the area's largest hospital or a loved one who lies in the area's largest cemetery.

The fact is, many things are depressingly out of scale these days—not just buildings but the institutions we deal with day in and day out. We are forced to transact nearly all the business of ordinary life under rules set by clumsy, impersonal behemoths: banks, drugstore chains, law firms, government agencies. A generation ago, nearly all of these institutions managed to present a human face to their clients and customers. Now they don't; they are too big. They are not necessarily monsters, but they are monstrosities, beyond comfortable human scale. People react against them.

Technically, it's not the institutions that have depersonalized our lives, it's today's technology. In a 1999 survey, 75 percent of respondents said that due to advances in technology, people are becoming less important and machines more important. This is reminiscent of the early industrial revolution, when people thought machines would replace them. Today's machines are different, however. Unlike their precursors, which were built to outperform a human physically, computers have the capacity to store and process so much information that it's mind-boggling. Consequently, people worry today that they will lose their jobs to machines. Some think it's only a matter of time.

Invisible and Inconsequential

In the smash Broadway show *Chicago*, the song "Mr. Cellophane" was a show-stopper. That's because most of the people in the audience could identify with its message. The lyrics lament that nobody ever pays attention to Mr. Cellophane, and this makes him feel "invisible and inconsequential."

With so many of today's workers fearing that the day will come when they will be replaced by a computer, a lot of us know what it's like to feel inconsequential. And who hasn't walked into a department store or an upscale boutique only to have a sales clerk look right through us as if we were invisible?

People feel insignificant when they read about billionaires such as Warren Buffett and Bill Gates. With a rise or fall of just an eighth of a point in Microsoft's stock price, Gates makes or loses millions of dollars—more than nearly all Americans could dream of earning in a lifetime. We conducted a 1999 survey in which 35 percent of Americans said they envied wealthy people such as Gates. Nor do they like knowing that a famous athlete receives millions of dollars for an appearance in a one-minute TV commercial. These are the same people who resent being ignored in a restaurant while a VIP gets royal treatment.

Feeling threatened by the wealthy is as old as wealth itself and knows no cultural barriers. The Kwakiutl, an aboriginal tribe of Washington State and British Columbia, practiced a tradition called a potlatch. The ritual was originally observed by coastal groups to establish political and economic superiority. The Kwakiutl would attempt to intimidate rivals by displaying their wealth in an unusual way. A Kwakiutl chief would present valuable gifts to invited chiefs from other tribes as a sign of his own wealth and power. Or he might set free his slaves or destroy his possessions or throw them into the sea, as if to say, "I am so rich, I can obliterate my property!"

Competing chiefs were expected to reciprocate and give even bigger gifts. To outdo one another, they'd not only give away or destroy jewelry, furs, or food, they might even set fire to their villages and fields. All this was to make other chiefs feel insignificant—not a good way to win friends and influence people, is it?

Relationship Marketing

Mary Kay Ash, founder of Mary Kay Cosmetics, said, "Whenever I meet someone, I try to imagine him wearing an invisible sign that says: 'MAKE ME FEEL IMPORTANT!'"

If you don't learn anything else from this trend, remember this invisible sign. Everyone wants to be treated as if he or she is important. This means pampering your customers and giving them incredibly good service. It also means praising your employees and showing you appreciate them. Don't take for granted they know this, tell them—again and again.

When customers enter your place of business, welcome them by name. If you own a business with heavy customer traffic, this won't be easy. You'll have to work at it. Ask your employees to do likewise. In time this will be part of your company culture.

If your company has voice mail, investigate how it serves outsiders. Or call your customer service number without identifying yourself, and see how your company treats its customers. Are customers getting results? Or a hassle? Speaking of telephones, do you return calls promptly? If not, shame on you.

Proactive companies have begun promoting "relationship marketing," a technique that involves reaching out to customers. Originally pioneered by airlines and automakers, tobacco companies are now doing it to quell negative press on their traditional advertising and promotions.

In September 1999, about 3,700 loyal Doral smokers were invited to R. J. Reynolds' largest factory in Tobaccoville, North Carolina, with a day of blackjack, live music by country group Alabama, and, of course, plenty of free smokes. The company sprang for lessons in line dancing and bowling and sponsored a tire-changing contest between NASCAR pit crews.

Philip Morris, the nation's largest cigarette maker, sent 1,300 sweepstakes winners to western ranches for whitewater rafting, horseback riding, and fly fishing as a promotion for its Marlboro brand. Another 250 went to race car–driving school. Smokers of the company's Virginia Slims brand, aimed at women, can win spa days complete with manicures, facials, massages, and even aromatherapy. British American Tobacco's Brown & Williamson unit tries to get closer to its customers by sponsoring bar nights and publishing magazines—a fashion glossy for smokers of its Misty, Capri, and Carlton brands and an outdoor sports journal for Kool and Lucky Strike regulars. Such promotions are an important weapon in the tobacco companies' cutthroat fight to protect their shrinking U.S. cigarette market. And they work.

In similar fashion, Harley-Davidson sponsors H.O.G. (Harley Owners Group) rallies. Thousands of bikers come from all over the country to enjoy weekend festivities reminiscent of a rock concert. These company-sponsored events have the atmosphere of a family reunion and work wonders to promote customer loyalty.

The importance of relationships is stated in the company's annual report: "At Harley-Davidson, we're in a relationship business, so we've long understood that being a worldwide leader in the motorcycle industry requires more than providing the best motorcycles and lifestyle experiences. It also requires having the industry's premier dealer network, because it is through our dealerships that lifelong customer relationships are built. Our long-term strategies call for us to continuously improve our working relationships with our dealers so they, in turn, can do the same with their customers."

The type of product a company sells doesn't matter; all good businesses are built on relationships. IBM understands this well. For years the company has traditionally invited customers to conferences ranging in size from fifty to a thousand participants. At these meetings, product planners, development engineers, and other key technical people mix and exchange ideas with key customers. Several times a year, specific industry groups—perhaps banking or the insurance field—are invited to discuss their industry's problems and assess how IBM products are meeting customers' expectations.

Perhaps the most exciting customer sessions conducted by IBM are its Chief Executive Officers Classes. Leaders from industry, education, and government are brought together in a classroom. The CEOs represent companies that do at least a billion dollars' business a year, the educators are presidents of leading universities, and the politicians are usually state governors.

Admittedly, few companies can attract CEOs and presidents of *Fortune* 500 companies. However, as the owner of a small business, you can invite customers to hear interesting speakers. You can include them in company parties or have customer appreciation days to show them you appreciate their business. Depending on your budget, you can hold events at your shop, lease a meeting room or invite people to your home. You can serve simple snacks or sit-down dinners with live music; you can host a cocktail party or an all-day event with golf and swimming. You can include giveaways, from T-shirts to gift certificates. Be sure your employees play a role in both the planning and the experience. Remember, you want to build strong customer relationships with your entire team—not just with you.

When you get right down to it, all great businesses are based on relationships. Successful stockbrokers build their client base through exceptional service. They stay in constant contact with their clients, informing them of both good news and bad news: "Joe, XYZ Company's quarterly numbers were less than expected. This was because . . ." He might conclude, "I recommend we accumulate more shares. The fundamentals are there, so I believe it's selling at a bargain." Or he might say, "Let's bite the bullet and bail out."

Likewise, a real estate broker must keep her clients informed about the sale of their property—otherwise, she'll end up with frustrated, disgruntled clients. It's not failure to perform that creates an unhappy customer; it's failure to communicate. Constant contact is how a relationship is built. A broker who stays in touch gets repeat business and referrals from her clients.

Observe any successful company, and you'll find it cares about its customers—and its customers know it. What's more, those customers care about the company and respond by being loyal. Nobody feels invisible. In summary, everyone wants to feel important. Your job is to make them feel they are—because they are!

Five Ways to Make Your Customers Feel Important

1. As a small-business owner, get into the habit of calling three to five customers every evening. Your reason for calling is to thank them for their business. Depending on the size of your company, some of your key managers should be encouraged to do the same thing. Do it in an organized manner, so you don't miss anyone. One manufacturer called to thank managers of accounts that paid their bills promptly, and that same year, the business of those accounts doubled.

2. Have special customer appreciation events to recognize customers and let them know how much their business means to you.

3. Learn as much as possible about your customers so you can send them cards and/or gifts on birthdays, anniversaries, children's graduations, and so on. We recommend signing cards personally as well as writing letters by hand. These are nice personal touches that customers appreciate.

4. Train your people to call customers by their names. It's not so difficult, especially when names appear on credit cards and personal checks. It's simply a matter of being alert and getting into the habit.

5. Train your employees to be observant to your customers' needs. For instance, a laundry employee should know which customers like or don't like starch in their shirts; a travel agent should know which customers like window seats and which like aisle seats; an interior decorator should know his client's favorite colors.

Each of the above is so simple to do that these should be standard operating procedure for every company. Companies that pay this kind of attention don't have invisible customers.

Home Offices and Telecommuting Are Redefining America's Workplace

Twenty years ago, when working people stayed home, it was called a strike. About the only people who worked in their homes were writers and artists. Today, home-based employment is one of the fastest growing segments of the workplace, thanks to computers, fax machines, e-mail, voice mail, and overnight couriers.

Now, one in every eight U.S. households has at least one adult working full-time at home, either for herself or for an employer. The number will rise to one in every five households by 2002, driven by a tight labor market, improvements in computer technology, and changing working values.

In late 1999, we surveyed people who had left a traditionally structured job to work out of their home. The results demonstrate how fast this trend is growing. Thirty-seven percent of those who had made the move had done so within the past two years; 24 percent had done it within the previous three years. This represents over a 50 percent increase from 1997 to 1998.

Notice how this trend indirectly relates to three other trends in this book. Despite having little discretionary time, the average American spends ninety minutes a day commuting, based on a 1999 survey by the Kensington Technology Group. This means that a full-time telecommuter or an at-home businessperson saves the equivalent of ten workweeks annually by eliminating the most time-consuming, stress-filled part of the day. No wonder millions of people want to work at home.

It is easier for the growing number of caretakers to be available for their elderly parents, especially if they live nearby or under the same roof. And with parents agonizing about leaving children to go to work, this trend is bound to influence their decision. Having one parent working at home may allow both to work full-time, thereby slowing the trend toward single-income families. For many women, this flexibility will be just what they need to keep them in the workforce.

According to the Bureau of Labor Statistics, in 1999, 70 percent of women with children age seventeen and younger had full- or part-time jobs. About one third of those women already worked at home. With these data, it would be easy to stereotype the home-based worker. But that would be a mistake.

The archetype of a home-based business is a female-owned enterprise providing day care or some other service so the owner can be near her young children. But according to a 1999 study, 59 percent of home-based workers are male, typically about forty-four years of age, married and employed in a white-collar profession such as marketing, sales, or technology. So much for stereotypes.

To dispel another common myth, people are not forced to work at home by their employers. On the contrary, only 7.3 percent, or one out of fourteen, are working for the company that previously employed them. In fact, only 36 percent are even working in the same field. And this will also come as a shocker: 94 percent of these people made their own decision to work at home. So they weren't squeezed out of the workplace by downsizing.

What's Driving This Trend?

Technology has given a new meaning to the term "home office."

"I can be anywhere and still run my company," a small home-based business owner said.

Although it's nothing new for people to work at home, never have so many done so as we've witnessed during the past few years. This trend is picking up momentum as we write. It's today's wonderful technology that is making it happen.

In a 1999 study, 59 percent of the people working in their homes said that today's technology made them more efficient. Only 24 percent said it didn't, and the remaining 17 percent weren't sure.

Telecommuting isn't for everyone. Some people have difficulty working in solitude; some need the company of coworkers; others need close supervision to be productive. In addition, we all need occasional face-to-face contact. Too much communication by e-mail, phone, and fax can lead to a breakdown of social skills. As people increasingly complain of feeling invisible, some telecommuters who lack interaction with company headquarters may begin to feel "out of the loop."

Amazingly, 95 percent of home-based workers we surveyed said that lack of personal contact does not affect their productivity or effectiveness. Sociologists claim that people are less productive when they work in isolation for sustained periods, but thanks to modern technology and, in particular, on-line communication, this feeling of isolation is absent for most home-based workers.

Fifty-eight percent of telecommuters said they are able to keep in touch with the office, thanks to the Internet. And 55 percent credited the Internet with providing them information to stay current.

There's No Place Like Home

Our 1999 survey showed that only 2.4 percent of all people who work out of their homes have any regrets about it.

People like working out of their homes because:

They can come and go as they choose.	65%
They can be closer to their children.	52%
It's easier to work at home.	50%
They can be there if needed by a family member.	49%
They can be there when the children come home.	45%

Autonomy is by far the number one reason people choose to work at home. One of the greatest benefits of having a home office is that there's no clock to punch. A morning person can start early; an evening person can stay up late.

Some comments we heard are "I can put in a full day's work and don't need anyone to manage the hours I put in—as if I were a child." "I know what I have to do, and I can do it at my own pace—and get the job done."

While managers express concern about what telecommuting employees are doing when not in the office, our studies show that only 5 percent of these workers claim that lack of personal contact has reduced their effectiveness.

What do these workers do with the commuting time they save? Do they simply work more? Fifty-three percent answered yes, while 47 percent said no. In a 1998 survey by Pacific Bell, if time wasn't used in work, the respondents exercised, did household chores or hobbies, or caught up on sleep.

Sixty-two percent of those surveyed said they have less stress because they work at home. Only 7 percent have more stress. The remaining 31 percent said it made no difference. In a society where so many complain of being stressed and starved for time, we think this trend will enrich many lives.

Women like telecommuting because they can coordinate it with domestic responsibilities. Women owned about 37 percent of our 9 million home-based businesses, according to data from the U.S. Census Bureau. As the number of home-based businesses increases, we expect that women owners will account for a larger percentage.

Financially, It's a Win-Win Situation

A common myth is that people choosing to work out of their homes risk taking a deduction in pay. Our survey reveals that only 27 percent earn less money at home. The other 73 percent earn the same or more. As people see their friends prosper, they become confident that they, too, can enjoy a similar lifestyle. Thus, this trend will build rapidly.

Thirty-five percent of those surveyed said they save between $200 and $400 monthly by working at home. More than 50 percent save at least $200 a month. Where did they save the most money?

Vehicle costs	44%
Child care	34%
Clothes	9%
Food	6%
Miscellaneous (dry cleaning, grooming, etc.)	7%

While 27 percent did take a pay cut, even most of those are still financially ahead because of these savings. The other 73 percent, who are making the same or more money, actually have more to take home.

When asked to name what was the most common expense incurred to set up a home office, people responded:

Computer	18%
Copy/fax machine	18%
None (incurred no additional expenses)	17%
Furniture (desk, chair, bookcases, etc.)	15%
Remodeling	14%
Phone lines	12%
Tools	4%
Extra groceries	2%

It's interesting that the two top categories are related to communication. In actual 1997 dollars, a home-based employee spent an average of $1,617 equipping his or her home office, according to the School and Home Office Products Association in Dayton, Ohio. Half of the people surveyed who set up a home office said that they needed to purchase one or more of the following: a computer, a fax/copier, or additional phone lines. These expenditures were necessary to provide them with a link to their business activities. These are onetime costs, in contrast to the recurring costs of daily commuting.

Integration

A buzzword we hear a lot is "integration." Simply put, home-based workers can mesh their work and personal lives; consequently, both areas of their lives are enriched.

We also hear the word "balance." As one father said, "Being able to have lunch with my kids is a special treat that I relish. What a wonderful way to take a break during a workday." We suspect the kids enjoy it, too, especially when Dad picks them up at school, takes them to a fast-food restaurant, and has them back at school before the lunch period expires.

Home-based workers enjoy greater flexibility of time than do their traditionally employed colleagues. While their eight hours' work may be done in thirty-minute segments, they can still accomplish the same work objectives.

Integration allows a parent to pick up children after school, take them to the dentist, or attend school or sports events with them. A mother can be available to nurse her infant at any time; a father can take a break to read to a toddler. One advantage of electronic technology is that workers are not limited to time zones and geographic boundaries. Voice mail and e-mail can be answered after the kids are asleep.

Watching Mom or Dad working in the home office also sets a good example for kids. Little ones learn to do their homework alongside their parents. Over time, this is bound to improve America's work ethic.

In a huge but mostly overlooked piece of the American child care picture, one third of all dual-earner couples with children under five work back-to-back shifts, said Harriet Presser, a University of Maryland professor and authority on shift work. While this facilitates parenting, it often impairs a couple's intimacy. Having one of these shift workers switch to telecommuting adds stability to the family unit.

Working at home also allows other family members to get involved. It may provide after-school employment for older kids, and it teaches them about business. An adult sibling or in-law may be inspired to begin her own home-based business after helping out over a weekend or two.

Still, like any job, working at home can present problems. For a workaholic, the temptation to work around the clock can be irresistible. And phone calls and faxes can come in at all hours—including the dinner hour.

Our 1999 survey showed that 56 percent of home workers say their proficiency and productivity increased. Those mentioning that they had interruptions said that 73 percent of the time it was family members who were their biggest distraction. Another 16 percent claimed that friends were their biggest distraction when they were interrupted from their work at home.

We asked, "If you are working at home, how often do you meet face-to-face with a supervisor?" Forty percent said they don't work for a company. Fifteen percent said they meet every second day; 15 percent said once a week; 12 percent said twice a week; 9 percent said once a month; and the remaining 4 percent said six times a year or less. As evidenced by this study, home-based workers are able to function effectively without much personal contact.

Make Telecommuting Work for Your Company

Employers must learn to accommodate employees who want to telecommute or risk losing them. There's an ongoing shortage of labor in the United States, and experienced, qualified people are hard to replace. Plus, turnover is expensive. Recruiting and training new people cost a bundle. In today's tight job market, a company might even have to pay a prospective employee a signing bonus.

Furthermore, telecommuting isn't a fad; it makes good sense for some people to work at home. And there are many companies that have benefited.

Once some managers believed that only slackers would want to telecommute. Supervisors feared they wouldn't be able to effectively manage people whom they couldn't see daily. But it's not the slackers who want to work at home.

A bank vice president said, "It's the best, brightest, and most mobile who want to telecommute. I expect several resignations soon if I don't agree."

If you calculate what your company spends per employee for such things as rent, utilities, and telephones, you'll realize there are substantial savings that will enhance your bottom line. So if one of your employees wants to work at home and it is feasible, welcome it as an opportunity to make an employee happy—and reduce your overhead.

Here are three tips: first, require home-based workers to participate in office meetings. Home-based employees must communicate regularly with supervisors and coworkers to prevent them from becoming too independent. Second, insist that mission and productivity are priorities that will be regularly scrutinized. Third, equip them with the proper tools. This means they'll require the same computers and on-line services that are available to them at the office. They'll also require special telephone services such as caller I.D. and conference calling, fax machines, pagers, and so on.

Business and Investment Opportunities

Like other trends that involve dramatic lifestyle changes, this one will affect America strongly. With millions of Americans working out of their homes and more to follow in the near future, there are many opportunities for investors and business owners.

Most obvious are the opportunities for those involved in selling products and services to home-based businesses and telecommuters. The 36 percent of setup expenditures going for computers, copiers, and fax machines represents billions of dollars. Since these costs are in the $3,000 range, we recommend that companies offer some type of deferred billing, such as no interest or no monthly payments for the first 180 days. Payment plans with nothing down will also appeal to these consumers. Likewise, companies can bundle products or services; computers loaded with software and Internet capability are popular. Professional technicians who service telephone equipment, copiers, and postage meters could mop up by offering a flat-price annual service contract for all in-home equipment.

Business furniture represents another 15 percent of setup spending. As home-based workers become acquainted with sciatica, headaches, and carpal tunnel syndrome, we anticipate demand for ergonomic office furniture. Executive chairs will be purchased for comfort and function rather than appearance. Smart retailers will stock loaner chairs so customers can determine what's right for them. Furniture retailers are responding to consumer demand by broadening their assortment of products and prices and by devoting greater floor space to home-office displays. Some have taken the category to the next level with dedicated freestanding stores. It seems just about every product designed for the home office is selling, from compact computer workstations to place in a corner of a dining room to full-blown, fully accessorized home offices that fill a spare bedroom.

Not everyone will have enough space for a dedicated home office. So designers of home-office furniture should develop: (1) products that can fit into small spaces; (2) products that can expand as more storage is needed; (3) products with doors or screens to conceal the workspace after hours; (4) products that harmonize with contemporary home decor.

As an example, Rolodex has designed some products specifically for its home-based customers. The new line will include new materials (brushed aluminum, light oak, and natural cherry) and colors (hunter green, burgundy, and cobalt blue). One of the first products in the new line has been a photo frame card file. When closed, the item looks like an ordinary photo frame, but it can be easily opened for access to the card filing system.

With its new line targeted to women, Rolodex has a new consumer advertising strategy. In June 1999, to reach home-based working women, the company began placing a series of ads in *Better Homes and Gardens, Working Woman,* and *Cooking Light.* We applaud this strategy and believe other equipment and supply companies would benefit from similar advertising.

Contractors that specialize in additions and remodeling will prosper from this trend. Many home offices require special lighting, wiring, and acoustical treatment to keep sound out as well as in. There will be a need for home-office consultants working with home remodelers as new home offices replace kitchens as the highest-demand remodeling projects. Some people will require extra storage capacity, so cellars and garages will have to be revamped. Or space will have to be rented and refitted.

Any business selling to first-time home-office consumers should help them manage costs. Other good selling messages will communicate "how to keep ahead of the curve" and "ways to compete with the big boys." People working out of their home will also appreciate products and services that save time and labor. The plain-paper fax machine obliterated the older thermal models because it was such a time-saver. Other new products will meet with similar success.

Owners of home-based companies will likely want to dispel the image of a hole-in-the-wall business, particularly if clients and customers never come to their homes. These entrepreneurs will purchase deluxe stationery and business cards, promotional items such as brochures and leave-behinds (pens, notepads, magnets, and so forth) and answering services that front as receptionists. Answering services will prosper if they advertise, "We get your messages right the first time, or your service fee is waived."

A word to the wise: quality should be stressed when selling to home-based customers. The value of service-free, top-of-the-line, quality equipment should be emphasized. Home-based business owners can't afford to have their equipment go down since they often have no backup. That's why they prefer products with "best service" ratings.

Telecommuters typically do not have a staff member or a service company to fix a malfunctioning office machine. It's a real hassle to wait around for a serviceperson or take a computer to a repair center. Most home-based workers are so dependent on their computer that they literally can't work without it. For this reason, we see good opportunities for companies that provide service contracts as well as full warranties for office equipment—especially for computers, copiers, telephones, and fax machines. It's also vital to provide loaners for customers to use while their own machine is in the shop. In like manner, we see opportunities for companies that rent and lease office equipment.

Highly specialized, rarely used machines are not practical for home-based office workers to own. Hence, on any given day, tens of thousands of home-office workers stop by a Kinko's store to use a high-resolution color printer or to find something else their home office does not have: other people. A visit provides face-to-face time with other telecommuters and possible networking opportunities.

Kinko's nine-hundred-plus stores include computer centers equipped for the Mac or Windows users who need access to high-speed Internet connections. Most of its workstations are loaded with popular applications and utilities, zip drives, and scanners. Also, at around $200 a session, a video conference can save hundreds in travel expenses, not to mention a lot of time.

In the future, we expect to see stores such as Kinko's offering one-stop services such as banking, legal assistance, and bookkeeping. And don't be surprised if they start serving bagels and coffee as well!

Today's Marketing Efforts Are Not Keeping Pace with Changing Consumer Demands

When we first collaborated on *Predatory Marketing*, published in 1997, we considered the title "Why Every Marketing Strategy Ultimately Fails." Our premise was that if a strategy is really good, the competition won't stand by idly. They'll copy the strategy and improve on it, rendering the original version obsolete. For this reason, a market leader must continually tweak a winning strategy—ideally when profit margins are high.

Every marketing strategy has a limited life span, which, in today's marketplace, gets shorter and shorter. Survival in business depends on constant change. Whatever information is available to us almost always exists for our competitors as well.

At the other end of the spectrum, today's consumer is empowered to make better-informed buying decisions. Never before have there been so many buying options. Throw in dwindling discretionary time, and the result is an intelligent and demanding consumer. So while the competition pushes to revise and redo its marketing strategies, the consumer is also screaming for change.

Profit margins shrink; it becomes difficult to top previous performances. Consequently, managers often react by cutting overhead. It's much easier to reduce payroll or advertising than it is to build market share. But that's only a partial fix. It's also a defensive posture. To stay healthy, you must fend off "corporate anorexia," a disease of decreasing inventories, closing stores, reducing budgets, and cutting back on customer services. All these are contrary to a healthy business. You must go forward, not back.

In past years, marketing efforts focused on sidestepping the competition. Today, the challenge is to keep one step ahead while continuing to satisfy consumers' demands. Most companies are falling behind.

The Changing Consumer

It's always more difficult to hit a moving target. With everything changing so incredibly fast, it's not surprising that the consumer is also changing.

Based on a survey we conducted in late 1999, 41 percent of American consumers believed that stores don't appreciate their patronage as they did five to ten years ago. Forty-one percent also stated that stores don't care about customers as they did a decade ago. We presented the following list of wants, asking consumers if the attitudes definitely applied to them.

1. "I want to be able to return purchases without a hassle."   68%

2. "I want to find easily what has been advertised."   55%

3. "I want a store with employees who can answer my questions."   54%

4. "I want to shop stores with thirty-day unconditional satisfaction guarantees."   53%

5. "I want the lowest price, period!"   50%

6. "I want signage in stores that directs me to what I want."   49%

7. "I want store employees to be visible
at all times."   48%

8. "I want to get what I want and leave."   47%

9. "I want new introductions to be
clearly marked."   41%

10. "I want a store that not only talks
about customer service but gives it."   41%

Notice at the top of the list is that consumers want a hassle-free return policy. It's a solid thirteen points ahead of number two. Even so, many stores are actually rescinding their no-questions-asked thirty-day return policy. Why? Because there's a small number of consumers who take advantage of it. Our studies show that 2.8 percent of all consumers are those jerks who buy something, use it, and then return it for a full refund within thirty days. We think that 2.8 percent is still pretty low and retailers shouldn't give up their return policy because of it. Note that number four, a thirty-day unconditional satisfaction guarantee, says that customers not only want such a policy, they want it in writing!

Lillian Vernon, a mail-order company, has an innovative way of soothing a dissatisfied customer. One man who ordered a humidor found his name misspelled on the nameplate. When the man called to complain, the serviceperson asked for the correct spelling and said, "We'll ship a new one to you overnight, sir, and we apologize for inconveniencing you." Then he was told, "Rather than having you repackage and return the humidor, we'd like you to donate it to your favorite charity."

We talked to David Hochberg, vice president of public relations, to confirm that this had really happened. He told us that this is standard procedure at Lillian Vernon. What a wonderful way to build customer loyalty! Of course, the company is saving the expense of the return shipping. Just the same, we don't know of another company with such a return policy, so we salute the Lillian Vernon Company.

A full thirteen points below number one, number two revealed that 55 percent of all consumers want the advertised merchandise in the store, and they want it to be easily located. People get steaming mad when an advertised product isn't available. Burger King learned this lesson the hard way in November 1999. The company had a $22 million Pokémon promotion, one of the largest in the history of the fast-food industry. Unfortunately, Burger Kings around the country ran out of Pokémon toys tied to the Warner Bros. hit movie *Pokémon: The First Movie,* just after its release, causing angry parents and crying children to storm out of its restaurants.

Whether you're giving away toys to children or a coupon for frozen food—you better have the product that you advertise in stock.

The remaining eight things that consumers want from retailers are directly related to time, to making a purchase reasonably quickly, and to getting a refund easily if the product turns out not to be what they wanted.

Referring to number ten, consumers want companies to back up their claims of customer service. We anticipate this will climb up the list in the near future. Banks especially have a lot of room for improvement here. While most promote personal service through advertising, few customers feel they receive special treatment. And it would be so easy. It surprises us that bank tellers rarely address customers by name. It's right there on their checks and deposit slips.

If you want your company to grow two to three times faster than your industry's rate, you must stretch your organization to give customers what they want. Three retailers excel in these areas. Wal-Mart comes closest, except that it has poor signage and stacks merchandise so high it creates a tunnel effect in some stores. Also, Wal-Mart is still short on open cash registers and slow at getting customers out. Wal-Mart does score high on good prices, and their greeters start customers off with a good shopping experience. Target has good signage, clean, well-organized departments, and wide aisles that make shopping easy. Home Depot staffs its stores with good people who are highly visible in orange shirts or aprons. Home Depot also excels in an area where most retailers don't—making sure customers know about new merchandise. Home Depot endcaps on the main aisle and stocks the shelves with new products or timely purchases. Music stores seem to be among the worst at displaying newly arrived merchandise. One small section of new arrivals typically just blends in with the other stacks or doesn't offer a wide enough or current enough selection.

The Consumer's Changing Perception

In 1988, ARG studied how Americans compared retailers and consumer product manufacturers to reveal which did a better job informing the consumer. Seventy-three percent said manufacturers were outperforming retailers in advertising and product education. In 1999, 59 percent of all consumers believed retailers did a better job. That's quite a reversal!

We believe television is the best vehicle for reaching and informing a mass audience about consumer products. Manufacturers are reducing their national advertising costs to maintain their profit margins. As a consequence, consumers' excitement about their products faded. Meanwhile, retailers got consumers excited about merchandise on sale. When influence over the buying decision switched from manufacturers to retailers, manufacturers lost big-time.

It's the manufacturers' job to establish constant awareness of their products. Retailers attempt to use price to get consumers to buy from them. Ideally, they'd like to sell their goods at the highest possible prices, but they can't when competitors across the street will undersell them. As retailers lower their prices to be competitive, their survival often depends upon buying from suppliers more cheaply. So manufacturers are forced to drop their prices.

In 1988, consumers said that American manufacturers communicated with them three times as well as retailers did. Now they're saying that retailers communicate with them slightly better than manufacturers. This illustrates how companies have changed over the years. When manufacturers forfeited their leadership to retailers, consumers' focus shifted to price. As a result, in our 1999 survey 43 percent of American consumers told us that manufacturers and retailers have not maintained the same level of quality as they did previously. Before 1990, fewer than 25 percent voiced this opinion. Now consumers are saying "I went to XYZ store to buy ABC brand, and I am disappointed. It's not as good as I expected."

When we asked consumers if retailers have maintained the same quality over the years, 42 percent said no. When we asked if manufacturers have maintained the same quality, 38 percent felt that brand products are inferior. As you can see, consumers blame both parties equally. Neither is willing to lead the way and stand for quality.

Next, we asked consumers if they felt that advertising is as truthful today as in the past. Twenty-nine percent said no. The real shocker was the response to this question: "Are you as motivated today as you used to be to shop a store based upon its advertising?" Of the respondents, 48.5 percent said yes, 48.6 percent said no; the rest didn't know. When half the population doesn't trust advertising, that's bad. In the same survey, 58 percent said they felt that companies routinely offer more in their advertising than they deliver.

Overselling in television commercials is rampant, with incredible offers at ridiculously low prices. A knowledgeable shopper knows they aren't genuine. For example, an auto dealer may advertise a late-model car with a sticker price far below its blue book value. When a customer inquires about it at the dealership, the salesman says it was recently sold or he can't find it on his inventory list. "But do I have a deal for you on this other car!" he declares, taking the customer by the arm.

Other complaints about advertising are: (1) The store has the item in stock, but only in odd sizes. (2) The store carries a poor assortment of colors. (3) The store is selling an outdated model. (4) The store has only a limited inventory. When customers discover that the advertising was misleading, they are in no mood to take a rain check.

We have discussed numerous problems consumers have with retail salespeople, from incompetence to scarcity on the floor. Our 1999 survey revealed another: 42 percent said salespeople are pushy today, compared to 14 percent five years ago. Eighty percent said they're more likely to leave a store without making a purchase when salespeople are overly aggressive. Sixty-two percent of consumers said they have stopped shopping where the quality of sales assistance has declined. To what do they attribute this decline? Sixty percent said that management was at fault due to inferior training. The other 40 percent believed that retail stores are simply hiring an inferior breed of salesperson.

We also learned from our 1999 study that 74 percent of today's consumers have strong objections to telephone solicitation. This is up from 56 percent in just five years. Since everyone is bombarded with phone calls of this nature, it seems unnecessary to elaborate.

The Basics Also Apply On-Line

There is some basic advice we think is appropriate to all businesses. Our recommendations focus on Internet companies but are applicable to all companies. Much of what we suggest is overlooked or disregarded by current management, and as a consequence, today's marketing is not keeping pace with consumer demands.

We chose to use an on-line company to illustrate our message because the Internet is becoming an integral part of so many businesses. Remember, too, that it's been predicted that in a matter of time, every business will be an on-line business.

For any Internet company to succeed, top management must be expert in that business. Your wonderful product may be ideally suited to market on-line, but unless you know a great deal about that product, you'll compete with a serious handicap. It's not enough to recognize, for example, that travel services are ideally suited to Internet selling; you also must have a lot of knowledge and experience in the travel industry. If you decide to be an on-line stockbroker, you must have expertise in the investment field. If you don't know your product and your market, the Internet is only one small step along a treacherous road.

You must identify your customer. You can't sell to everyone, so ask yourself, "Who will buy my product?" Are you after the haves or the have-nots? Male or female? Generation X or AARP? See the point?

Also, be aware of your competition. No matter how well you can sell books on-line, you may want to avoid taking on Amazon.com and barnesandnoble.com. On the other hand, if you're in a small niche and your customers are spread across the country or around the globe, the Internet might be just the right vehicle.

Consider, too, that the presentation of a product on-line differs from displays in a brick-and-mortar store. Product illustrations have the same limitations on-line as they do in a catalog.

In surveys conducted in mid-1998 and mid-1999 by the Strategis Group, consumers said they would buy the following items most often on-line :

Item	Mid-1999	Mid-1998
Books	41.1%	24.3%
Computer hardware/software	16.8%	31.7%
CDs/music	17.3%	14.9%
Travel services	15.2%	11.4%
Computer hardware	14.7%	31.7%*
Clothing	12.7%	6.4%
Office supplies	8.1%	1.5%
Car parts	7.1%	2.0%
Flowers and cards	5.1%	5.9%
Collectibles	5.1%	3.0%

*Computer hardware and software were combined in the mid-1998 survey.

Not everything will sell well on-line. Shoppers may prefer to examine clothing and furniture before buying. Product size and durability are factors in fulfillment, warehousing, distribution, and shipping. Selling ice cream or tropical fish via the Internet would be tricky. But as quickly as we say it can't be done, someone is sure to find a way to do it.

A Critical Difference

Whether you begin an Internet company or a traditional brick-and-mortar enterprise, you must address an important question: Why?

Maybe it's simply what you want to do. That's okay, to a point. You should definitely enjoy your work, but this alone will not justify investing in a new venture. The world is full of enthusiastic men and women who have failed in business. You must also find a market for your product or service. For instance, if your life's ambition has always been to open a bagel shop but you put it in a mall that already has three bagel shops, you are not meeting a need.

Such a small independent business can still succeed against the national bagel shops because it has a distinct advantage: the owner. Special relationships form between the owner and the customers. Our research reveals that when a business's owner is directly involved with a customer, there is an 83 percent chance of repeat business. This compares to a mere 16 to 38 percent of repeat business with a mass marketer. Research proves that customers feel there is no greater honor than to be waited on by the owner. No other retail experience can duplicate that special feeling.

It's important to realize that personal attributes go only so far. You can't duplicate the success by opening more bagel shops because you can be in only one place at a time. To operate on a large scale, every business must have a critical difference—something that persuades the consumer to shop at your store instead of at the competition.

Increase Your Marketing Efforts to Stay Ahead

The opportunist understands that today's consumer is unlike his counterpart of yesteryear. Several trends discussed in this book explain changes in spending that will have a ripple effect on business in the future, primarily Americans' limited time. This affects every facet of their lives. Each trend nourishes and sustains other trends; all impact consumers' behavior measurably.

Success in business requires venturing into uncharted waters, seeking new challenges in an ever-changing marketplace. As consumer demands change, marketing efforts must adapt correspondingly. Innovative marketing must be implemented. No one can sit on the sidelines; consumers' behavior patterns must be closely monitored for the slightest deviations and what they suggest.

For example, in the furniture industry, high-income markets were always targeted for high-end products. No one with an ounce of common sense ever disputed this fact. However, a two-year ARG study revealed that there was only a 65 percent correlation between high earnings and big-ticket furniture purchases. The same study showed only a 53 percent correlation between the value of a consumer's home and the furniture purchased. And when it comes to better-educated consumers (college and graduate-school levels), there was only a 38 percent correlation with these purchases. In fact, the study revealed that the number one factor that determines the best prospects for big-ticket furniture items is how often people entertain at home.

For the purposes of this study, entertainment was defined as a party where invited guests are served a home-cooked or catered meal. For many Americans, this happens on Thanksgiving and Christmas and perhaps two or three other occasions during the year. Twenty-nine percent of all Americans entertain four or five times a year. And just 20 percent of all Americans entertain six to nine times a year. Those hosting ten or more events make up only 6 percent of the total population. This small, select group of people are the most desirable prospects for high-end furniture.

Once information of this nature is known, it's important to know what to do with it. Innovative furniture manufacturers and retailers reacted quickly to reach the prime prospects for pricey furniture. They pulled their ads from *Architectural Digest* and *Home*

Beautiful and instead placed them in *Gourmet* and *Bon Appétit*—where there was more bang for their advertising buck. Those who refused to break with their old mode of advertising lost market share. This is a profound example of successfully identifying consumer patterns, analyzing them, and following up with an effective marketing strategy.

Another trend that ARG has been following for the past two decades involves large appliance or electronics purchases. In 1980, we concluded that American consumers expected to shop at 3.5 stores to make such a purchase. In 1990, they visited 2.8 stores, and only 2.1 stores in 1995. Our most recent studies show that the average consumer will shop at 1.3 stores in the year 2000 when purchasing appliances or electronics. This is crucial information for a retailer: it's essential to be the first store shopped. Being second means you're in serious trouble; being third or fourth puts you out of business.

In 1985, an ARG study revealed that the exterior of a retail store accounted for 33 percent of its image. Today, it accounts for 45 percent. We determined that consumers react favorably to a store with a strong exterior presentation. When shoppers are impressed with the outside of a store, they presume they'll be impressed inside. Therefore, retailers that occupy older buildings should consider remodeling or accept the fact that their customer base will get older and older.

Television advertising is yet another criterion used by today's consumer to measure the quality of a product. Retailers who use a local production company to make a commercial are unlikely to have the success of a nationally produced spot. So we recommend spending the extra money for a high-quality commercial. The extra expense will generate a better image for your company.

At a time when customers are rushed and require more service, it seems foolish for retailers to reduce frontline staff. This is not a good place to cut overhead. Today's consumers want answers. As gauged by the University of Michigan index, customer service satisfaction has dropped steadily the last few years. The rate of satisfaction among the 200,000 shoppers interviewed remains far below what it was in 1994. Claes Fornell, a professor of business administration who oversees the American Customer Satisfaction Index, said, "You have fewer people serving more customers."

With less sales help available in retailing, customer loyalty is a thing of the past. As a consequence, the number of years a company has been in business is no longer so important in influencing consumers. Satisfaction guarantees have replaced longevity. Sadly, however, many manufacturers and retailers fail here, too. They aren't listening to their customers.

Today's consumers are driving shorter distances to shop. As a result, savvy retailers realize that more stores will be required in large metropolitan areas to reach customers.

Successful marketers are innovative—and problem solvers. J. Crew CEO Emily Woods, for example, came up with a simple yet unique way to capture a particular market: "I think we were the first company that introduced tops and bottoms for bikinis that you could buy separately (by size). This had always been an issue for me growing up," she explained. Woods offered some solid advice on meeting the demands of consumers: "Stay current—it's about reading the right materials and watching the right movies and listening to the right music and staying involved with younger people."

Do you remember your Shakespeare: "That which we call a rose by any other name would smell as sweet." We're sure that when William Shakespeare wrote *Romeo and Juliet,* he wasn't thinking about marketing. However, in today's marketplace, there's a lot riding on having the right name. Ask yourself, "What does my company's name tell the consumer?" Even more importantly, what does it tell your noncustomer? Does it mislead them?

Sometimes a company's focus on the bottom line is a trap. Mattel, the world's largest toymaker, got into trouble in 1999 because company CEO Jill Barad tried to squeeze additional profit from Barbie. At a time when Barbie sales were declining, Barad produced more high-margin collector Barbies that sold for between $50 and $100. This enraged Barbie collectors who purchased the dolls as limited editions. Customers who complained to Mattel said they were ignored. "A lot of it was an obsession with the bottom line, and they were riding on their high horse and not listening to their customers," one retailer said. "Not listening to the dealers and customers is now a major part of their problem."

Lillian Vernon is a CEO who listens very carefully to her customers. Her photograph appears inside every catalog with a personal letter. Her message is always the same: she thanks her customers for their business and tells them she'd like to hear from them. All letters go to her, and her office responds to each. The company listens carefully to customer suggestions, many of which have been implemented. What a wonderful way for a company to plug into its customer base.

The Internet is an excellent vehicle for assessing customers' needs. For example, Oldsmobile sees Internet marketing as a way to reinvent itself in the eyes of younger, Web-savvy customers. Advertising and sales director Mike Sands explained that the company also wants an Internet-driven database that measures a customer's past habits against current interests and then serves it up in a profile.

Today most companies fail to meet the demands of the American consumer. It doesn't have to be this way. You must listen to your customers. Likewise, you must listen to your employees. Give them credit for knowing your business. All the while, watch your competition. And remember, no matter how good your marketing strategy, sooner or later it will fail. Why? Because the other guy can think, too. Don't wait. Be proactive. Change your current strategy while it is still working.

A Mock Session

If it's within your budget, we recommend you hire a reputable, established firm to identify trends pertinent to your business, to interpret and analyze what consumers are saying. As a novice, you may misinterpret what you hear or allow personal bias to influence you.

If you don't want to employ an outside firm, you can collect information on today's shopping patterns that will help you implement a proactive marketing strategy and stay a few paces ahead of the competition.

Reserve a meeting room in a nice hotel or conference center, away from your place of business. Invite thirty people who represent your target market. Be sure to have an employee present to take notes. Then ask them a series of questions about how their buying habits have changed over the past twelve months. Inquire through conversation rather than interrogation. Here's a sample script:

> "Thank you all for joining us. The purpose of this meeting is to learn how you, our customers, are changing, so we can better meet your needs. We are always looking for ways to better serve you.

> "We will ask you some questions; just say how you feel. There are no right or wrong answers. Use the pad and pencil in front of you; write down your answer. What is the biggest change you have made in the way you buy things? It could be a recent change, or one in the last three to six months, or in the last two years."

When everyone is finished, continue: "Who'd like to begin? What have you noticed in your shopping behavior that's different today? Please introduce yourself by your first name."

> "My name is Debbie. I think my biggest change is that I shop less often than I did two years ago."

> "Thank you, Debbie. What do you think caused this?"

> "My mother is older, and I take care of her."

Ask if others have noticed a similar pattern.

> "I'm Jeff, and I shop more on the Internet because I don't have enough time to visit the malls."

> "My name is Jon, and I work two jobs."

"I'm Nancy. My two daughters work, and I take care of four grandchildren."

Then ask those remaining for their answers and their reasons behind the answers.

"What else can somebody tell me about his or her changes?"

"I'm Sarah, and I buy more brand-name products today than I used to."

"Why do you buy more brand names, Sarah?"

"I'd have to say it's because of my job. I'm a physical therapist, and my employer cut back by letting several of the other therapists go. Now I'm working an extra six hours a week to make up the slack. I don't have the time to compare prices, so I buy the products I know. They're always good, no surprises."

"I'm Elizabeth. I quit work to stay home with my son and started clipping coupons and entering sweepstakes. My husband and I charge everything on credit cards that give us frequent-flyer points. We also buy less because we just have Bob's salary. But we still shop at better stores once in a while where we know we get top quality."

"I'm Bruce. We used to take a cruise trip every summer. But since Nancy had the twins, we can only get away for a few weekend trips now and then. We cash in frequent-flyer miles for free lodging."

Continue changing the subject as conversation dries up or becomes repetitive. Ask about buying store brands and generic products when making purchases over $200. Ask what they look for in a company today that's different from two years ago. Ask whether they're happy with the level of service they receive and what changes they'd like to see.

Wrap up with comments reviewing what you've heard. "What I'm hearing is we all have less time to shop. We are more likely to buy name brands. We like stores where there are no-hassle returns. We like companies that are involved in the community. And we like companies that pay attention to us when we come in their stores. Have I missed anything?"

Thank them generously for their attendance and show your appreciation with a $100 gift certificate from your store. Especially thank them for spending their time with you.

Consider having similar sessions every quarter. Be sure to do your homework and prepare your questions in advance. In time, you'll observe patterns in what your customers tell you. You will spot trends. You'll have all you need to stay on the cutting edge of your business, ahead of your competition.

Trend 1 Americans Have Less Discretionary Time

16 In survey after survey: Lauren R. Rublin, "Too, Too Much!" *Barron's*, March 9, 1998, p. 33.

16 How we reconcile: Ibid.

18 Hours worked at all jobs: Survey. Families and Work Institute.

19 The National Study of the Changing Workforce: Families and Work Institute, Ceridian Performance Partners 1998, *The Orange County Register*.

19 both sexes feel stressed: "Couples Dismayed at Long Workdays, New Study Finds," *The Columbus Dispatch*, January 22, 1999, p. 5A.

21 "For anyone who wants to be successful": Dr. James B. Maas, *Power Sleep: The Revolutionary Program That Prepares Your Mind for Peak Performance* (New York: Villard, 1998), p. xvii.

23 With a record 32 percent: Sue Shellenbarger, "Business Travelers Reshape Work Plans in Rush to Get Home," *Wall Street Journal*, March 18, 1998, p. B1.

25 the single most important factor: Paco Underhill, *Why We Buy* (New York: Simon & Schuster, 1999), p. 37.

25 The more shopper-employee contacts: Ibid.

29 At the Ritz-Carlton in Boston: Jane Wolfe, "What Seminar, Dad? It's Play Time," *New York Times*, April 23, 2000, Business section, p. 13.

31 Not long ago, drive-thru was a hole: Jennifer Ordonez, "An Efficiency Drive: Fast-Food Lanes Are Getting Even Faster," *Wall Street Journal*, May 18, 2000, p. A1.

31 The chain that most consistently offers: Ibid.

32 NPD Vice President Harry Balzer: Associated Press, "Americans Eat Fewer Meals in the Home," *Columbus Dispatch*, January 2, 2000, p. 6H.

33 "Consumers now see eating": Dirk Johnson, "Snacking Today: Anytime and Anyplace," *New York Times,* July 31, 1999, p. A1.

33 The automobile: Ibid.

36 While the average consumer: Turball Lornet, "A Perishable Commodity," *The Columbus Dispatch,* June 6, 1999, p. 1H.

37 grocery ordering and delivery: Ibid.

37 "Coffee and food": Robert Johnson, "So Far, Cybercafes Fail to Deliver on Their Initial Buzz," *Wall Street Journal,* June 8, 1999, p. B1.

37 "They can check e-mail": Ibid.

Trend 2 The Gap Between the Haves and the Have-Nots
Is Widening

41 increased from 3 million: Edward N. Wolff (New York University economist), *New York Times,* September 20, 1998, Business section, p. 4.

42 While the net worth: Louis Uchitelle, "More Wealth, More Stately Mansions," *New York Times,* June 6, 1999, Business section, p. 5.

42 The median wealth level: Louis Uchitelle, "The Have-Nots, at Least, Have Shelter in a Storm," *New York Times,* September 20, 1998, Business section, p. 4.

43 Whatever savings Americans do have: Robert B. Reich, "When Naptime Is Over," *New York Times Magazine,* January 25, 1998, p. 33.

44 forty wealthiest Americans: Melanie Warner, "The Young and the Loaded," *Fortune,* September 27, 1999, p. 78.

45 Entertainers' earnings for the calendar year 1998 appeared in several articles in *Forbes,* March 22, 1999, written by Ben Pappas, Peter Kalfa, Robert La Franco, and other staff writers.

46 CEOs' pay increased almost 30 percent: Bethany McLean, "Where's the Loot Coming From?" *Fortune,* September 7, 1998, p. 128.

47 "the typical married-couple family": Bob Herbert, "The Baker's Slice," *New York Times,* September 6, 1999, p. A17.

47 "The booming economy": Ibid.

47 "If you look at the business cycle": Ibid.

48 Mr. Crystal looked at: Adam Bryant, "Executive Cash Machine," *New York Times,* November 8, 1998, sec. 3, p. 1.

48 His salary was just a shade: Luisa Kroll, "The Top-Paid CEOs," *Forbes,* May 18, 1998, p. 224.

49 From 1984 through 1998, Farley was paid: David Barboza, "Taking the Starch Out of an American Icon," *New York Times*, March 19, 2000, Business section, p. 1.

50 Many companies in the Dow Jones Industrial Average: Bryant, "Executive Cash Machine."

50 Options are sometimes used: Ibid.

51 Envy among the affluent: Jonathan Kaufman, "Amid Economic Boom, Many of the . . . 'Haves' Envy the . . . 'Have-Mores,'" *Wall Street Journal*, August 3, 1998, p. A1.

51 "So-and-so got acquired": Warner, "The Young and the Loaded," p. 105.

52 "When you go to a company": Ibid.

53 Unions in most industries: Steven Greenhouse, "U.A.W. Deal: For Almost Everyone?" *New York Times*, September 23, 1999, p. C1.

55 "I can't write this doctoral paper": M. R. Kropko, "Executive Sticks to His Principles When New Employer Comes Calling," *Columbus Dispatch*, September 8, 1998, p. 1F.

56 Never before have there been: Blaine Harden, "Molding Loyal Pamperers for the Newly Rich," *New York Times*, October 24, 1999, p. 1.

56 When the Census Bureau: Ibid.

57 cars lasted longer: Keith Bradsher, "Today's Cars and Drivers Can Grow Old Together," *New York Times*, February 15, 1998, Business section, p. 1.

Trend 3 Community Involvement Enhances a Company's Reputation

70 According to a 1999 Cone/Roper: Dick Silverman, "Every Going Concern Should Get Its Concerns Going; Supporting a Worthy Cause Translates to Greater Sales and Stronger Customer Loyalty," New York *Daily News Record*, July 21, 1999, p. 48.

71 Wal-Mart, which has mounted: Ibid.

Trend 4 There Is a Growing Obsession with the Internet

74 The personal computer: Thomas Stewart, "A Nation of Net Have-Nots? No," *Fortune*, July 5, 1999, p. 185.

74 The e-mail devices look like souped-up beepers: Andrea Petersen, "Messaging Miss Manners . . . Wireless Devices Let Users Get E-Mail Anywhere, Anytime—and They Do," *Wall Street Journal*, April 26, 2000, p. B1.

74 According to Nielsen: Marc Gunther, "The Internet Is Mr. Case's Neighborhood," *Fortune*, March 30, 1998, p. 69.

74 A word to the CEO: Stewart, "A Nation of Net Have-Nots? No."

75 "the ultimate medium for business": George Anders, "Buying Frenzy," *New York Times*, July 12, 1999, p. R6.

76 About 51 percent: Saul Hansell, "A Former Television Executive Enters a Deal to Provide Content for Web-Faring Women," *New York Times*, September 16, 1998, p. C6.

77 "The traditional media": Ibid.

77 According to a 1999 survey: Bob Tedeschi, "E-Commerce Report," *New York Times*, July 12, 1999, p. C4.

77 the number of small businesses on-line: Eleena De Lisser and Dan Morse, "More Men Work at Home Than Women, Study Shows," *Wall Street Journal*, May 18, 1999, p. B2.

78 Grandma and Grandpa: John Hughes, "Companies Help Seniors to Tap into Online World," *Columbus Dispatch*, May 18, 1999, p. E2.

78 A 1997 survey: Jim Carlton, "Web Sites, Other PC Wonders Draw Crowds of Retirees," *Wall Street Journal*, January 29, 1997, p. B1.

80 The percentage of total Internet sales: "Internet Retail Sales in '99 Are Expected to Double," *New York Times*, May 18, 1999, p. A4.

81 The reasons behind: Anders, "Buying Frenzy."

82 According to the Mortgage Bankers Association: June Fletcher, "Should You Get a Mortgage Online?" *Wall Street Journal*, June 11, 1999, p. W12.

83 outsourcing companies such as nFront: Rick Brooks, "Bank One's Strategy as Competition Grows: New Online Institution," *Wall Street Journal*, August 25, 1999, p. A1.

83 opening its popular Web site: Leslie Kaufman, "Amazon.com Plans to Reposition Itself as Internet Bazaar," *New York Times*, September 30, 1999, p. A1.

83 Most existing search engines: George Anders, "Amazon Opens Online Mall of Small Stores," *Wall Street Journal*, September 30, 1999, p. B1.

84 Manufacturers and merchants: Anders, "Buying Frenzy."

84 Analysts say most B2B exchange revenue: Richard A. Oppel, Jr., "The Higher Stakes of Business-to-Business Trade," *Wall Street Journal*, March 5, 2000, Business section, p. 3.

85 "There is probably at least a trillion dollars in market cap": Ibid.

85 Business-to-business e-commerce: Ibid.

87 Estée Lauder: Andrea Petersen, "Getting Noticed," *Wall Street Journal*, July 12, 1999, p. R16.

88 According to a 1999 study: Timothy Hanrahan, "Price Isn't Everything," *Wall Street Journal*, July 12, 1999, p. R20.

88 Web shoppers, according to Internet business evaluators: Mary Ethridge, "Returning a Gift Bought Online? You might E-rupt," *Columbus Dispatch*, December 26, 1999, p. 1.

89 Live video on the Net: Lisa Napoli, "The Post-Lewinski Winner Is the Web," *New York Times*, September 28, 1998, p. C7.

90 in January 1998, 17 percent: Jerry Useem, "For Sale Online: You," *Fortune*, July 5, 1999, p. 67.

91 These days, even old-line industries: Claudia H. Deutsch, "Internet Strategy Becomes a Must at the Top," *New York Times*, October 20, 1999, p. C8.

91 Once on-line, older computer users: Mike McNamee, "Where Silver-Haired Surfers Browse," *Business Week*, July 20, 1998, p. 94.

92 Amway joined the ranks: Lisa Singhania, "Amway Enters Realm of Cyber-sales," *Columbus Dispatch*, October 2, 1999, p. B8.

93 "Today we are preoccupied": Anders, "Buying Frenzy."

Trend 5 American Companies Can't Expect Employee Loyalty— They Must Earn It!

96 Continual restructurings: Aaron Bernstein, "We Want You to Stay. Really," *Business Week*, June 22, 1998, p. 70.

96 Not long ago, most people: Peter T. Kilborn, "Help Desperately Wanted, So the Help Can Be Fussy," *New York Times*, November 6, 1999, p. A1.

96 With turnover near 20-year highs: Sue Shellenbarger, "To Win the Loyalty of Your Employees, Try a Softer Touch," *Wall Street Journal*, January 26, 2000, p. B1.

97 Fifty percent of junior technical employees: Matt Richtel, "Need for Computer Experts Is Making Recruiters Frantic," *New York Times*, November 18, 1999, p. A1.

99 Just as companies have: Jennifer Laabs, "The New Loyalty: Grasp It. Earn It. Keep It," *Workplace*, November 1998.

100 the turnover rate for companies: Adrian Wooldridge, "Come Back, Company Man!" *New York Times Magazine*, March 5, 2000, p. 82.

100 The new notion of loyalty: Bernstein, "We Want You to Stay. Really."

100 Perceiving that employees: "Loyalty in Business Is a Two-Way Street," *USA Today*, May 1999, magazine, p. 6.

103 Many companies claim: Sue Shellenbarger, "Companies Declare Lofty Employee Values, Then Forget to Act," *Wall Street Journal*, June 16, 1999, p. B1.

104 At brokerage firm Edward Jones: Shelly Branch, "The 100 Best Companies to Work For in America," *Fortune*, January 11, 1999, p. 118.

105 American Century: Every employee gets: Robert Lervering and Milton Moskowitz, *Fortune*, January 10, 2000, p. 82.

106 On the principle: Branch, "The 100 Best Companies to Work For in America."

106 The American Board and Kennel Association: Rebecca M. Knight, "Day Care for the Dog, Peace for the Owner," *New York Times*, September 26, 1999, Business section, p. 14.

106 "Our goal is to keep": Fisher, "The 100 Best Companies to Work For in America."

107 When the company's CEO: Hal Becker, *At Your Service* (New York: John Wiley & Sons, 1998), p. 229.

108 The typical 100-best company: Levering and Moskowitz, "The 100 Best Companies to Work For."

109 In a similar approach: "Profits from Loyalty," *Time*, November 9, 1998, p. 122.

109 Reflecting this demand: Louis Uchitelle, "Jobless Rate Drops to 4.1% as Wages Rise by 1¢ an Hour," *Wall Street Journal*, November 6, 1999, p. B1.

111 Calico has made a concerted effort: Alex Berenson, "In Silicon Valley, Loyalty Means Paying a High Price," *New York Times*, May 28, 2000, Business section, p. 1.

112 Young companies often share: Ibid.

112 The total annualized stock market return: Levering and Moskowitz, "The 100 Best Companies to Work For."

113 A recent survey of 1,544 employers: Marilyn Chase, "Healthy Assets," *Wall Street Journal*, May 1, 2000, p. R9.

114 particularly in management consulting: Rob Duboff and Carla Heaton, "Employee Loyalty: A Key Link to Value Growth," *Strategy & Leadership*, January–February 1999, p. 8.

115 Being a tough guy might have worked: Amy Zipkin, "The Wisdom of Thoughtfulness," *New York Times*, May 31, 2000, p. C1.

115 Some old-economy companies are training: Ibid.

Trend 6   Consumers Are Reluctant to Pay Full Retail Price

122 today's consumers have: Wendy Liebmann, "How America Shops," *Vital Speeches of the Day,* delivered to Nonprescription Drug Manufacturers Association, Rutherford, N.J., March 12, 1998.

123 Why are consumers so: Wendy Liebmann, "Given a Choice Between a $15,000 New Car"; Keith Bradsher, "Today's Cars and Drivers Can Grow Old Together," *New York Times,* February 15, 1998, Business section, p. 1.

125 Since salespeople can exert: C. Britt Beemer with Robert L. Shook, *Predatory Marketing* (New York: William Morrow, 1997), pp. 86–87.

126 a $30 million plan: Laurence Zimmerman, "United Airlines to Offer Its Coach Passengers More Legroom," *New York Times,* August 6, 1999, p. C1.

127 Surveys have shown: Beemer with Shook, *Predatory Marketing,* pp. 184–85.

128 "That's more important": Sarah Hale and Kevin Helliker, "Celebrated Jewelers Go National, but the Locals Won't Be Pushovers," *Wall Street Journal,* August 5, 1999, p. A1.

Trend 7   More Americans Are Caring for Their Aging Parents

133 25 percent of the U.S. wage: James Bond, Ellen Galinsky, and Jennifer E. Swanberg, "The 1997 National Study of the Changing Workforce," Families and Work Institute, 1998.

133 "Well, that's how I feel": Joyce Brothers, "Are You Caught in the Middle?" *Parade,* June 28, 1998, p. 4.

134 When Martha Jan Thompson's husband: Sue Shellenbarger, "More Children Start Making Plans Early to Care for Elders," *Wall Street Journal,* July 8, 1998, p. B1.

134 caught in the sandwich generation: Rimer, "As Centenarians Thrive, 'Old' Is Redefined."

134 Most Americans: Ibid.

135 The number of Americans aged eighty-five or older: Laura Pedersen-Pietersen, "Should Octogenarians Walk on the Wild Side?" *New York Times,* July 12, 1998, p. 5.

135 Americans over age sixty-five: Michael Moss, "Leon Black Bets Big on the Elderly," *Wall Street Journal,* July 24, 1998, p. B1.

135 As America ages: Ellen Graham, "Two Generations, One Nursing Home," *Wall Street Journal,* May 13, 1998, p. B1.

136 These responsibilities average: Bond, Galinsky, and Swanberg, "The 1997 National Study of the Changing Workforce."

144 Policy trading is: American Council of Life Insurance; Life Insurance Marketing and Researching Association; Viatical Association of America.

145 as it loses: David Jones, "Elder Care Time Bomb Imperils Productivity," *Business First,* January 8, 1999.

Trend 9   Dual-Income Families Are Becoming Single-Income Families

162 66 percent said they long: "The Balancing Act: Home Versus the Office" *Ladies' Home Journal,* October 1, 1997, p. 67.

162 It's no wonder they're feeling: Ibid.

162 In a 1998 survey: Diane Lore, "Atlanta Metro Poll: The Parent Trap," *Atlanta Journal-Constitution,* September 6, 1998, p. A1.

164 Do you ever feel: "How to Make the Most of Two Paychecks," *USA Today,* November 1997, magazine, p. 6.

164 to buy and prepare food: Mark Jenkins, "Do You Really Need Two Incomes?" *Men's Health,* April 1998, p. 94.

166 "The places you used to think": Erica Cheek, Elizabeth Angell, Sherry Keene-Osborn, and Donna Foote, "The New Age of Anxiety," *Newsweek,* August 23, 1999, p. 39.

166 the near-universal response: Editorial, "Safer Places of Learning," *Christian Science Monitor,* August 20, 1999, p. 10.

166 "education of school-aged children": Ibid.

166 Brian D. Ray: Ibid.

167 64 percent of parents: Cheek, Angell, Keene-Osborn, and Foote, "The New Age of Anxiety."

Trend 10   Frequent-Buyer Programs Have Come to Govern Consumer Spending Habits

171 no fewer than 3.6 trillion miles: Melynda Dovel Wilcox and Lynn Woods, "Desperately Seeking Seats," *Kiplinger's Personal Finance Magazine,* July 1999, p. 88.

171 "The whole pace of travel activity": Ibid.

174 5,000 to 10,000 bonus points: Louise O'Brien and Charles Jones, "Do Rewards Really Create Loyalty?" *Harvard Business Review,* May–June 1995, p. 77.

179 customers must perceive value: Ibid.

186 Harrah's has invested more than $100 million: Andrew Pollack, "In Search of Frequent Gamblers," *New York Times,* December 26, 1999, Business section, p. 2.

186 For example, knowing that many of its loyal customers: Seth Lubove, "The Odd Couple: A Dignified Corporate Lawyer and a Harvard Business School Prof Figure to Shake Up the Casino Business," *Forbes,* September 7, 1998, p. 52.

187 Loveman's ultimate goal is to make: Ibid.

Trend 11 Today's Consumer Wants Brand-Name Products

191 Branding is a hot topic: David Court, Mark Leiter, and Mark Loch, "Branding Leverage," *McKinsey Quarterly,* no. 2, 1999, p. 101.

198 nearly all chicken and turkey: Ann Merrill, "Jumping on the BRAND-wagon: Companies Seek Increased Name Recognition, Profits," *Star Tribune* (Minneapolis), May 11, 1998, p. D1.

198 the number of students: Ethan Bronner, "For '99 College Applicants, Stiffest Competition Ever," *New York Times,* June 12, 1999, p. A1.

200 Found in 97 percent of households: H. J. Heinz Company, Web site.

202 Drugstores mark up: Elyse Tanouye, "Steep Markups on Generics Top Branded Drugs," *Wall Street Journal,* December 31, 1998, p. B1.

202 Markups on some generics: Ibid.

203 "Oprah stands for": Tim Jones, "Oprah Is a Brand unto Herself," *Columbus Dispatch,* August 1, 1999, p. 1H.

204 Winfrey has succeeded: Ibid.

204 "The company needs to change": Diana B. Henriques, "The Cult of Personality vs. Needs of the Market," *New York Times,* October 12, 1999, p. C1.

204 "But history suggests": Ibid.

206 grunge is hardly a newcomer: Rebecca Quick, "True Grit, or How Sights Denim Makes Money in Dirty Jeans," *Wall Street Journal,* October 12, 1999, p. A1.

206 Of the 150,000 pieces of clothing: Ibid.

207 prices of particular CDs varied: Lisa Bransten, "The Bottom Line, If They Build It, Will Profits Come?" *Wall Street Journal,* July 12, 1999, p. R8.

207 Burma Shave, Brylcreem, Pepsodent: Brian Wansink, "Making Old Brands New," *American Demographics,* December 1, 1997, p. 53.

208 Bay Rum might remind: Ibid.

208 "We want to put all our resources": Ernest Beck, "Unilever to Cut More than 1,000 Brands," *Wall Street Journal,* September 22, 1999, p. A17.

209 a slew of new products: Kathryn Kranhold, "FAO Schwarz to Add Kids' Lifestyle Line," *Wall Street Journal,* October 19, 1999, p. B8.

210 "One of the hallmarks": Constance L. Hays, "Pulp Fiction," *New York Times,* May 19, 1999, p. C1.

211 "In the world of marketing": C. Britt Beemer with Robert L. Shook, *Predatory Marketing* (New York: William Morrow, 1997), pp. 151–52.

212 like many small shopkeepers: Joel Kotkin, "Helping the Little Guy Fight the Big Guy," *New York Times,* October 24, 1999, Business section, p. 7.

212 He decided to take aim: Ibid.

213 Jeans didn't go out of style: Bruce Upbin, "Beyond Burgers," *Forbes,* November 1, 1999, p. 219.

216 The free samples: Thomas M. Burton, "Why Generic Drugs Often Can't Compete Against Brand Names," *Wall Street Journal,* November 11, 1998, p. A1.

216 baby formula makers have nurtured: Michael Brick, "Formula Fight: A Generic vs. the Giants," *New York Times,* September 26, 1999, Business section, p. 1.

216 For nearly thirty years: Sam Hill and Glenn Rifkin, "Customers Tuning Out? Try an Alternative Approach," *Wall Street Journal,* December 28, 1998, p. A14.

Trend 12 Gaming Casinos and Lotteries Have Joined America's Mainstream

220 Gambling is as American: George F. Will, "George Washington Bet Here," *Washington Post,* June 28, 1999.

220 betting is socially stratified: Jacob Weisberg, "United Shareholders of America," *New York Times Magazine,* January 25, 1998, p. 29.

226 A Maryland study: "Lady Luck Is a Tramp," *Wall Street Journal,* October 15, 1999.

227 About a third: Douglas Frantz, "Top Sweepstakes Promoter Settles Suits for $4 Million," *New York Times,* May 29, 1999, p. A9.

229 It showed a war veteran: Skip Wollenberg, Associated Press, October 28, 1999.

230 A $25,000 winner-take-all competition: C. Britt Beemer with Robert L. Shook, *Predatory Marketing* (New York: William Morrow, 1997), p. 210.

234 Once the domain of science fiction: Reed Karaim, "Better Book Your Moon Orbit Now," *USA Weekend,* October 8–10, 1999, p. 4.

234 Recent studies indicate: Ibid.

Trend 13 People Today Complain of Feeling Invisible

239 It doesn't take a genius: Britt C. Beemer with Robert L. Shook, *Predatory Marketing* (New York: William Morrow, 1997), p. 98.

240 an authentic psychological encounter: Edward M. Hallowell, "The Human Moment at Work," *Harvard Business Review,* January–February 1999, p. 58.

241 when human moments are few: Ibid.

242 many things are depressingly: Alan Ehrenhalt, "If You Build It, They Will Yawn," *Wall Street Journal,* October 13, 1999, p. A30.

244 "Whenever I meet someone": Mary Kay Ash, *Mary Kay on People Management* (New York: Warner, 1984), p. 15.

245 Philip Morris: Gordon Fairclough, "Dancing, Blackjack and Free Smokes," *Wall Street Journal,* October 25, 1999, p. B1.

245 The importance of relationships: Harley-Davidson 1996 annual report.

246 At these meetings: Buck Rodgers with Robert L. Shook, *The IBM Way* (New York: Harper & Row, 1986), p. 55.

Trend 14 Home Offices and Telecommuting Are Redefining America's Workplace

249 Today, one in every eight: Sue Shellenbarger, "Families, Communities Can Benefit from Rise in Home-Based Work," *Wall Street Journal,* May 13, 1998, p. B1.

249 the average American: Alice Bredin, "Time Saved Commuting Can Be Put to Good Use," Tribune Media Services, August 16, 1998.

250 The archetype of a home-based business: Eleena De Lisserand and Dan Morse, "More Men Work at Home Than Women, Study Shows," *Wall Street Journal,* May 18, 1999, p. B2.

252 One of the greatest benefits: Harriet Webster, "Would You Like to Work at Home?" *Reader's Digest,* March 1998, p. 128.

253 a home-based employee: Rodney Ho, "From Desk Lawns to Bed Desks: Exotic Items for the Home Office," *Wall Street Journal,* November 11, 1998, p. B1.

254 In a huge but mostly overlooked: Sue Shellenbarger, "For the Burseks, Best Parent Regimen Is Back-to-Back Shifts," *Wall Street Journal,* February 25, 1998, p. B1.

256 A bank vice president: Marilyn Moats Kennedy, "How to Manage an Empty Office," *Across the Board,* March 1999, p. 67.

257 Furniture retailers are responding: Lee Buchanan, "Keeping the Home (Office) Fires Burning: From RTA to High End, Home Office Products Are Hot," *HFN: The Weekly Newspaper for the Home Furnishing Network,* March 29, 1999, p. 32.

257 The new line will include: Kristen Bryceland, "Rolodex Heads Home: Company Introduces Female-Friendly Files for the Home Office," *HFN: The Weekly Newspaper for the Home Furnishing Network,* April 5, 1999, p. 68.

259 on any given day: Laurie J. Flynn, "For the Officeless, a Place to Call Home," *New York Times,* July 6, 1998, p. C1.

Trend 15 Today's Marketing Efforts Are Not Keeping Pace with Changing Consumer Demands

264 Burger Kings around the country: Greg Hernandez, "Pokémon Promotion Turns into Snarling Monster for Burger King," *Columbus Dispatch,* November 13, 1999, p. G1.

269 when a business's owner: Britt Beemer with Robert L. Shook, *Predatory Marketing* (New York: William Morrow, 1997), p. 185.

271 University of Michigan index: Constance L. Hays, "Service Takes a Holiday," *New York Times,* December 23, 1998, p. C1.

272 "I think we were the first": Wendy Bounds and Rebecca Quick, "The Secret of Ursula Andress's Bikini," *Wall Street Journal,* November 11, 1999, p. B1.

273 Customers who complained: Gretchen Morgenson, "Barbie's Guru Stumbles," *New York Times,* November 7, 1999, Business section, p. 1.

273 Oldsmobile sees Internet marketing: Jess McCuan, "Auto Companies Head Online in Search of Sales Leads," *Wall Street Journal,* July 6, 1999, p. A20.

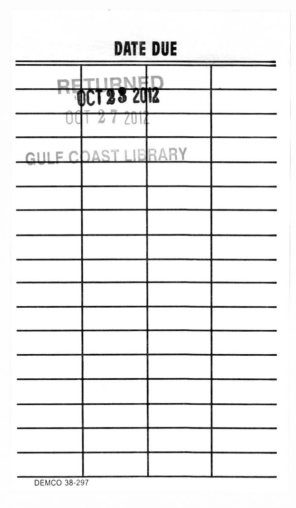